A TASTE FOR FREEDOM

A TASTE FOR FREEDOM

The Life of

ASTOLPHE

de

CUSTINE

Anka Muhlstein

TRANSLATED BY TERESA WAUGH

Helen Marx Books

NEW YORK

Originally published 1996,
Editions Grasset & Fasquelle, France

Copyright © 1999 Helen Marx Books

LCCN 99-74049
ISBN 1-885983-41-7

Design and composition by
Wilsted & Taylor Publishing Services

Published in association with Turtle Point Press

Printed in Canada

FOR ILARIA AND STÉPHANE

ACKNOWLEDGEMENTS

This book owes its existence to chance and to friendship; a chance conversation with Bernard Minoret who suggested I read *Aloys*, at a time when I was looking for a new subject for a biography. I would like to thank him here.

I owe a debt to Olivier de Luppé who, with unusual generosity, allowed me to consult his archives, some unpublished letters of Delphine de Sabran and his own work.

I wish to thank Helen Marx for her enthusiasm and clear-eyed advice.

Thank you also to Thierry Bodin, Manuel Carcassonne, Robert Dujarric, Georges Liébert, Cécile Muhlstein, Eve Sourian and, once again, François Nourissier.

Finally, the curiosity and critical sense of my friend Louis Begley have been a constant support.

CONTENTS

FOREWORD

Out of the turbulent cauldron of political and social change that was France in the first half of the nineteenth century many extravagant talents survived with undiminished reputation long after their mortal days were over. No one ever forgot Napoleon, Tocqueville, or Balzac, or such resident foreigners as Chopin and Rossini. But others who achieved a certain fame or notoriety at the time soon passed into an oblivion from which a later and more sympathetic age had to rescue them. The Marquis Astolphe de Custine was one of these. In 1843 he had published, to broad international attention, a riveting and not very friendly account of a journey to Russia in 1839, but when he died in 1857 he was best known, if at all, for litigation over his modest estate. The Tsar had banned his work in Russia, and after editions in various European languages that were estimated to have run to more than 200,000 copies the name of Custine all but disappeared from the historical record. Yet this ardently romantic writer with a keen eye for the world around him is both a mirror of the rapidly changing European scene in the half century after the French Revolution and, at the same time, one of us. His life and his work seem strangely contemporary.

Not surprisingly the rediscovery of Custine began in Russia itself. An abridged Russian translation of his once famous *Russia in 1839* appeared in 1910. After the Russian Revolution the work was then formally suppressed a second time. Any astute reader could readily perceive the most astonishing parallels between the Russia of Nicholas I and the Communist state. But gradually excerpts came to the notice of western diplomats in Moscow in the 1930s and 1940s, and in 1951 an abridged English translation was published with a preface by Walter Bedell Smith, who had been United States ambassador to the Soviet Union in the late forties. The translation itself was done by Phyllis Kohler, whose husband was to hold the same post in the sixties. Meanwhile, in Monaco of all places, the first biography of Custine appeared on the centenary of his death from the hand of the Marquis de Luppé. In the previous year the same publishing house in Monaco had produced a small collection of texts on Custine with a brief biographical preface. The revival of Astolphe was well under way.

My colleague at the Institute for Advanced Study, George F. Kennan, himself a former ambassador to the Soviet Union, wrote the first substantial study of Custine's Russia in any language. His book *The Marquis de Custine and His Russia in 1839* appeared in 1971, and it was from that book and from personal conversation with its author that I acquired my own enthusiasm for the extraordinary marquis. I learned that his father and his grandfather had both been guillotined in the French Revolution, and that his maternal grandmother had practiced the politics of the boudoir with a skill that was only exceeded by her daughter, the beautiful Delphine, whose name was immortalized in the title of Mme de Staël's novel of 1802. The courageous widow brought up her son Astolphe in an environment of eroticism and culture best exemplified by Delphine's eminent lover, the statesman and writer Chateaubriand. Inevitably traumatized by the events of his early childhood, as related to him by his mother, and confined to predominantly female companionship, the boy longed to find a friend, an intimate male friend in whom to confide. Remarkably he did find such a friend in the person of an expatriate Englishman, Edward Sainte-Barbe, born of Hampshire gentry that traced its origins to the Norman Conquest. Sainte-Barbe spent over thirty years living with Astolphe and providing the kind of emotional support that would nourish his literary talent.

It was Anka Muhlstein who directed me to Custine's first novel, *Aloys*, when she was at work on the important biography that is now appearing here in English translation. This novel, romantic and sad, contains much of its author's own life in a coded but perfectly comprehensible narrative. The hero finds himself unable to marry because he is more attracted to the mother of his prospective bride than to the poor young girl. *Aloys* is a kind of lavender *Adolphe*, a forgotten pendant to the far better known novella of Benjamin Constant. When I read the work, I realized at once that a full biography of Custine would illuminate the Europe of his day just as vividly as Custine himself had illuminated Russia. Astolphe had connections all over Europe. He had traveled in Italy, England, and Spain, and his close intellectual ties with the German writer Varnhagen von Ense strengthened a predisposition for nordic romanticism. Ample citation of the correspondence with Varnhagen makes Anka Muhlstein's presentation of Custine particularly compelling.

We see the marquis for the first time free of the accumulated prejudices of a century and a half, during which his homosexuality impaired the judgment even of those who admired his work on Russia. A public scandal in 1824 had made known Custine's tastes, and he himself had subsequently done nothing to conceal them. But if there was any malicious gossip about the domestic relationship with Edward Sainte-Barbe, Anka Muhlstein has successfully demonstrated that Custine's household was generally accepted with an openness and unconcern that would not be matched until our own time. She sees the scandal, brutal and unpleasant as it was, as the liberation of Custine. He went on to win the respect of Balzac and to enjoy the glittering company of Polish exiles who came to Paris in the early 1830s. Among them were the pianist Frédéric Chopin, the poet Adam Mickiewicz, and a flamboyant figure of evident bisexuality, Ignace Gurowski, who moved in with Custine and Sainte-Barbe to set up a *ménage à trois*.

Foreword

The presence of the Polish exiles together with the publication of Tocqueville's *Democracy in America* in 1835 appears to have ignited a desire in Custine to see Russia. The Poles in Paris could have had nothing good to say of the Russians, and Custine had nothing good to say of Tocqueville's idea of democracy. In 1838 Custine had published his book *Spain under Ferdinand VII* to great acclaim, notably from Balzac, and he may have recognized that travel literature suited him far better than novels or poetry. His memorably unsympathetic response to Russian culture may be attributed in part to his ignorance of Russian (Tocqueville, after all, had mastered English), but if he failed to appreciate the genius of Pushkin he had a sharp eye for character and custom. That is presumably why his work seemed as threatening to the Stalinist government as it was to that of Tsar Nicholas I. Ignace Gurowski had a brother living in Russia and may even have harbored an ambition to go there himself, but after Custine had published his devastating account of the realm of Nicholas the imperial wrath drove Ignace's brother out of Russia and ultimately into the United States. Once again the life of Custine is linked to the great events of his century: Adam Gurowski became a translator for the U.S. State Department and, through published letters on the Civil War, a considerable vexation to Abraham Lincoln.

Anka Muhlstein has constructed a biography of Astolphe de Custine that is eloquent, searching, and sympathetic. It describes the formation of a temperament that produced in *Russia in 1839* a travel book like no other in modern times. It has the vast sweep of the marquis' own life, which was played out in many countries among some of the most creative and influential persons of the day. Yet we can see that after an anguished youth the center of Custine's life was his unbroken relation with Edward Sainte-Barbe, "my best friend," as he wrote in his will of 1852, "who for thirty years did not leave me, and who in every circumstance gave me proofs of the sincerest devotion." In the title for her final chapter Anka Muhlstein draws from a letter of Astolphe that reaches back to classical antiquity to evoke his friend as "half of myself." This is Horace's tribute to Virgil, *animae dimidium meae.* Amid the terror, the scandal, the notoriety, and the polemic that encompassed Astolphe a quiet dignity and decency reigned at the heart of it all.

GLEN BOWERSOCK

A TASTE FOR FREEDOM

Introduction

Many writers slide into oblivion, but only a small number come out of it again to earn the respect and fame that eluded them in their lifetime. Astolphe de Custine is one of the lucky few.

Born in the middle of the Revolution, Custine died in 1857, under the Second Empire. As a novelist, poet and travel writer, he met with a respectable, if fleeting literary success. Even the account of his journey to Russia in its many editions was eventually forgotten with the passage of time. For sure, he belonged to a generation of literary geniuses—novelists, playwrights, poets—who elbowed each other for room, and it was not easy to compete on their own ground with Balzac, Hugo, Stendhal, Lamartine or Dumas. The name of Custine lingered on in people's memories because it evoked both Astolphe's mother, the beautiful Delphine, remembered for having been celebrated by Chateaubriand, and his grandfather, a hero of the American War of Independence and revolutionary general, executed under the Terror by the government he had served . . . but Custine, the writer, was forgotten. At the beginning of the twentieth century no one would have given credence to the survival of his work. It needed the Cold War and the threat posed by the ever increasing power of the U.S.S.R. for his best book, *La Russie en 1839*, known only to a few specialists, to come once more into its own.

As a travelogue, a confession and the study of a society, it is an unclassifiable masterpiece that owes more to a sense of foreboding than it does to historical research. If it attracts the attention of the contemporary reader, it does so primarily because of its application to the Soviet Empire. In the nineteenth century, the Russian philosopher Herzen called it the most intelligent book about Russia; in the twentieth, the American diplomat George Kennan declared it to be an excellent book, no doubt the best, on Russia and Stalin. It is this paradox that has long formed the basis of interest in any study of Custine. But there is more to Custine and his work than that.

The Revolution had robbed Custine, the aristocrat, of his property, shaken his initial confidence in the world with which he was familiar and destroyed the society from which he sprang. But it gave him, in exchange, the assurance that he had a right to freedom and the conviction that he was accountable neither to the old order nor to the new. "I am not a revolutionary but I have been revolutionised," which he proved by living precisely as he intended.

Astolphe de Custine was homosexual. There was nothing new about that. At the time of his marriage—of short duration—and despite the fact that his friend Sainte-Barbe lived with him, Custine kept up the appearances of a conventional way of life. After the death of his wife, his mother was not offended by the constant presence of his companion; nevertheless Custine waited for her death before he founded a household openly with Sainte-Barbe. For thirty years Custine and Sainte-Barbe led a respectable conjugal life, marked, if not by complete faithfulness, at least by absolute loyalty. The nature of their relationship became quite clear as soon as Custine was freed from family constraint. The two men lived together, received company together, and if they did not always go out together—no couple did in the nineteenth century—Custine would never have allowed Sainte-Barbe to be excluded for reasons of propriety or morality. Strangely enough, this unyielding attachment to personal liberty is inseparable from Custine's literary success.

Custine's posthumous career has been most unusual: not only has his work been retrieved from oblivion—following the success of *La Russie en 1839*, his novels and other works were all reprinted—but in addition, his personal life has justifiably become a subject of curiosity. Custine has caught up with his brilliant relations and overtaken them: today the name belongs to him.

I

A Life of Ease

At the time of his birth, on 18 March 1790, the people of France were still smiling; especially so in a liberal family like the Custines, open as they were to new ideas. So happy were they, that they baptised the child Astolphe. His grandmother, knowing her Ariosto and somewhat worried about the first reforms, hoped that, like his namesake, her grandson would bring some phials of good sense back from the moon.

What was there to prevent good humour from prevailing in the family château of Niderviller in Lorraine? The child, Armand de Custine's second son, was born twenty years to the day after his mother, the pretty marquise. According to Mme de Sabran, his maternal grandmother, he was born to the sound of the peasants rejoicing on the estate.

"I must tell you," she wrote the following day to her lover, the chevalier de Boufflers, "that my good fat little mother[1] has just given birth to a fine handsome boy whom I received into my lap (as the old wives say) and whom I kissed all over once he had been washed. This event has excited the entire village and my grandmotherhood was announced by a cannon that could be heard for two leagues round. More than a hundred and fifty peasants commanded by Captain Pèdre came with their muskets on their shoulders and all the necessary gravity to lead me to the church with the child . . .

"At last, by dint of our able captain's skilful manoeuvres, we came to the end of our labours. The greatest order was re-established at the church porch: the silvery voices of the bells rang out; the parish serpent, the organ, the hautboys and horns all vied with one another as to which could make the most noise; the curé and the schoolmaster baptised my poor godson in such good conscience and with so much salt and water that he vomited like a wretch over all the curious people and developed an inflammation which causes him for the moment to be blind in one eye."[2]

The tone is set. All the gaiety, the fantasy, the somewhat absurd vivaciousness—and all the correspondence—are to be found on

1. The Sabran family language sometimes lent itself to confusion: thus Mme de Sabran called Delphine "my fat mother" and Delphine referred to her mother affectionately as "little mé."

2. Gaston Maugras and P. de Croze-Lemercier, *Delphine de Sabran, marquise de Custine* (Plon, 1912), pp. 64–65.

the Sabran side. The Custines were more reserved and, despite an unquestionably ancient lineage, were of less distinguished descent. The Sabrans were far more brilliant. This illustrious provincial family included several saints and was connected to all the reigning heads of Europe since the thirteenth century. In fact Gersende de Sabran's son, Raimond Bérenger IV, comte de Provence, married one of his daughters to Henry III, the Plantagenet king of England, another to Saint Louis and the third to Charles of Anjou, the king of Naples. Yet, despite a glorious name and a considerable fortune, the young Delphine was tenderly raised in quiet intimacy by a mother who was a devout follower of Rousseau and who treated love as a serious matter.

Delphine's mother, Françoise Eléonore de Jean de Manville, was born in 1750. At a time when, doubtless, the happiness of children was barely considered, the unfortunate Eléonore had a particularly bleak childhood. She suffered every misfortune: a mother who died in childbirth, a terrible stepmother, an imbecile older sister, a rogue of a half-brother and a frighteningly strict grandmother who, to make matters worse, broke off all relations with her son-in-law. As soon as Eléonore left her convent, various suitors presented themselves, but one of them had only to meet with her father's approval for her grandmother to oppose him, and vice versa.

Determined to be free, the young woman decided to take control of her own destiny. In her grandmother's salon there was one person who had always treated her with great kindness. This was an elderly gentleman of nearly seventy, a lieutenant general in the navy. He listened to her, treated her as a favourite granddaughter and told her stories. In battle he had single-handedly withstood an attack by four English ships and when he returned to Versailles after this great act of bravery, Louis XV presented him to the queen with the words: "He is one of our cousins." The young Eléonore was well aware that he would never dare to ask for her nineteen-year-old hand in marriage. But wouldn't that be the best—in fact the only way of escaping from her family? She took the initiative and begged her father to tell the comte de Sabran that she would willingly marry him. Such an alliance was too good for her father and grandmother not to agree to it. The old officer accepted joyfully and the pretty Eléonore married him, thus yielding to a "very sweet sentiment" such as she had for her father and grandfather, "and which satisfied [her] heart . . . [since], loving nothing, everything [to her] seemed worthy of love."[3]

Rejuvenated by his marriage, Joseph de Sabran gave his young wife two children, a daughter, Delphine, born in 1770, and four years later in the year of Louis XVI's accession, a son, Elzéar. The two children were named after the family saints, Elzéar and his wife,

3. *Correspondance de la comtesse de Sabran et du chevalier de Boufflers 1778–1787*, ed. E. de Magnieu and Henri Prat (Plon, 1875), pp. 286–287; letter dated 31 July 1787, the day of her daughter's marriage.

Delphine, whose marriage was remarkable for its total chastity, the young bride having consecrated her virginity to God. They were both canonised in 1369.

The comte de Sabran, having fulfilled his dynastic duty, died shortly after the birth of his son, leaving his wife in the enviable position of a pretty young widow, who was rich to boot, well received at court, and respected and admired in society. She lived in Paris, on the rue Saint-Honoré. There, the charm of her house lay in a huge garden that ran down to the Champs-Elysées. The house, which would have stood between the present British Embassy and the rue de l'Elysée, no longer exists. In summer the young widow spent several months at Anisy, the episcopal seat of the bishop of Laon, a relation of her husband's. The bishop, although no kill-joy, was a virtuous man. Mme de Sabran jokingly recounted how, with him, she lived surrounded by bishops who could no more do without her than they could do without their crosses. No one could have taken exception to her behaviour. She had no lovers and devoted herself entirely to the education of her children; to amuse herself she painted and spent several hours a day studying Latin. But an encounter in 1777 was destined to upset this peaceful existence.

The maréchale de Luxembourg's salon was sought after by all the most elegant people. There, according to Rousseau, the conversation was of an exquisite delicacy "which never made any impression, but which always pleased."[4] Mme de Sabran frequented the salon, as did the maréchale's nephew, the chevalier de Boufflers, whenever he was in Paris.

The chevalier was renowned for his wit, the suddenness of his amorous advances, his passion for horses and his love of travel. He was teased so much about this that a friend meeting him one day on the highway hailed him with, "Chevalier, I am delighted to find you at home." His perpetual restlessness may well have come from the fact that he was born in a coach on the road to Nancy. His amorous temperament came from his mother, the ornament of King Stanislas's court who, true philosopher that she was, composed her own epitaph:

> *Ci gît, dans une paix profonde*
> *Cette Dame de Volupté*
> *Qui, pour plus de sûreté,*
> *Fit son paradis de ce monde.* *

As the youngest son of an illustrious family—an ancestor was one of Louis XIV's grand marshals—he was destined for holy orders which he flatly refused to take: *Lasciare le donne?* Never. He was not

---

*Here lies in deep peace Lady of Sensual Pleasure, who, to be on the safe side, made her Paradise in this world.

4. Jean-Jacques Rousseau, *Confessions* (Paris, Bibliothèque de la Pléiade, Gallimard, 1951), pp. 510–511.

prepared even to pretend to make the sacrifice. Instead he agreed to become a Knight of Malta, thereby acquiring sufficient, if not vast income, and went on to pursue an honorable military career. His unparalleled rudeness was tempered by indescribable charm.

He was thirty-seven when he met the comtesse de Sabran. Ten years older than she, and with an experience of women, the world and of love, quite inconceivable to the chaste young comtesse, ignorant as she was of the trouble so small a thing as a glance might cause. As she later wrote, she had hitherto known only serene days and tranquil nights. In his usual manner, the chevalier attacked immediately by visiting her the following morning, but he soon realised that a campaign based on the classic rules of libertinism would not succeed. He was disarmed by the unaffected way in which the comtesse received him, inviting him into her somewhat untidy house where her children crushed her crayons, her guitar lay casually about and her inkwells were always empty. He was disarmed too by the sight of her unruly hair, which showed a lack of coquetry, and fell totally in love. Too cheerful to succumb to sentimentality or to forgo his wit, he paid court light-heartedly and in verse, with references to her unkempt beauty and uncoiffed hair.

Fully aware that she would not yield with the ease to which he had become accustomed, he suggested, not a love affair but a brother and sister relationship. In fact the brother and sister—for this was how they soon described themselves—wrote to each other nearly every day, either short notes or long, chatty, familiar, loving letters. They became friends, real friends who told each other the most intimate details of their lives before they finally became lovers.

> *I really need to talk to you today, my brother, to cheer me up and to distract me from a certain visit which I have just made, and what a visit! A visit which one makes only at a certain time, at the knees of a certain man, to admit certain things which I won't tell you. I am still weary from it and full of shame. I do not like that ceremony in the least.*[5]

To which the chevalier immediately replied:

> *What, charming little Magdalene, did you leave the confessional where you said so much that you won't say to me, when I would tell you so many things that my confessor will never know! My God! How offended I am to have counted for nothing in your discourse! And what did this man say who saw you at his knees? If only I were your confessor! If only I had been your sin! If I might only be your penitence!*
>
> *Farewell, my sister, I have a cold in the head and on the chest; I am coughing like a wolf and weeping like a calf. Had you had the same, it would have served you well at the tribunal of penitence.*[6]

---

5. Gaston Maugras, *La Marquise de Boufflers et son fils, le chevalier de Boufflers* (Plon, 1907), p. 296; letter dated 25 April 1778.

6. Ibid., pp. 296–297.

Nevertheless, on 2 May 1778,[7] in the bishop's large château at Anisy, the comtesse at last succumbed with delight to pleasures that she never came to regard as guilty. But the tranquility of her days had ended. Along with pleasure she discovered jealousy, anxiety and the deathly boredom of being subjected to the company of people who prevented her from thinking about her lover, of re-reading his letters and of composing replies in her head. In order to please Boufflers, who was an excellent Latinist, she set herself the task of translating Lucan and Ovid. He enquired at once about the results; "I see you from here working at polishing and adjusting your lines, like a dentist working on uneven teeth."[8] Sometimes he would have preferred her to be less proper. Her lines, he wrote, "are very pretty, very sweet, very well done but they are a little too like my mother's soup which is never salty enough."[9] Then she took it upon herself to forbid him to address her by the familiar *tu*.

But he wouldn't go along with that: "This *vous* freezes me; it seems to me that nothing which you inspire in me is in accordance with it. It is as if I had to always bow to you instead of embracing

7. *Correspondance de la comtesse de Sabran*, op. cit., p. 230, letter dated 2 May 1778: "Above all remember the second of May, it will be forever memorable in my calendar."

8. *Lettres du chevalier de Boufflers à la comtesse de Sabran* (Plon, 1891), p. 43, letter dated 30 August 1778.

9. Ibid., p. 113.

you. Withdraw your defence, dear Sabran, if you make me polite, you make me false and cold, and above all gauche. Love is a badly brought up child."[10] Clearly a classic liaison could not satisfy Boufflers. Neither did he want it to: he aspired to be brother, lover, the children's "best friend," in short, a husband—and a loving husband. He surprised himself by his need to abandon the chase both literally and figuratively: "I stopped yesterday at Luzancy, with the comte de Bercheny, and for the first time I surprised a feeling of jealousy in myself. I saw him taken up with his wife, and with his land, happy in such good fortune as I have always desired, but will never have. He does delightful things; he spends his time enjoying his life, congratulating himself on it and making plans. His wife seems to participate in everything and to love the countryside as much as he does. I asked myself: what good has that man done to be so well treated by fate, and what crime have I committed to be so ill-treated? This is the poison that slid into my veins and is still active there."[11]

Marriage seemed impossible to him because it would have deprived him of the income provided by the Order of Malta. For sure, the comtesse was rich enough for two, but he refused to bring to the marriage nothing but poverty and his white hairs: "If I were young, if I were rich, we would long since have borne the same name; but

10. Ibid.
11. Maugras, *La Marquise de Boufflers*, op. cit., p. 301.

14

only scant honour and respect could allow my age and poverty to be forgotten."[12] The situation was all the more exasperating because the comtesse minded about her reputation and, more importantly still, she was embarrassed by the way her daughter, "the imposing"[13] Delphine, looked at her.

Delphine was a young person of very strong character whose boldness was tempered by a great shyness in society. From the age of ten she expressed the most trenchant opinions especially in the field of literature. "I am reading with *maman*," she wrote to Boufflers, "the tragedies of Corneille. I have read *Polyeucte* and *Cinna*; they amuse me greatly because I find them ridiculous; above all when Emilie says: *Tout beau, ma passion devient un peu moins forte.*"

At such an early age she was already so flirtatious with the chevalier that her mother's irritation is easy to understand. On thanking him for a little dog he gave her, the child wrote, "She is most amiable, but nevertheless, not more so than you; I think it is hard to be as amiable as that."[14] Although the decision made her "as sick as a beast,"[15] the comtesse decided on the chevalier's advice to put the little girl in a convent before she began to show hostility towards her mother.

12. Ibid., p. xi.
13. *Correspondance de la comtesse de Sabran*, op. cit., p. 51.
14. Maugras, *Delphine de Sabran*, op. cit., p. 11.
15. Ibid., p. 20.

There followed several years of freedom for the lovers—the presence of Elzéar whom Boufflers regarded as a son in "all but the making" did not trouble them. But eventually the chevalier tore himself away. In November 1785 he accepted the post of Governor of Senegal, this seemingly the only way in which he could acquire sufficient distinction and money to be able finally to marry his comtesse.

He returned to France only once during the three years that he stayed in Africa, where both Europeans and Africans were surprised by his judgement. The French government, too, was astounded by the resources he discovered in the colony and by the opportunities he discovered for establishing trade. "From his hideous, dilapidated house, no door of which would shut, no plank of which was solid, all of whose rooms were furnished by rags covered in dust," and from "his poor head which resembled a château abandoned by its caretaker, with everything soon to become topsy-turvy,"[16] he managed to write cheerful optimistic letters to his "dear heart," to send her love birds and to send little black slaves to all his friends.

Delphine and Elzéar received a little boy, "no higher than a boot ... and as black as ebony," whom they called Friday. According to their mother, the poor child "resembled one of those cats with a curling paper attached to its tail: he turns, he looks at himself, he

16. *Correspondance de la comtesse de Sabran*, op. cit., Journal du chevalier, pp. 402–403.

16

dares not move for fear of soiling himself."[17] He presented the duchesse d'Orléans with a girl of two or three years old who, he said in a letter to the comtesse, "is as pretty, not as the day, but as the night. Her eyes are like little stars and her bearing so sweet, so tranquil, that I feel myself moved to tears on thinking that the poor child was sold to me like a little lamb. She does not yet speak, but understands what is said to her. Should you see her at the Palais-Royal, do not fail to address her in her own language and to kiss her, thinking that I too have kissed her and that her face is the meeting point for our lips."[18] Another little girl was sent to the princesse de Beauvau. This child, Ourika, was the subject of a novel written during the Restoration by the duchesse de Duras who in fact used both the little Senegalese girl's first name and her pathetic life history. Despite an excellent education, intelligence and wit, Ourika, who was in love with her mistress's grandson, could find no place for herself—let alone a husband—in aristocratic society which was the only society she knew, and she died of tuberculosis at the age of twenty.[19]

Meanwhile Delphine came home to her mother, "prodigiously larger and fatter . . . considerably uglier . . . having lost all her ele-

17. Maugras, *Delphine de Sabran*, op. cit., p. 27.

18. *Correspondance de la comtesse de Sabran*, op. cit., Journal du chevalier, pp. 413–414.

19. Nicole Vaget Grangeat, *Le Chevalier de Boufflers et son temps, étude d'un échec* (A. G. Nizet, 1976), p. 69.

gance."[20] This return occasioned one of the chevalier's most sensitive letters: "But let us speak of Delphine; she is, then, at last with you; you cannot imagine how relieved I am to think it. Her presence is a sweet distraction during a cruel absence; I say cruel because I feel it so keenly for myself which is to feel it for you. But the looking after of her, the care, the vigilance, even the anxiety will all alleviate your grief; you imagine moreover that we will no longer enjoy the same freedom, that ease, that absence of constraint to which we were so well accustomed. We would have to meet less often, it would be a great nuisance; even when we met we would have to do so with greater circumspection; it would be a considerable loss of pleasure and we would have difficulty in accustoming ourselves to it; or, if by chance, we yielded too easily to our invincible fondness for one another, if we were to fight too feebly against this sweet and oh, so strong habit which we have of one another, it would mean for both of us, but above all for you (who are more worthy than I) a perpetual recurrence of regret which would expose the least of our faults to the microscope."[21] The chevalier was all the more right by virtue of the fact that the moment had come to marry Delphine.

The young woman soon regained her figure and natural elegance so that when she was presented at court "she was praised with one

20. Maugras, *Delphine de Sabran*, op. cit., p. 16.

21. *Correspondance de la comtesse de Sabran*, op. cit., Journal du chevalier, p. 369.

voice."[22] From 1786 a plan began to be made for a marriage between Delphine and Armand de Custine. Mme de Sabran—now only too aware of the disadvantages of a much older husband—was pleased by his youth, his sweetness of character and his reputedly fine fortune. For inexplicable reasons the arrangements dragged. Eighteen months after the idea was brought up, the marriage was no further advanced than it had been on the first day. Then, in June 1787, Armand's father, a permanently complaining widower, announced that he had a pain in the leg and talked of "making a journey to take the waters, which would put everything off until doomsday."[23]

Infuriated by the role of mother-in-law, Mme de Sabran got angry with General de Custine. "This father-in-law is a scourge sent from heaven to put an end to me. He doesn't know what he wants, he doesn't know what he says, he no longer knows what he does . . . Our father-in-law tires me . . . I know not where to find words with which to reply to him, nor ears with which to hear him; I would willingly give a pint of my blood to be rid of it all. I am sometimes tempted to pack and to make my escape as fast as my legs can carry me . . . I grow thinner as you look at me, and if it isn't all over soon, a funeral not a marriage will be taking place in this family."[24] In the end she cornered him. Thanks to the duc de Polignac's intervention,

22. Maugras, *Delphine de Sabran*, op. cit., p. 26.
23. *Correspondance de la comtesse de Sabran*, op. cit., p. 251.
24. Ibid., pp. 262, 258, 251.

the difficulties were ironed out and on 10 July, she announced to the chevalier that the contract would be signed in a week.

The *little betrothed*, as she called the young couple, seemed to grow daily more attached to one another and the girl's character to become gentler. Mme de Sabran watched her daughter's heart "soften and melt in the fire of this redoubtable god."[25] And although she told the chevalier everything she could find out about the political situation at a time when "the sovereigns of Europe had never been so busy," and although she railed against the boldness and insolence of Parliament which rejected all taxation, she always came back to the subject of Delphine's happiness which so preoccupied her. "If one can count on happiness, I have every reason to believe that she will be happy; but when I think of all the ingredients necessary to the composition of this happiness and of the multitudinous circumstances which throw themselves in the path of such perfect harmony, like comets in the middle of the universe to disrupt the order . . . I tremble, and I see that much must be left to chance whatsoever precaution we might take to restrain it."[26]

At last the great day arrived. The marriage was to be celebrated by the bishop-uncle at Anisy on 31 July 1787. Both mother and daughter spent a restless preceding night. The mother took advan-

25. Ibid., p. 269.
26. Ibid., p. 284.

tage of these last moments of intimacy to explain the mechanics of a wedding night "without positive instruction . . . but in an attempt to prepare her in such a way as to avoid the turmoil which is unavoidable when one is taken by surprise."[27] But she only succeeded in frightening the girl so much that she developed a fit of shaking and the pair of them spent the night in the same bed without either of them sleeping a wink. Nevertheless the bridegroom appeared at eight o'clock in the morning with his father, his little sister and an "otherworldly" look.

Just as they had been about to set out, the young man was struck by a terrible toothache. He was determined to have "this bad tooth" extracted for he "would have begrudged it his wife on their wedding day since love never triumphs over pain." It was impossible to find a dentist. The fashionable one, Saillant, was in the country as were his colleagues. Eventually a M. Catallan was found, who, "on extracting the tooth, removed part of the jaw; this resulted in appalling pain, sadness and disappointment, on top of which a swollen cheek made a very bad impression." So the entire family went back to bed until one o'clock, the time fixed for the ceremony.

The procession advanced in the gloomiest silence; Mme de Sabran was so deeply moved by witnessing "this famous yes which, once pronounced, can never be revoked however much one may some-

27. Ibid., p. 286.

times wish it so" that she burst into floods of tears. Delphine did not cry "but her little face was so long and neither was her husband very confident . . . When the ceremony was over M. de Custine took hold of my daughter, and I of his son and we left with the same order and the same gravity as when we arrived, to go to the drawing-room where a very good breakfast awaited us."[28]

The afternoon was spent in dancing, with songs from the village fiddlers and ended with a splendid meal hosted by the bishop. But it was eventually time to think about the dreaded night again. Mme de Sabran, showing she had the ability to see things through, took M. de Custine aside to persuade him that it was his turn to talk to his son. "Never in my life have I felt so foolish; I think that I will still be blushing about it tomorrow. But there they are together . . . If only I were now in my daughter's place, and that you were in my son-in-law's, having obtained, as they have, the Church's permission; for otherwise it is *a work of the devil who puts us in hell both in this world and the next, according to Saint Augustine.*"[29]

Of course she woke at dawn, sick with impatience. A look on Delphine's face reassured her. The young son-in-law had behaved perfectly. The little darling was wonderfully well. "Love is not so wicked as one thinks; it is a pretty little monster which neither bites nor scratches, and my little Delphine, apart from a modest pinkness

28. Ibid.; the three extracts are from the same letter of 31 July 1787, pp. 285–289.
29. Ibid., p. 289.

. . . seems the same as ever."[30] What's more, her confidence didn't seem threatened since her family wagered that it would take her no more than a fortnight to dominate her husband. "She controls him more despotically than she does her brother. I do not know how long it will last."[31] It was to last for three years.

Three years during which political events increasingly prevailed. But the private lives of the Sabran-Boufflers-Custines mustn't be forgotten. Just a year after the wedding, the chevalier, now aged fifty, finally returned from Senegal. Would the comtesse find him too old? He was sufficiently self-confident to be able to write to her: "Was I not forty-nine last year, and did you not love me then? I ask it of your beautiful blue bed which I have not lost from sight since I left it very much against my wishes";[32] to which she replied, "I am so troubled that I would not know what else to say, if not that I await you, with suffering or with pleasure I do not know which, so agitated am I by a thousand different feelings."[33] She barely had time to question herself: family events and politics crowded in.

In September, Delphine gave birth to a baby boy, Gaston. The men in the family could no longer think of anything but politics; so much so that the chevalier and General de Custine, both supporters

30. Ibid., p. 290.

31. Ibid., p. 306.

32. Quoted by Jeannine Delpech, *L'Amour le plus tendre* (Librairie Académique Perrin, 1964), p. 114.

33. *Correspondance de la comtesse de Sabran*, op. cit., p. 362.

of the new ideas—the General having fought in the American War of Independence—were elected to the States General. Armand, the young husband, also threw himself enthusiastically into the fray. Mme de Sabran was the least enthusiastic of them all. The fall of the Bastille confirmed her fears. She abandoned the whole clan and, to Delphine's dismay, left for Switzerland with her son, Elzéar. Delphine was living in Lorraine, in the château de Niderviller where the general had started a china and earthenware factory. The young woman, pregnant again, was in fact counting on her mother to support her during the last months of her pregnancy.

Boufflers, showing great good sense, refused to be carried away by political passion and sided entirely with Mme de Sabran. "I do not understand the imperious madness of the good fat Delphine wanting you to come to her in a country where, from one moment to the next, anything might happen, instead of going to find you with your good Swiss people who have surely already taken you to their hearts."[34] It is true that riots were breaking out in the provinces; some châteaux had been pillaged, but the Custines could not imagine that their peasants might turn against them, and Mme de Sabran did join her daughter in time for the birth of Astolphe. She shared her darkest forebodings with the chevalier—"Every brake which should control the multitude is gone now and the people will take advantage of the liberty, in which they were supposed to re-

---

34. Maugras, *Delphine de Sabran*, op. cit., p. 62.

joice, to cut all our throats, not in one Saint-Barthélemy, but in ten thousand"[35]—but unable to bear the idea of being far from her family, she nevertheless returned to Paris with the young couple in September 1790. But there was already a distinct shadow cast over the joy caused by Astolphe's birth.

35. Agénor Bardoux, *Madame de Custine* (Paris, Calmann Lévy, 1891), p. 66.

2

The Hard Life

Delphine did not share her mother's pessimism. On the contrary, she was busy discovering Paris and, since being married, thoroughly enjoying herself there. And Paris now on the threshold of revolution remained a city "where one laughs about everything, where one is afraid of nothing, where one suffers everything, and without which one does not care to be."[1] She felt free to collect admirers, and not realising how deeply she hurt her husband, had a great many. Too young or too proud to take her away from her lovers, Armand soon stopped treating his wife with the tenderness to which she had grown accustomed during their long, solitary sojourns in the country. The couple rapidly be-

1. *Mémorial de J. de Norvins*, 3 vols. (Plon, 1896), I, p. 240.

came detached from one another and Delphine threw herself whole-heartedly into society—a society that was never better described than by a "slim sub-lieutenant" to whom she paid not the least attention when he was introduced. He was the brother-in-law of her best friend, the marquise de Chateaubriand. Flitting about, Delphine took advantage of what the young François-René was to refer to later in his *Mémoires* as the "redoubling of life" which arises in times of crisis.

"In a disintegrating society which is trying to remake itself," he wrote with admirable precision and subtlety, "the struggle between two genii, the collision of the past with the future, the mixture of the old manners with the new give rise to a transitory combination which does not allow for one moment of boredom. Passions and liberated dispositions manifest themselves with an energy they do not have in a well-regulated city. Infringement of the law, exemption from duty, from custom and seemliness, and even danger, all add to the interest and disorder. The human race on holiday walks about the street, freed from pedagogues, briefly restored to its natural state, and it will feel the need for social restraint once more, only when it bears the yoke of a new tyranny begotten of licence . . . In every corner of Paris there were literary gatherings, political societies and spectacles . . . There passed and passed again in the streets committees of the people, cavalry pickets and infantry patrols. Behind a man in a French coat with a powdered head, a sword at his side, hat under his arm, in pumps and silk stockings, walked a man with short-cut, unpowdered hair, wearing an English frock coat and an American cravat . . . There were countless duels and love affairs, liaisons made in prison, political brotherhoods, mysterious meetings among ruins under a serene sky, surrounded by the peace and poetry of nature; walks in out-of-the-way places, silent, solitary, mixed with promises of eternal love and ineffable tenderness, to the dull din of a fleeting world, to the distant noise of a crumbling society which, by its fall, threatened the bliss that depended on events. If you lost sight of someone for twenty-four hours, you could never be sure of finding them again. Some were engaged on the path to revolution, whilst others meditated on civil war; some left for Ohio having forwarded plans for châteaux to be built among the savages, others went to rejoin the Princes . . ."[2]

In fact, Delphine's circle soon disintegrated. Mirabeau's death on 2 April 1791 ignited a spark of anxiety among all those who, like the Custines, still hoped to survive the crossing, however hazardous it might be, between the old and the new France. Mirabeau had managed to create a neutral territory around himself; people who would have insulted each other elsewhere shook hands in his house. But with his disappearance, all hope of collaboration between the different trends was dashed. "With me I take all mourning for the monarchy, whose wreck will become prey to the different factions,"

2. Chateaubriand, *Mémoires d'outre-tombe* (Paris, Bibliothèque de la Pléiade, Gallimard, 1951), bk. V, chap. 14, pp. 181–183.

he said on his deathbed.[3] In April 1791, Mme de Sabran finally decided to emigrate with Elzéar. At the invitation of Frederick the Great's brother, Prince Henry of Prussia, she went to his beautiful château at Rheinsburg, set in a landscape of lakes and forests eighty kilometres from Berlin. Delphine watched with regret as her confidantes and friends departed: the marquise de Chateaubriand left to spend the summer at Malesherbes and the comtesse de La Rochefoucauld at whose house Delphine had made friends with Alexandre de Beauharnais and his wife, the gentle Josephine, took refuge in Brussels. Armand de Custine rejoined his regiment on the Rhine. "Here am I as sad as a night-cap," she wrote to her brother. "I spend my day at the piano, singing sad ballads, the blackest that I could find. That is all my pleasure."[4]

She lived at this time in what was the rue de Bourbon, the present rue de Lille, opposite the hotel de Salm, now the museum of the Legion of Honour. Lafayette was living at what is now number 81 and the chevalier de Boufflers, who had been elected to the Constituent Assembly, was with his cousin, the duchesse de Biron, at number 127. To amuse herself Delphine often took her elder son, little Gaston, to call on the chevalier. She went as a neighbour, "without a footman." "One day," she wrote to her brother, "on passing in front of the grenadier who mounted guard for M. de Lafayette, [Gaston]

3. Norvins, op. cit., I, p. 254.
4. Maugras, *Delphine de Sabran*, op. cit., p. 85.

pulled me by the hand, shouting that he wanted to embrace the grenadier, with me trying quietly to deter him from so incredible an idea and everybody stopping and looking . . . 'I love the grenadiers very much,' he shouted. 'I am a good citizen.' He is a mad democrat. But I will no longer dare to take him walking; in the end the grenadiers might think that it was I who wished to embrace them.'[5] She may well not have been tempted by the grenadiers, but from the surprisingly frank confidences made to her brother, Delphine seems to have allowed herself to be easily embraced.

The sickly, delicate little Elzéar had considerable influence over his sister. She sent him copies of her letters, particularly of her love letters. Sometimes, appalled at her indiscretion, he passed them on to his mother who took up her pen to remonstrate: ". . . it is a dangerous game that you are playing . . . I wish you were a little more coquettish and above all prouder. That is the safeguard of our poor sex. If we do not respect ourselves, we are respected but little and respect is worth more than love in the century in which we find ourselves . . ."[6] More especially since the closing century offered no guidelines on matters of behaviour.

In September 1791 the Constituent Assembly split to make way for the Legislative Assembly in which the revolutionary parties had a much greater influence. Thus freed from his obligations and

5. Ibid., pp. 85–86.
6. Ibid., p. 93.

greatly perturbed by the turn of events, the chevalier de Boufflers left for Prussia to rejoin Mme de Sabran. It is worth noting that in so doing he demonstrated more sense and better political judgement than his clever friends, Custine, Biron or Beauharnais, all liberal officers who were employed by the Revolution "so long as it remained of moderate proportions . . . once grown, it abandoned with disdain these frivolous apostates of the throne."[7] These departures did not appear to affect Delphine in Paris, "where life is so peaceful and where one amuses oneself so much."[8] And in case Elzéar should fail to understand the extent of her pleasures, she sent him an explanatory letter: "I have so much to tell you, where shall I begin? Let's talk first of Victor. He is more amiable than ever . . . Secondly, I see M. d'Esterno . . . Thirdly, the chevalier de Fontanges . . . amiable and above all quite extraordinary . . . Fourthly. Ah! Here is something wonderful, incredible and interesting. The comte Antoine de Lévis has returned to Paris. He came to see me and *subito* he contrived to have the *air* no doubt of being greatly in love with me . . ."[9] And as for her husband? What became of him in all of this?

Despite Custine's extreme youth, Louis XVI's ministers, Narbonne and Delessert, yielding to joint pressure from Mme de Staël and Talleyrand, had entrusted him with a curious diplomatic mis-

---

7. Chateaubriand, *Mémoires d'outre-tombe*, op. cit., bk. V, chap. 15, p. 185.
8. Maugras, *Delphine de Sabran*, op. cit., p. 109.
9. Ibid., p. 108.

sion. He had to persuade the duke of Brunswick, commander-in-chief of the Prussian Army, to refuse command of the coalition against France. He arrived too late, Brunswick having already accepted, but an unforeseen incident obliged him to stay on and go to Berlin. At the beginning of 1792, France's international position was not at all clear. According to the Constitution of 1791, the king ruled, but having suffered the humiliation of the flight to Varennes, he was isolated, captive, unhappy and without authority. His brothers and a considerable number of emigré aristocrats were clamouring for war, thus putting all their hopes in a military intervention to reestablish the kingdom. The king's position was even more complicated by his patriotism, which revolted against the idea of a foreign invasion of France; besides, he realised full well that the Allies couldn't remain in the kingdom indefinitely and that as soon as they left, the rebellion would reassert itself. So at the beginning of 1792, France's ambassadors were still trying to maintain the peace, or at least to weaken the unity of the Allies. This put them in open opposition to the emigrés.

Therefore, when the comte de Ségur arrived in Berlin to try to persuade Frederick-William of Prussia to leave the coalition, he was violently attacked by his compatriots who had taken refuge at the court, and had so poisoned the king's mind that he refused to speak to him. Ségur asked to be recalled to Paris and suggested that Custine, who was in Brunswick, be sent to Berlin to act as ambassador.

He felt that the presence of Mme de Sabran and her popularity with the king would make the young man's position easier. In addition to unusual diplomatic skills, solid support was needed for anyone to keep afloat in the troubled waters of the court. The confusion is exemplified by the fact that, to add weight to his mission, Paris gave Custine the title of minister, but the Prussian government refused to recognise him as more than a *chargé d'affaires*. Although Custine, too, failed in his efforts for peace, he stayed more than six months in Berlin, kept there as a hostage by the Prussians who were worried about the safety of their ministers in France.

Meanwhile, the situation in Paris had worsened. The regime was collapsing. In 1792 it would have been obvious to anyone that in the eyes of the revolutionary government aristocratic origins constituted an unforgivable stain. Nevertheless, despite being in favour of the reforms and loyal to the new government, the Custines, the Birons and the Beauharnais exposed themselves to appalling risks by virtue of their names alone. The venerable jurist Malesherbes was aware of it by 1790: "If I were younger," he advised Chateaubriand, "I would spare myself the spectacle of so many crimes, such cowardice and such folly."[10] Chateaubriand emigrated, but Custine, despite the attention he should have paid to Malesherbes, never understood the absurdity of applying his own code of honour in a revolutionary

10. Chateaubriand, *Mémoires d'outre-tombe*, op. cit., bk. V, chap. 15, p. 188.

situation. Deaf to the reproaches of Mme de Sabran and the chevalier, embarrassed by Delphine's refusal to join him in Prussia with
the children and reassured by his father's position as Commander of
the Army of the Rhine, Armand de Custine announced: "I have
been sent here by this government; it is my duty to return and give
an account of my mission to those who charged me with it; I will do
my duty."[11] He reached Paris on 22 June 1792.

Two days earlier the people had overrun the Tuileries, destroying
anything which stood in their way. Louis XVI had donned a red cap.
The monarchy had teetered. This public catastrophe was echoed by
private misfortune. After a great deal of indecision, Delphine decided to have her children inoculated against smallpox, a precaution
already available for several years, the illness being a much greater
risk. Astolphe, the younger child, survived without problems but his
older brother, the vigorous little boy who so loved the grenadiers,
was inexplicably carried away within a week. Sorrow did nothing to
unite the grieving parents, but Delphine became aware of the generally disastrous situation. The Commune was declared on the night
of 9–10 August 1792; the Tuileries was invaded again on 10 August,
the Swiss Guard wiped out and the monarchy suspended; in September, political prisoners were massacred. "The gates of Paris are
closed," Delphine wrote at the time to her brother, "and I do not

11. Maugras, *Delphine de Sabran*, op. cit., p. 129.

know when it will be possible to leave, we are living in terrible times."[12]

At last, aware of the threat that hung over them, Delphine and Armand realised that they must seek protection; so at the invitation of M. de Malesherbes who was gathering his children, grandchildren and great-grandchildren around him, they left with Astolphe on 15 September to take refuge with Malesherbes near Orléans. Events were escalating: on 20 September came Valmy, the first big revolutionary victory; two days later the Republic was proclaimed, after which the king was formally charged with crimes that included treason. Armand, too impatient and too anxious to do nothing, joined his father and the army. Meanwhile M. de Malesherbes, taking a risk of which he was perfectly aware, asked for the honour of defending the king at his trial. Thus he came back to Paris in December 1792 accompanied by his family, Delphine and Astolphe.

The charming Delphine was little influenced by her long stay with so thoughtful a man. She resumed her correspondence with Elzéar but naturally did not write in detail about the lives and opinions of friends who had remained in Paris; to do so would have been criminally imprudent; nevertheless, the catalogue of her lovers is surprising. She could think of nothing but love, the young woman's energy in this field being admirable: "One person alone consoles me

12. Ibid., p. 134.

. . . he is a new admirer . . . I think I told you that I made his acquaintance at the time of the troubles on 10 August; he is my husband's friend, M. de Grouchy, . . . He is simplicity itself, virtue and sincerity personified . . . he is deeply in love with your poor sister . . . I am sure that you would like him a good deal, he is simple and good. But your poor sister is too bad to be attached to these two qualities alone. An amiable, seducing coxcomb has more power over her . . . It is horrible, I know, but with you, I do not fear to speak openly."[13]

Armand de Custine was meanwhile still serving with the revolutionary army. At his father's request he had come back to Paris to explain his plan of campaign to the Committee of General Defense and was living with his wife but "although quite tender towards one another . . . were more disposed to live as brother and sister than husband and wife," Delphine wrote to Elzéar. The establishment of a revolutionary Tribunal worried Armand sufficiently for him to insist on his wife leaving Paris with Astolphe, to go first to her friend Mme de La Rochefoucauld at Mello and then to stay with her sister-in-law, Mme de Dreux-Brézé at Les Andelys. There she was bored of course, and at the end of a month, unable to stand it any longer, she escaped to Le Havre on the pretext of seeing the sea. She left alone, with her maid, but without Astolphe. There was no question of taking him to play on the beach since his mother was really going to join "le Sigisbée," otherwise known as M. de Grouchy. It was an

13. Ibid., p. 151.

exquisite trip: "I have been here for six days now . . . I can easily count them as among the happiest since we were separated. His love is tender and respectful, he is good and sensitive . . . he was touched by my journey: in fact he had good reason to be for it was a high-spirited folly."[14]

It was to be the last.

On returning to the Dreux-Brézés at Les Andelys, she learned of her father-in-law's arrest on 22 July 1793. She did not hesitate. She left Astolphe and her maid, Nanette, with her prudent sister-in-law who, not wishing to attract the attention of the revolutionary Tribunal, remained in Normandy, and returned to Paris to be with her husband and the general. "She had difficulty leaving her son, for she was a true mother," Astolphe was to write later, "but misfortune always took first place in her large heart."[15] Enter the heroine. She was twenty-two years old.

Later Astolphe was to point out that his mother's family had "quarrelled several years earlier [with the general] because of the opinions he had expressed since the beginning of the Revolution."[16] Mme de Sabran, who was the first of her family to predict the excesses of the Revolution, certainly had scant respect for the general's political

14. Ibid., p. 159.
15. Astolphe de Custine, *La Russie en 1839*, 2 vols. (Solin, 1990), I, p. 46.
16. Ibid., I, p. 37.

ability; added to that, he had not adhered scrupulously to the financial agreements undertaken at the time of his son's marriage and, above all, she had not forgotten the difficulties he had caused over the engagement. But, as we have seen, Delphine was not in the least concerned with politics and, despite her distant relationship with her husband, she happily received the general in the rue de Bourbon whenever he returned from the army. The general was a bold man and sincerely attached to the principles of the Revolution, always outspoken and never hesitating to censure either ministries or ministers. When Bouchotte, the Minister for War, made a remark he regarded as inept, he replied, "The time is no longer when generals regard ministers, however imbecile, as gods. I have never been one of those men without character. A republican before the Republic, every time I have encountered these ministerial idols, I have impressed them by my scorn."[17] He would have had to be invincible indeed, not to fear the vengeance of the Committee men. Unfortunately for Custine, after the victories of 1792, he suffered a series of defeats. By the unanimous wishes of the troops he was nominated Commander-in-Chief of the Army of the North, leaving General de Beauharnais in command of the Army of the Rhine, but he was unable to redress a catastrophic situation. The besieged Condé surrendered on 12 July 1793 and three days later the Committee of Pub-

17. Maugras, *Delphine de Sabran*, op. cit., p. 164.

lic Safety summoned Custine to Paris. He was arrested before the end of the week and taken to the Conciergerie on 28 July.

Disgusted by such injustice, and clearly understanding nothing of the mechanics of revolutionary government, his son had printed and posted all over Paris a defense of General de Custine's military and political actions. The authorities reacted instantly: he was arrested and locked up in La Force. So Delphine was left to face the agony of the trial on her own, a trial which aroused considerable emotion in Paris.

The general, nicknamed *Moustache* by the public, was a popular man. Only a few days before his arrest, he was still being cheered on appearing at the Palais-Royal. His wit, repartee and courage were so admired that many members of the public offered their assistance in defending him; but the person who attracted the most attention was a young blonde woman with long hair who sat at the feet of the accused. So lovely was she that, seduced by Mme de Custine, the judges were said to have dragged the proceedings out for the pleasure of being able to continue to admire her.

To appreciate the attention Delphine attracted, it is important to realise the extent of the courage needed for such devotion as hers. Her sister-in-law, Adelaide de Dreux-Brézé, always refused to join her. "She was persuaded by religious devotion," Delphine declared, "that she owed more to her husband and her child (for she is pregnant) than to her father, which meant that throughout the whole unhappy affair, and despite the awful turn of events, despite my entreating her to come at least to embrace her unfortunate father, nothing could decide her; she did not believe she could expose herself to fear, for it would not have been to danger."[18]

Delphine, however, arrived at the Palais de Justice in a hackney cab with a friend of her husband's, Guy de Chaumont-Quitry, the only one to support her. He did not go in but stayed and waited for her in the street. In her letters to her brother she nicknamed him "Misfortune's friend," "a friend who is a little in love, but we don't mention that."[19] Dressed as a man of the people in a *carmagnole*— a narrow coat with several rows of buttons, made fashionable by the delegates from Marseilles—and with his hair cut short like the Emperor Titus, he hoped not to draw attention to himself. But she had to pass through the crowd standing in front of the Palace, a terrifying obstacle according to the *Mémoires* of the comte de Beugnot: "The stairs of the Palace were crowded with women who seemed to be sitting in an amphitheatre awaiting a favourite spectacle. As I descended from the carriage, the whole amphitheatre rose to its feet and let out a long cry of joy. The clapping of hands, the stamping of feet, convulsive bursts of laughter all expressed the ferocious delight of these cannibals at the arrival of a new prey. The short way I had

18. Ibid., p. 181.
19. Ibid., p. 185.

to go on foot was still long enough for me to receive a shower of filth thrown at me from every side and, from my reception on arrival, I was able to assess what awaited me on my departure."[20] The travails Delphine had to undergo each day are described in a contemporary journal: "The day before yesterday you could read in the *Gazette française* of 21 August 1793 that this woman, interesting by virtue of her sensibility and filial piety, left the Palais de Justice surrounded by a crowd; she had a smile on her lips; they thought she was laughing. Some women, untouched by the situation, began to shout: 'She's laughing, but she won't be laughing long. She's Custine's daughter: her father will soon be playing hot cockles.'"[21]

Later she was to tell her son about the worst incident of that time, to which he referred nearly fifty years after it happened in the first chapter of his book about Russia. "Shy and untamed as a hind, [my mother] had instinctively, all her life, an unreasonable fear of crowds..." After one of the last of the Tribunal's sittings, she stopped, trembling, at the top of the perron and looked down "this long, quite narrow flight of steps entirely overrun by the crushed ranks of an angry populace, moved by rage and gorged with blood, too experienced already and too used to acquit its own conscience of

20. Extracts from *Mémoires du comte Beugnot* in *Revue française*, October 1838, pp. 28–34.

21. Maugras, *Delphine de Sabran*, op. cit., p. 170.

detestable deeds, for it to recoil before one more murder ... My mother believed herself to be lost: 'If I falter, if I fall like Mme de Lamballe, that will be the end of me,' she thought to herself as the angry crowd grew ever more dense around her path: 'It's the Custine woman! The traitor's daughter-in-law!' they shouted on every side ... How could she proceed? How cross this infernal multitude? Some stood with swords drawn in front of her, others, without coats, their shirt sleeves rolled up, were already pushing the women aside—preliminary indications of an execution; the danger was increasing; she told me that she was biting her hands and tongue until they bled in the hope of preventing herself from blanching in anguish. At last, on looking around, she noticed the most hideous fishwife ... with a baby in arms. 'What a pretty child you have there,' she said with a sudden flash of inspiration. 'Take him,' the mother replied, 'and give him back at the bottom of the steps.' "[22] Mme de Custine took the child, embraced it and peacefully descended the steps of the perron amidst the astounded populace; she crossed the Palace courtyard and went towards the square without being touched or even insulted. She reached the gate, returned the child to the woman who had lent him, and fled.

The next day, quite unmoved, she returned to her accustomed place. On 28 August, after a session lasting twelve hours, the general

22. *La Russie*, op. cit., I, p. 41.

was found guilty of high treason and condemned to death. His daughter-in-law came to see him for the last time that evening. She was surprised to find him in a lighter cell. "They have moved me," he explained, "to make room for the queen since my first lodging was the worst in the prison."[23] In the small hours he made his confession, wrote to his son, refused to read the last letter Delphine had sent for fear of upsetting himself, was led to the door behind which they cut the prisoners' hair (which was thrown, according to colour, into large wicker baskets to be sold to the Parisian wig-makers), and climbed onto the tumbril. "To the gallows, to the gallows," snarled the crowd. "We're going, we're going," he replied.

Delphine was no ordinary woman. The timid, frivolous person she acknowledged herself to be developed an intelligent boldness when confronted by real danger. Although she behaved perfectly, taking the initiative in soliciting help from members of the Committees or the Tribunal and braving humiliation, and while she missed her little boy whose presence would have cheered her, her old preoccupations still concerned her, and the letters she exchanged with her brother at the time, "thanks to a beneficent being," are fired by both courage and self-love: "Our letters are like those of two tender lovers; do you know that it has sometimes occurred to me to regret that I cannot love you in that fashion! We suited each

23. Maugras, *Delphine de Sabran*, op. cit., p. 177.

other so well . . . at least you suited me . . . My God! What folly! I am telling you fairy tales!"[24] Did she dream of a relationship with Elzéar like that of their holy ancestors, dispensing, nevertheless, with the vow of chastity? But as Elzéar was far away—and in any case little interested in amorous adventures—she consoled herself "by living the most constant, the most tender and the most interesting romance" with "le Sigisbée," and by making new conquests "since they rain in from every side."[25] But she never allowed a romantic encounter to interfere with visiting hours at La Force where her husband was incarcerated.

La Force had been used as a prison since 1780. It was a debtors jail. La Petite-Force, where women were kept, looked out on the rue Pavée, whereas the men's wing, known as La Grande-Force, had its entrance in the rue du Roi-de-Sicile. The front of the prison could be seen from the rue Saint-Antoine, down the end of a stinking blind alley lined with miserable hovels. Once across the threshold, there were two more wicket-gates—three-foot openings made in larger doors—through which to go, bent double for safety of one's head, before reaching the inner courtyard. Delphine arrived in a hackney cab with, like most visitors, some letters hidden in the fold of a handkerchief or the hem of a cravat, her pockets filled with a few

24. Maugras, *Delphine de Sabran*, op. cit., p. 188.
25. Ibid., p. 191.

sweets, and spent long hours with Armand in the large garden used by the prisoners. His wife's loyalty caused him to "fall in love as he had never done before but [she] had only the tenderest friendship for him, nothing more."[26]

Convinced that he would inevitably be condemned to death, she concentrated all her efforts on planning his escape: "To be arrested was to be condemned; now one was only judged for the sake of form."[27]

Since the death of the general, Delphine went out in full mourning. "She always wore a black hat and a black veil although such a custom was dangerous in the street, for in these disastrous times the advertisement of grief did not go unpunished."[28] With a combination of charm and generosity, she managed to win over the gatekeeper's daughter who promised to help. The plan involved disguising Armand, who was "delicate [with] enough youth still, and a pretty enough face to be dressed as a woman without attracting attention," in his wife's mourning clothes whilst she should wear Louise's things and Louise should escape by another door. But, on the eve of the chosen day, the Convention declared that anyone helping a political prisoner to escape did so on pain of death and Armand had the newspaper in which this law was published under his

26. Ibid., p. 196.
27. *La Russie*, op cit., I, p. 42.
28. Ibid.

nose. When Delphine arrived he flatly refused to attempt to escape for it would have put both his wife and the girl in danger. Two days later she came back to say good-bye. He had been condemned to death. He was twenty-five years old.

There is an account of this last visit in their son's book. So precise and moving an account that it evokes only too powerfully the tragic nostalgia of the child, the adolescent and the man as he turned these memories, which were not his, over and over in his mind.

My mother approached my father calmly, embraced him in silence and for three hours sat beside him. Throughout this time not one reproach was voiced. Death was there. The perhaps too generous sentiment which had brought about this catastrophe was forgiven, no regret was expressed: the unfortunate man needed all his strength to crown his sacrifice. Few words were exchanged between the condemned man and his wife; my name was pronounced several times and this name broke their hearts . . . My father asked for mercy . . . my mother spoke no more of me.

In heroic times, death was a spectacle where the victim staked his honour on not bending before his executioners; in the heart of my father, so young, so handsome, so full of soul, of spirit and not long since so happy, my poor mother respected the need to preserve all his courage for the next day; this last test of a noble character had become his first duty even in the eyes of a naturally timid wife. So true it is that the sublime is always within reach of sincere souls! Midnight drew near; fearing she might feel unwell, she was going to rise and withdraw.

The condemned man had received her in a hall which served as an entrance to several of the prison bedrooms. This communal room was quite big, low and dark; they were both seated by a table on which a candle burned; there were windows one side of the room through which could be seen the figures of the guards.

All at once they heard the opening of a small door that they had not noticed until then; a man came through it with a dark lantern in his hand: this man, so strangely attired, was a prisoner on his way to visit another. He was dressed in a little gown, or rather a kind of under-waistcoat, a little long, and edged with swanskin, even the name of which was ridiculous; white drawers, stockings and a large cotton bonnet, its point adorned by an enormous flame-coloured bow, completed his outfit: he advanced across the room slowly, with small steps, sliding the way Louis XV's courtiers slid, without picking up their feet as they crossed the gallery at Versailles.

On drawing near to the couple, this figure looked at them for a moment without saying a word and continued on its path; they noticed then that the old man was wearing rouge.

This apparition, watched in silence by the two young people, surprised them in the midst of their despair; without dreaming that the rouge had not been put there to paint a withered face, but that it might be meant to prevent a brave man from blanching on tomorrow's scaffold, they both broke out in a terrible burst of *laughter; for a moment nervous tension triumphed over the soul's anguish.*

The effort they had long been making to hide their thoughts had irritated the fibres of their brains; a sense of the ridiculous found them defenseless and took them by surprise. It was doubtless the only emotion for which they had not been prepared; thus, despite their efforts, or rather because of their efforts to remain calm, they gave way to uncontrolled laughter which soon degenerated into terrifying spasms. The guards, whose revolutionary experience had enlightened them on the phenomenon of sardonic laughter, took pity on my mother . . . These men came into the room and took my mother away whilst she was suffering from a fit of nerves that manifested itself in ever recurring bouts of laughter, whilst my father remained alone, overcome by the same convulsions.[29]

The next day, undaunted, he went to his death.

29. Ibid., I, pp. 46 ff.

3

The Terror

So Delphine found herself completely isolated in a town para-lysed by terror, where it was no longer safe even to express pity for the victims. One word of commiseration as the tumbril passed was enough to attract attention or to be arrested. The law on suspects made every excess permissible. You couldn't write to your family, as smugglers would no longer take letters abroad. In these fearful, silent times the only way of hearing the daily news was one forbidden to single women, since it meant going into a theatre (many new ones had sprung up since the Legislative Assembly had abolished the restrictions of the Ancien Régime), "sitting in the stalls where a lot of old habitués were gathered, all naturally communicative among themselves and who indicated to each other the people in front of whom it was safe to talk."[1]

Occasionally Delphine turned to Mme de Staël who, thanks to her husband's position as Swedish ambassador, was able to help. "People hurried to see her by night to beg her to convey to absent friends news of those who were dear to them, and also to stipulate absolute silence on their part. For every letter from the emigrés carried death with it."[2] In any case, Mme de Staël took no letters with her when she went to Switzerland; with her prodigious memory she could remember all her friends' and acquaintances' news by heart.

Delphine was especially alone by virtue of the fact that, because of her father-in-law's and her husband's opinions which she had adopted, the circles in which she used to move had rejected her. The "pure aristocrats" hated the reformers' party so much that they refused the widow Custine "the consolation of weeping together."[3] General de Custine had served the State after the fall of the monarchy, after Louis XVI's execution. According to his old friends he was guillotined on the false pretext of betraying the Republic; in fact there had been a betrayal, but it was a betrayal of the Ancien Régime. His son, who, in April 1792, had written to Condorcet

1. Jean Tulard, *Joseph Fiévée, conseiller secret de Napoléon* (Fayard, 1985), p. 35.
2. Norvins, op. cit., II, p. 83.
3. *La Russie*, op. cit., I, p. 51.

to complain of the behaviour of a king "habitually influenced by priests, by women (of what a kind) and by inferiors,"[4] was likewise barely mourned by the aristocracy.

So Delphine, in her misfortune, was unable to count on the few old friends still in hiding in Paris. She sent for Astolphe, whom her sister-in-law did not want to keep any longer, and, whether through fecklessness or courage, didn't move, but remained in her second-floor apartment in the rue de Bourbon, at number 509. (At the time houses were numbered by district as they still are in Venice, the present system being introduced by Napoleon.) The name of the street was soon changed in honour of the town of Lille. Delphine was running out of funds and worried about having to live off her capital. The Custines' assets had been confiscated, in addition to which the peasants were bringing a case against them to claim an estate near Sarrebourg with a château and six farms. Meanwhile, besides Nanette, the household consisted of a nursemaid, a lady's maid, a valet, a cook and his wife. Although abroad people imagined Parisians "covered in blood, dressed in rags with all the trappings of poverty,"[5] in fact life went on: the cafés were overflowing, the women well dressed and Mme Broquin still sold "her flesh-

4. Collection Lovenjoul, D867, Bibliothèque de l'Institut.

5. Sébastien Mercier in *Le Nouveau Paris*, quoted by Jean Robiquet, *La Vie quotidienne au temps de la Révolution* (Hachette, 1938), p. 97.

coloured ointment for dying red or white hair chestnut or black at one sitting."[6] But Delphine had been too much in evidence, too compromised at the time of her father-in-law's trial and her husband's, not to be suspect; in fact, the police of the Grenelle ward had her apartment searched and put her under house arrest. The cobbler at the corner was appointed guard and caretaker. Then she decided to escape and began to make an elaborate plan.

The first requirement for such a plan was as rare as it was indispensable: a friend. Despite the difficulties of the times, Delphine found one with disconcerting ease. The friend was called Bertrand; she had met him on her visits to La Force where he had shared a cell with Armand. Arrested without reason, he was likewise inexplicably and fortuitously released, whereupon he immediately went to call on the beautiful Mme de Custine with whom he had fallen deeply in love. She took him into her confidence: it would be impossible for her to wait patiently to be arrested. She had to leave France, but how could she do it without the necessary passport? Bertrand had connections and acquired papers for her in the name of a lace merchant who went to Brussels on business. But what about Astolphe? Delphine decided to entrust him to Nanette whose absolute loyalty had caused problems on her return to Paris. She had made so bold as to join the crowd during the general's trial and to defend him fiercely with little regard for her own danger: "He's worth more than you

6. *Moniteur,* 15 August 1792, quoted by Robiquet, p. 97.

. . . if he had wanted he would have prevented your miserable Revolution, and now you would be licking his feet instead of insulting him, you cowards,"[7] she shouted to the violent opposition, before running away as fast as her legs could carry her.

Once, however, she was nearly caught. On crossing the place du Carrousel with little Astolphe, she stopped in front of the revolutionary altar erected in Marat's honour to look at the kneeling women making the sign of the cross and paying homage to the new saint. Infuriated by what she saw, Nanette turned on one of the new faithful and hurled insults at her. The pious harpy replied by accusing her of sacrilege, so from words they came to blows. A crowd gathered around the fighting women; there was no doubt which side it took. Before long Nanette was threatened from all around by calls for her death: "Hang the aristocrat from the street lamp!" She was already being pulled by the hair towards the lamp in what was then called the rue Nicaise. One woman had snatched away little Astolphe whom Nanette had been holding tightly to her, when a man, seemingly even angrier than the others, cut through the crowd and momentarily pushed the relentless aggressors away from their victim. "Pretending to pick something up off the ground, he whispered in her ear: 'You are mad, you are mad, listen to me carefully or you will be truly lost . . . fear nothing for your child, I will bring him to you, but act the imbecile, or you are dead!' So Nanette began to sing

7. *La Russie*, op. cit., I, p. 56.

and to pull all kinds of faces. 'She's a lunatic,' someone said, and other voices immediately replied, 'She's mad, she's mad, you can see she is. Let her go!' Taking advantage of the means of escape offered her, she ran off, dancing, crossed the Pont Royal, stopped at the entrance of the rue du Bac and there, as she received the child from the arms of her liberator, began to feel ill.'"[8] After this incident Nanette became more discreet and Delphine decided to trust her. In any case, she had no choice.

So Nanette was to leave with the child; since she spoke German better than French, she would pass for an Alsatian peasant. She was to take the stage to Strasbourg and then find her way to Westphalia, there to rejoin Delphine. They would go on to Berlin where Mme de Sabran would meet them. As it was out of the question to let the other servants into the secret, Delphine was unable to prepare any luggage. She entrusted to Bertrand who came to dine every evening little parcels of linen, of clothes and shoes that she felt she could not do without.

The departure date was fixed for 2 ventôse, or 20 February 1794. Bertrand was to wait for Delphine at nine o'clock in the evening at the gate of the Maison-Blanche. Nanette, carrying Astolphe hidden in a shawl, left after nightfall at the time when the caretaker-guard was eating his meal and made her way to the office where the coaches left for Alsace. Modestly dressed, Delphine waited her turn.

8. Ibid.

She intended to creep out through the carriage entrance, but had bought a rope ladder to tie to her sitting-room window to prove that she had escaped without her servants' knowledge, thus protecting them from suspicion.

Sitting on her large sofa in her drawing-room, she was shredding papers. "In the box and the drawers that she was busy emptying, there was enough to have her guillotined within twenty-four hours, and fifty people with her."[9] She threw the most dangerous letters in the fireplace and those she thought she could keep she put away in a chest. The Sabrans—Delphine and Elzéar as much as their mother—attached great importance to their letters and, as far as possible, were never separated from them. Suddenly she heard a noise at the door that opened from the dining-room into the sitting-room. "I have been denounced," she said to herself, "they have come to arrest me," and without hesitation, realising that it was too late to burn the mass of papers surrounding her, she picked them up in armfuls from the table, the sofa, the box and threw them with the casket untidily under the sofa, the legs of which were luckily quite high and covered by a valance that reached to the floor.

Having completed this task with the "speed of fear," she rose with her usual good manners to welcome the people she saw coming into the room. Men from the ward accompanied by members of the Committee of Public Safety had come to arrest her.

9. Ibid., I, p. 53.

*These figures, as horrible as they were ridiculous, surrounded
her in a moment: swords and guns flashed all around her; she
could think only of her papers which she finished pushing with
her foot under the sofa, in front of which she was still standing.*

"You are arrested," the President of the ward told her.

She remained silent.

*"You are arrested because you have been denounced as an
emigrée by intention."*

*"It is true," my mother said, on seeing that the president was
already holding her portfolio and her false passport which had
just been taken from her pocket; for the first thing the members
of the Committee had done was to search her. "It is true, I wished
to leave . . ."*

*"Which prison would you like to be taken to?" a member of
the Committee asked. "You are free to choose."*

"It doesn't matter."

"Come along then."

*But before leaving the apartment, they searched her again;
they opened cupboards, drawers, desks, they turned the bedroom
upside down, but no one thought to look under the sofa! At last
she left and climbed into a cab with three armed men.*[10]

She had been betrayed by her maid who had come across the little
parcels her mistress had been preparing for several days, and in-

---

10. Ibid. Anatole France was so struck by what happened that he recounted the
whole incident in *L'Etui de Nacre*.

formed the ward. Meanwhile, Bertrand was waiting at the gate. When Delphine didn't come, he was sure she had been arrested. Leaving one of his brothers at the rendez-vous, just in case, he rushed to the stage-coach office to prevent Nanette from leaving. He arrived just in time. Nanette and the child returned to the rue Bourbon. Delphine had disappeared, like the servants who had gone off with the linen and the silver. All the doors in the apartment were sealed except for the door to the kitchen where Nanette installed herself with the child. "The house was empty, unfurnished; it was as though there had been a fire: a thunderbolt."[11]

To understand the irony of the question put to Delphine about her place of detention, it has to be appreciated that there was no more room in any prison in Paris. It was not unusual for a cab carrying suspects to go from prison to prison before finding a clerk willing to accept them. Delphine was at first shut up in Sainte-Pélagie and then sent to Les Carmes. There she found herself amongst her own kind and felt a certain relief, if only because she could once again say what she thought and say it in the form to which she was accustomed. Conventional good manners, along with the polite form of *vous*, forbidden by the Revolution, were current in prison. In his *Mémoires*, the chancellor Pasquier describes how soothed he felt when taken to the same prison as M. de Malesherbes, the whole Ro-

11. Ibid., I, p. 55.

sambo family and a great many of his friends. Such was his sense of relief that M. Pasquier sent a letter to his son in which he "advised him to reflect on his situation, to see if the life he was leading, and which he knew from experience, was not a hundred times worse than his own; then imagining a situation in which I might take a stand that would lead to my arrest, he acquainted me with an arrangement he had made with the prison caretaker whereby the room he occupied would be kept for him alone for several more days so that we might lodge together."[12]

Behind the bolted doors people found themselves in society, surrounded by relations and friends, able to see each other without constraint and to talk freely among themselves. Besides, before the great judicial massacres, there appeared to be safety in numbers. There were so many detainees that the danger for any individual seemed quite remote. It felt safer in prison than outside, where every knock on the door might herald commissioners from the revolutionary Committee and arrest.

By the time Delphine went to prison, the guillotine presented a far greater threat, but the warmth of rediscovered, open friendship was all the more comforting. She shared a paid room with eighteen other people, including two old couples, for men were occasionally allowed to remain with their wives.[13] If one had what in prison slang

---

12. *Mémoires du chancelier Pasquier*, 6 vols. (Plon, 1893), I, pp. 92–93.
13. Dauban, *Les Prisons de Paris sous la Révolution* (Plon, 1870).

were known as *sonnantes*, gold coins, one could avoid the straw of a dungeon floor and sleep in a bed, albeit a trestle bed without curtains, on a mattress like a fluffed omelette, but still a single bed, standing next to others of its kind. It cost 27 *francs*, 12 *sous* for the first month and a little less for succeeding months. But the money had to be paid a month in advance, so at the height of the Terror a bed was a good investment since one person rarely occupied it for a whole month. Delphine, Joséphine de Beauharnais, who was arrested a few weeks later, Mme de Lameth and an English woman of good society, who shared their views on cleanliness, drew their beds together. "There was a jailer called Roblâtre," according to the *Mémoires* of Mme de Lameth's daughter. "He was not fierce; he loved the juice of the vine, thanks to which he sometimes agreed to take me to my mother where I spent a part of the day . . . a quantity of letters and papers would be carefully concealed in my corset for these poor women were not allowed them. They took care to ask me at the door whether I was bringing in anything suspect and I affirmed that I was not."[14]

It was also possible to have what one needed brought from home. Thus Nanette sent a pillow, some sheets, bedcovers, a change of clothing and reassurances about Astolphe. She was camping with the small boy in the kitchen, the only room in the house which

14. Olivier Blanc, *La Dernière Lettre, prisons et condamnés de la Révolution 1793–1794* (Hachette, 1986), p. 76; extract from Mme de Nicolaï, *Mercure de France*, 15 March 1939, p. 619, and Souvenirs, *Nouvelle Revue*, 1894, p. 475.

wasn't sealed, living at first off the little money which had been put aside for the journey and then from articles of clothing which she sold one by one at a time when, despite the introduction of ration cards for bread and then meat, despite vegetables being planted in both public and private gardens, the famine was really beginning to be felt. In the town where an ox jaw cost 10 *sous* a pound, a siege mentality was building up.

Delphine adapted herself immediately to life in Les Carmes, characterised as it was by the prisoners' casual courage—a courage that sometimes manifested itself with such daring in both men and women that it verged on bravura and on a total disdain for both death and the executioners. Countless anecdotes tell of the impassivity of the condemned and of the elegance with which the prisoners said good-bye when summoned to the tumbril. The men often played a game called prisoners' base; if some unfortunate fellow was in the middle of a game, he said a quick good-bye to his companions, and the game went on. When the handsome Biron's hour came, he asked only for permission to finish the oysters he had ordered for his last meal.

Contemptuous frivolity took the place of high morality or of the Christian precepts lacking in so many. "Our national failing, levity, at this moment became a virtue."[15] The bravery of those persecuted

---

15. Chateaubriand, quoted in Baldensperger, *Le Mouvement des idées dans l'émigration française, 1789–1815* (Plon, 1824).

accorded with their fierce and absolute determination to continue to live by their usual standards: the importance of dress and of good form remained paramount. The women changed, or at least put a ribbon in their hair, for the evening meal which they ate with the men. The food was not necessarily bad.

Provisions were brought in from outside, either from private houses or by a caterer. One prisoner specified to his wife, Citizeness Boileau of the rue Révolutionnaire, formerly rue Saint-Louis, that he wanted ". . . a good lettuce salad seasoned, or rather the wherewithal to make it; we have some terrines, but try to see it is fresh and plentiful . . ." One wife sent her husband "a pigeon, some red currants, some apricots, a bottle of wine; yet another sent a pigeon, an artichoke, a bottle of wine and a handkerchief."[16] Legs of lamb were hung in the windows to keep them fresh before being carved up and cooked on small portable stoves installed in the passages. One prisoner, the poet Roucher, was given permission for his five-year-old son to join him.

To allow for conversation between the sexes in prisons where men and women lived separately, dinner was served on summer evenings in the courtyard—provisions were always shared—with the tables set on either side of the dividing grille; rhymes and verses were made up, just as they would have been in a *salon*. And love blossomed within the walls. In Les Carmes, for instance, men and

16. Blanc, op. cit., p. 71.

women could meet as they pleased in the large garden; a discreet cell mate and a screen allowed for a few moments of intimacy. Delphine perfectly exemplified this prison culture by showing herself to be totally unmoved in the face of danger and by abandoning herself openly to passion.

"A unique set of historical circumstances were needed for the formation of a woman such as my mother; the combination of greatness of soul and of sociability produced in her by the elegance and good taste of conversations heard in her mother's, or in Mme de Polignac's salon, and by the supernatural virtues acquired, by anyone with a heart, on the steps of Robespierre's scaffold, will never be found again. All the charm of the French spirit from the good times, all the sublimity of characters from antiquity were united in my mother."[17] The same Delphine who prevented herself from sleeping "so long as she did not feel strong enough to sacrifice her life,"[18] so as not to risk showing signs of weakness were she ever woken with a start to be led to the Conciergerie, which meant death—that same Delphine allowed herself to be carried away by love for Alexandre de Beauharnais.

She had met him with her friend, Mme de La Rochefoucauld, and she noticed him at Les Carmes where they arrived at the same time in March 1794. The freedom which seems to have been enjoyed in-

17. *La Russie*, op. cit., I, p. 57.
18. Ibid., I, p. 57.

side the prisons is hardly surprising if one considers how inadequate they soon became to house the thousands of suspects arrested. In 1794 there were more than fifty detention centres used by the government: convents, barracks, palaces like the Luxembourg and the Quatre-Nations (which today houses the Mazarine library and the Institut) into which were crammed two thousand people; private houses too, and nursing homes were made into rudimentary prisons. In convents, like Port-Royal whose name had been changed to Port-Libre, Les Carmes or L'Abbaye, the cells could be locked from the inside but not from the outside. The prisoners were quite able to organise their leisure as they pleased. At Port-Libre they started a string quartet. "Nothing was less like a prison than that house; there were no bars, no bolts, the doors were closed by a simple latch only. There was good society, excellent company and women were respected."[19] The guards were hardly professional and often the job of guard would be given to the former gate-keeper. The one at L'Abbaye was so sympathetic to the prisoners that his wife was the subject of flattering rhymes.[20] Visitors could easily slip inside without being searched, and yet there were very few escapes from revolutionary prisons, partly for the sake of accomplices who if discovered would be condemned to death, but mainly because, paradoxically, people often thought they were safer inside than out.

19. Blanc, op. cit., p. 39.
20. Ibid., p. 37.

Beauharnais, who, like Custine, had fought in the American War of Independence with Rochambeau, and who shared his advanced ideas, had replaced Custine in command of the Army of the Rhine. He resigned in 1793 and retired to the country where he was unable to escape arrest. At Les Carmes he found Delphine, dazzling in her widow's weeds, with her Greuze complexion and her Greek profile;[21] a Delphine who had lost none of her charm or her psychological subtlety and who confided in Alexandre her excessive love of her brother, whilst yielding willingly to his desire. A month later, on 21 April 1794, Easter Day, it was Joséphine de Beauharnais's turn to be arrested. Thus she shared a cell with Delphine and they performed "the services of lady's maid"[22] for each other in the yard where they washed and dressed.[23] Since there had been no intimacy with her husband for many years, she wasn't worried by the lovely Delphine's emotions and when not busy telling her fortune with cards, or crying—to her companions' indignation, the timorous Joséphine wept openly—she had her beautiful eyes turned on General Hoche to whom she wrote notes of such passion that she tried to get them back when she married Bonaparte in 1796.

At the beginning of Thermidor,* conditions in the prisons wors-

---

*The month that was going to be marked by Robespierre's execution and the easing of the Terror, July 1794.

21. *La Russie*, op. cit., I, p. 58.

22. Ibid., I, p. 57.

23. Dauban, op. cit., p. 185.

ened. Executions multiplied. The law of 22 prairal allowed the accused to be condemned without interrogation, without witnesses, on simple moral grounds. The whole of M. de Malesherbes's family, including his granddaughter who had married Chateaubriand's older brother, was guillotined at this time. The prisoners knew exactly what was happening because the jailers left around copies of *Le Moniteur*, the back page of which carried a list of the previous evening's executions. In May 1794, the guillotine had been removed from the Place de la Révolution—the future Place de la Concorde. The blood no longer drained and the district was becoming infected. Those who still had the nerve to joke described a certain shade of red blood as Parisian mud. By now the tumbrils passing in the narrow streets gave rise to little enthusiasm from the residents. The scaffold was at first moved to the Champs-Elysées, and then in June to a more working-class district, the Place Antoine (formerly Saint-Antoine and the future Place de la Bastille). Four days later the machine was taken to the Place de la Nation, known then as the gateway to the overturned Throne, where, according to Michelet, "it would no longer be surrounded by the crowd. It was the emancipation of the guillotine. It would breathe a great dying gasp to take it out of the civilized world, having nothing left to blush for."[24] This move was a bad idea: the lugubrious procession of tum-

---

24. Michelet, *Histoire de la Révolution française*, 9 vols. (Marpon & Flammarion), IX, p. 257. In Thermidor, the guillotine was returned to the place de la Ré-

brils through the interminable suburb shocked the people. The extreme youth of some and the frailty of others caused hearts to constrict. The smell of blood could no longer be tolerated. "What no one would have dared to say in the name of humanity, was said in the name of hygiene and health."[25]

The nervousness of a government that continued to condemn people to death manifested itself in the suppression of all favourable treatment within the prisons. Everyone was obliged to eat "from the porringer," which meant being served "a disgusting soup, vegetables swimming in water . . . and some pork mixed with cabbage in a large vase or tin porringer."[26] Telescopes were confiscated: a great many prisoners had acquired these so as to exchange signals with people outside.[27] And on 4 Thermidor, Citizen Beauharnais was summoned to the Revolutionary Tribunal, which meant death. He had time to write a beautiful farewell letter to Joséphine and to give Delphine "as a souvenir of himself" an Arab ring set with a talisman. Alexandre was condemned as an accomplice of Custine's treachery. Since women were treated with as much severity as men, could Delphine escape death?

---

volution for Robespierre's execution. It was eventually moved to the place de Grève—the present place de l'Hôtel-de-Ville—where it was in use until 1830.

25. Ibid.

26. Dauban, op. cit., p. 226.

27. Ibid., p. 228.

During her detention, she was taken home to the rue de Lille three times in order to continue the search for her papers. There she was able to embrace Astolphe before having to assist with the sacking of her apartment. Her desks were smashed so the secret drawers could be searched, the parquet floor was lifted but still no one thought to look under the sofa. It is easy to imagine the terror of a four-year-old child on seeing his mother surrounded by these loutish men who addressed her with familiarity and insulted her. Twelve men took part in the search, including a hunchback cobbler "as evil as he was ugly"[28] who discovered a shoe made of English leather—and all imports from England were banned. It was a serious offence. Delphine defended herself, speaking clearly and quietly; she managed to convince all her interrogators except the cobbler. Whilst they deliberated, she picked up a pencil and began to sketch the scene. A mason and ardent Jacobin called Jérôme snatched the sheet of paper and passed it around. Everyone recognised himself and they burst out laughing at the caricature of the hunchback, standing on a chair, waving the incriminating shoe. The drawing was confiscated and deposited with Delphine's dossier; after the Revolution, Fouché gave it back to Delphine but it was lost many years later in a move. Jérôme, the workman, who had never been near a woman whose courageous gaiety, unaffected charm and natural grace could com-

28. *La Russie*, op. cit., I, p. 62.

pare to that of the accused, did as many others had done before. He fell in love with the marquise. Unlike the others, he saved her life.

Being too careful to allow anything of his feelings to show, he continued to address her angrily, to insult her and to push her around, but having free access to the office of Fouquier-Tinville, the public prosecutor, he went there every evening. He opened the box in which the detainees' dossiers were kept. Every day during the months leading up to Thermidor, Fouquier grabbed twenty, thirty or forty dossiers from the top of the pile to provide for that day's executions. Jérôme leafed quickly through the bundle, found the Custine woman's papers and put them back at the bottom of the pile. It would have been too dangerous to remove them, as Fouquier was a scrupulous official who knew how many dossiers there were. Better still, he helped Astolphe by giving little sums of money to Nanette, under deepest oath of secrecy.

At last, on 9 Thermidor, Robespierre was overthrown, thanks to a plot led by Barras, Tallien and Fouché. It was the end to the Terror. Two days later the prisons began to empty. The first person to leave Les Carmes was Joséphine. Then Mme de Lameth and Mme d'Aiguillon left. Everybody—that is to say, all of high society—regained their freedom little by little except for poor Delphine. Her friends and relations were all far away. Her humble protector, Jérôme, had had to hide. Had he not been one of Robespierre's most enthusiastic partisans? Nanette of course came to see her, but what could Nanette do apart from giving her news of Astolphe who was at last cured of a malignant fever thanks to the care of the three "best doctors in Paris" whom she had succeeded in dragging into her kitchen? Delphine later told her son that this was the hardest test she was put to because now her companions in captivity had been replaced under lock and key by her enemies. She had been forgotten. Nanette, however, managed to save her.

Her father had been employed for years at the Custines' porcelain factory. In 1793 the factory had been confiscated and the workshops closed. Thus some fifty men came looking for work in Paris, among them Nanette's father. Nanette got Delphine to sign a request for liberty which she had her father and his friends sign and seal, then she took it herself to the butcher, Legendre, who presided over the office where such requests were vetted.

Legendre's negligence was well known. He threw the petition in a corner and forgot about it. One evening, on 13 Vendémiaire, three young men who worked for him came back from a good dinner, knocked over the boxes where the requests were accumulating and one of them, on picking up a paper at random, insisted that his boss sign it that very evening. The petition was Delphine's. What a godsend to save the "lovely Custine"! Legendre went home, drunk as usual, and the three boys hurried to Les Carmes. They had the door opened and were shown the former marquise's cell where they knocked with such enthusiasm that she was frightened and refused to let them in. They had to come back the following morning when Delphine, reassured by the daylight, pushed open the door and finally walked out of the prison.

She came home to find a wrecked apartment and to discover the horrible cupidity of some—one of her female relations came to ask for 30,000 francs which she claimed she had spent on bribes to get her out of prison—and the inexpressible devotion of others, and fell ill. An appalling jaundice kept her in bed for five months. On recovering, she questioned Nanette. What were they living off? She must have sold the silver? No, there wasn't any left. The linen then? The jewels? But no, there was nothing left, and then Nanette told her how Jérôme had not only saved her life and seen to it that her child had enough to eat, but how still, from his hiding place—since he had been obliged to disappear after Thermidor—he continued to subsidise them. He added, Nanette pointed out, "the express order to say nothing to Madame, but now that she can make amends, I am telling. I have kept an exact record, here is the account."[29] Delphine, who had retrieved a little money from the small part of her husband's confiscated lands which had not found a buyer, helped Jérôme to leave Paris and gave him all he needed to embark for America. There he made a fortune and returned to France under the Consulate. Astolphe, who had been told the story a hundred times,

29. *La Russie*, op. cit., I, p. 70.

70

remembered his mother's affection for Jérôme and Mme de Sabran's enormous gratitude. But Jérôme, a Bordelais whose conversation consisted of nothing but a cascade of curses, always came to see Delphine when she was alone. He didn't want to be stared at by her friends as if he were "a strange animal."[30]

Delphine moved and settled in the rue Martel, near the rue du Paradis, and it was there that her mother managed to reach her again. A meeting in Switzerland was planned, but Delphine, who wanted to recover a few scraps of her fortune, was reluctant to leave Paris until her affairs were in better shape. What her brother described as "the victors of Beauharnais's memory" were beginning to assemble, amongst them Boissy d'Anglas, who after Thermidor had been elected President of the Convention. She had met him through Joséphine and with her habitual ease had captivated him. He set out to help her by procuring a passport authorising her to take the waters at Baden near Zurich. Unfortunately the passport didn't allow her to take Astolphe with her. Thus she resigned herself to leaving him in the good care of Nanette in Niderviller in Lorraine.

Her reunion with Elzéar and her mother took place in Zurich. Delphine told them of the horror of her husband's and her father-in-law's executions, of the ruin of so many friends, the devastation

30. Ibid., I, p. 71.

of their world, but as soon as she found herself alone with her brother, she returned to her favourite subject—her love affairs. Not the current ones, which might shock the delicate young man—she was seeing a good deal of a Venezuelan adventurer, called Miranda, who had served successively in the Russian, English and Republican armies—but she spoke of Beauharnais's tragic passion. She had brought with her the letters he had written her in prison, to reread them and to discuss them with Elzéar. He, in his exalted way, wished to convince his sister "that after Alexandre's love, all other love would be a degradation."[31] How little he knew his sister.

Dismissing the idea of a quiet family life in a pretty corner of Germany, refusing to give way to her mother's altogether well-founded fears of a return of trouble in France, and with the excuse of having to attend to her affairs, Delphine prepared to return to France, to her son . . . and to several lovers. Then Astolphe, who had just turned five, sent her a letter—his first. "I wish you good day, my dear little mother—come back soon. They made us some muffins, if you had been here, you would have had a feast.—I love you as much as you love muffins, that means a lot— . . . I eat well, I run well and I drink well—I like wine. My hair falls nicely over my forehead, and I have a little rat's tail. Farewell, Mama, I embrace you with all my heart."[32] How could she resist the temptation to go to

31. Maugras, *Delphine de Sabran*, op. cit., p. 273.
32. Ibid., p. 285.

the child? Delphine left and, by an act of extreme generosity to her mother and her brother, manifested her confidence in the future. She left them a box which she made them promise not to open until after her departure. It contained her diamonds. In December 1795 she was back in Paris.

4

A Circle of Friends

In families rallying to Bonaparte, the boys all wanted tuppenny coloured prints from which to cut out the generals of the Army of Italy. The confidence encapsulated by the figure of a young general gave them a sense of courage, they were dazzled by the spectacle of a parade, and they envied the glamorous uniforms of the victorious officers; conscious of living in extraordinary times, they were very much aware of the country to which they belonged. What they were told about the Ancien Régime and the Revolution—and usually only the servants talked to them about the good old life and the Terror—gave them a sense of history. But it was the past now, and of that, too, they were aware. Their imagination was excited by victory and they no longer looked back to the cruel years.[1] But when parents rallied only half-heartedly, children continued to be tormented by vague nightmares of the Revolution.

Astolphe de Custine belonged to the second category. "My family's mourning, the clumsy reserve of the servants when I questioned them about my father, the mysterious accounts with which my troubled spirit had been nurtured, all contributed to striking my imagination with a vague sadness and I already wept for misfortunes about which I knew nothing as yet."[2] He recovered from his illness, but would he ever recover from the horrible memories that marked his childhood? His mother hoped so without being convinced, and always treated him with a rare gentleness and understanding. Astolphe had regained his strength, but he was a nervous, anxious, amazingly attentive child, ever on the watch, in whom an awareness of his mother's strength, courage and indomitable resilience had taken on exceptional proportions. He was to say later that he considered her "as a *second* Providence particularly enjoined to watch over [his] fate."[3] A providence of such extreme sweetness and so readily available that he added: "I recognised myself, from my tenderest years, as the sun in my little universe, and, on opening my

1. Charles de Rémusat, *Mémoires de ma vie* (Plon, 1958). See vol. I, chap. I, "Enfance et Jeunesse (1797–1815)."

2. Astolphe de Custine, *Aloys* (Toulouse, Editions Ombres, 1994), pp. 17, 21.

3. Marquis de Luppé, *Lettres de Custine au marquis de La Grange* (Presses françaises, 1925), pp. 81–83.

eyes, I could see that everything revolved around me. I sensed all my importance well before I suspected my nothingness; and this sentiment would have made me unbearable, had the tenderness which accompanied it not exalted my sensibility which in turn modified it and acted as a counterbalance."[4] And it might have been the case, if Delphine had concentrated exclusively on her child. She did no such thing. She never let her love for him interfere with her relationships with men. But the seriousness with which she treated him, the pleasure she took in bringing him up and perhaps the repeated failures of her love life meant that Astolphe never questioned either his own importance or his equality with his mother. This was symbolised by their reciprocal use of the familiar *tu*. Once the Revolution ended and the manners of the Ancien Régime were no longer proscribed, it was unheard of for a boy of the nobility, the bourgeoisie or even the peasantry to address his mother as *tu*. Thus it really was a sign of openness and remarkable intimacy.

So the little family settled in the rue Martel on the right bank, in a beautiful apartment with a studio where Delphine spent as much time as she could, for she had taken up painting again. She had not, however, forgotten the lessons learnt from her lengthy imprisonment: if she didn't look after her own interests, no one else would do it for her. With no one she could naturally depend on, it was up to her to act to make sure she would have some resources. And she

4. Ibid.

needed money. For sure, she held all the aces. For one thing, she hadn't emigrated; and for another, her relationship with Joséphine de Beauharnais had remained excellent, and Joséphine, having married her little Corsican general, was now at the centre of things. The new dispensation sought to treat the old nobility with tact. Finally, Delphine knew how to make useful friends. But the competition was harsh. It seemed as if all France was busy soliciting.

Some victims of the Revolution, like Delphine's mother, wanted above all to be erased from the list of emigrés. Others wanted to reclaim whatever property of theirs had not been sold during the Revolution as a national asset and which therefore remained at the government's disposal; those who had made a profit wanted reassurance that their newly acquired riches were theirs forever. "Not everyone had been ruined by the Revolution, although they all claimed that they had, even those who had helped to cause it, those who had never possessed anything, and above all those who were already ruined when it happened. The year 1801 in which many wounds were healed allowed to see the contents of many wallets . . . one discovered the owners of shameful fortunes made one way or another—from the scaffold, from proconsulates, or from the violation of safe deposits, from the abuse of power of attorney for emigrés, abuse of redemption or from blood money . . . had also . . . cast off their fears, to face the daylight under the umbrella of the law."[5]

5. Norvins, op. cit., II, p. 299.

Delphine's strongest suit was her charm, which she was to use shamelessly. First of all she captivated Boissy d'Anglas, an influential member of the Council of Five Hundred, the newly elected legislative assembly. Unfortunately their letters, "which were not of a kind to be published,"[6] were destroyed. Next she made sure of the affectionate and extremely efficient support of Barthélemy, a man of the Ancien Régime, a protégé of Choiseul,* ambassador to Switzerland under the Directory and subsequently a Director himself. True to her passion for nicknames, she mockingly called him the *pale friend*. Finally she made friends with Fouché, the most powerful of protectors, Fouché the regicide, Fouché responsible for the slaughter in Lyons. The nasty, pock-marked Fouché with his cold, serpent's eyes, his mean mouth and scraggy neck to whom the princesse de Vaudémont said, on leading him to a looking-glass in her *salon*, and taking him familiarly by the chin, "My God, my little Fouché, how like a weasel you look." The same Fouché who didn't hesitate to receive his new lady friends with his feet stuffed into a pair of frayed greenish slippers.[7] Was it possible? Everything was possible, if not probable, under the Directory.

Fouché had betrayed Robespierre on the eve of 9 Thermidor, just

---

*The duke of Choiseul (1719–1785) was Louis XV's most powerful minister. He was in power from 1758 to 1770 and simultaneously Minister of Foreign Affairs, Minister of War and Minister of the Navy.

6. Maugras, *Delphine de Sabran*, op. cit., p. 296.

7. Norvins, op. cit., II, pp. 318 and 320.

in time to make himself indispensable to both Tallien and Barras. After a few months of purgatory, he found himself back at the centre of things, knowing everything, with a hold over everyone, weaving new webs. He needed the salons of the aristocracy; and so he dangled carrots, particularly in the shape of his ability to strike names off the emigré list. The habitués of the salons, hoping to gain much from his support, bowed like lackeys before him. Some pertinent advice concerning people and things earned him the gratitude of several society women, amongst them the princesse de Vaudémont, an old friend of the Sabrans, and Delphine herself. In exchange for his services he asked nothing except that they should pass information to the royalist camp about the help he had given. In the first place Fouché, a defrocked Oratorian, was married to a wife whom he adored despite her fearful ugliness, and he was a good father. Paternity was said to be his finest—indeed his only—virtue, but he was, above all, far too prudent to leave himself open to possible blackmail. Delphine soon kissed her dear *Chéché* on both cheeks and received him as a confidant and adviser, telling him as much about her financial worries as about her affairs of the heart. For Delphine, true to herself, was in love again.

Another general, twenty years her senior, whose life resembled a turbulent serial, gave her back a taste for life. Born in Caracas, Francisco Miranda became an officer in the Spanish army, fought in the American War of Independence and travelled to Europe and on to Russia where he was said to have had a brief affair with Catherine the Great, which allowed him to return to France with a Russian passport. So enthusiastic was he about the Revolution that on 10 August he joined the French army. He was made a general and left for the front, where he distinguished himself in several engagements, but he came under suspicion as a result of General Dumouriez's betrayal in 1793. He was recalled, tried by the revolutionary Tribunal and acquitted. Delphine met Miranda just at the time of Custine's trial at which he was a witness. Miranda was arrested for a second time and not released until Nîvose, five months after Thermidor; then he met Delphine again and their liaison began in March 1795.

She visited him in the morning, in his little house at Ménilmontant; back at home she wrote him affectionate grateful letters: what would happen to her without her "political compass," how could she thank him enough for taking so much trouble to recover not only her property, but also—which was more difficult—Mme de Sabran's? Sometimes she affected a rather embarrassing humility, "Tell me which day you want me in the morning?" or "I came to see you. I am so sad not to find you."[8] One would like to think that this was a form of flirtation, yet she was clearly yielding to that lack of self-respect in her relations with men that her mother had earlier tried to combat. When, after a few months, Miranda began to avoid

8. Parra-Perez, *Delphine de Custine, belle amie de Miranda* (Grasset, 1950), p. 188.

her, she clung to him. Had it not been for her son, she would have
given way to despair.

But all the heartbreak, the money problems, creditors' proceedings and the efforts on behalf of her mother did not prevent her from
organising Astolphe's life. One of the great problems of the times
was the collapse of the schools and the difficulty in finding teachers
for children. Delphine discovered a young German of about thirty,
"full of merit and amiability."[9] Berstoecher was a very gentle man,
quite susceptible to her charm and capable of making up for the neglect of the little boy's education. More importantly perhaps, he
took root in their midst. Soon he became more than a tutor, more
than a help. Loyal, indispensable, always ready for anything, and
faithful as a dog, he earned the nickname of *Médor*. Not only did
he lend Delphine money when she ran out, but he quickly came to
arbitrate between mother and son who, while adoring each other,
had frequent furious confrontations.

"The tenderest love for his mother did not prevent [Astolphe]
from sometimes behaving towards her with violent obstinacy: he
confided everything in her and never disguised how thwarted she
made him feel, openly discussing with her his character as well as
hers."[10] This friend "placed between [their] two characters as if to

9. Maugras, *Delphine de Custine*, op. cit., p. 329.

10. Astolphe de Custine, *Lettres à Varnhagen d'Ense* (Geneva, Slatkine Re-
prints, 1979), introduction by Auguste Varnhagen d'Ense, p. xiv.

blunt the angles" was to form Astolphe, to become respected and loved by him and to lend support to Delphine until her death. Astolphe seems to have accepted, without the slightest irritation, the permanent presence of a man who was clearly in love with his mother. Berstoecher is referred to quite simply in Astolphe's correspondence as *the friend*. The tender love he nurtured for this beautiful, graceful, kind, flirtatious young woman could not pass unnoticed. Their understanding was such that Chateaubriand paid the young man the compliment of appearing a little jealous. "Love me at least as much as M.B.," he wrote to Delphine in 1803. The absolute devotion of Jérôme, Nanette and Berstoecher contrasted with the detachment and inconstancy of Delphine's lovers. Astolphe explained it by "the sweetness with which she exerted her power which made it irresistible" precisely to those who might suffer from it, and the simplicity with which she treated people. She knew nothing of condescension; differences of rank and birth were unimportant to her. Affectation was alien to her. She was genuinely natural in a way that never ceased to enchant her son.

The year 1797 would be another agitated year for the Sabrans and the Custines. Mme de Sabran, fearing that she had abused the Prussian prince's hospitality, accepted an estate which he offered her in Poland and off she went with the chevalier de Boufflers to play the farmer in Winislow—the little town which came to be known as Winislow-le-Français in her memory. In very Catholic Poland they were finally to marry. Delphine can almost be heard clapping her hands at the news. For one thing a change of name might facilitate her mother's return, and then she wondered gaily whether it was really too late for the new wife "to present her with a pretty little sister."[11] Neither did she want her dear stepfather to forget Astolphe, who was now his grandson. Would Astolphe call him "grand-steppapa"? No. Grandpapa would do. As for herself, could she not also get married? To the *pale friend*, for example, always so perfect in his dealings with her? What did her mother think? Unfortunately the moderate wing of the government, represented precisely by Barthélemy, was overthrown by the coup d'état of 18 Fructidor. The unfortunate Director was sent to Guiana, there was a violent antiroyalist reaction in France, and all Delphine's plans were upset. The measures in favour of emigrés were nullified. It was to be another two years before, thanks to Bonaparte's political victory, 18 Brumaire gave all French people a feeling of safety and permanence.

Delphine returned to her campaign for the damages due to her, and for her mother and stepfather's return to France. Mme de Sabran's house on the faubourg Saint-Honoré had been bought by General Beurnonville, a man who had taken advantage of the Revolution rapidly to further his career. Born in 1752 as a wheelwright's son in the small town of Champignol, despite his great intelligence his only hope was for a career in the Church. Thus he entered a sem-

11. Maugras, *Delphine de Sabran*, op. cit., p. 317.

inary, but in 1766 he escaped to join the army. At the beginning of the Revolution he was stationed in Lunéville as a militiaman. In 1792, his advanced opinions earned him the post of general in the Army of the Centre, then Minister for War twice over. He was sent by the Convention to enquire into Dumouriez's conduct, but handed over by the latter to the Austrians. Imprisoned at Olmutz, he made friends with La Fayette and he stayed there until 1795 when there was an exchange of prisoners. The Austrians freed a group of detainees, including Beurnonville, in exchange for Louis XVI's daughter, the future duchesse d'Angoulême, who had been shut up in the Temple since 1792. On his return to France, the general judiciously aligned himself with Bonaparte's camp.

Delphine saw him several times. The house had been sold at a very low price—30,000 francs[12]—for which she could envisage buying it back. Beurnonville, who became increasingly friendly and understanding, suggested a solution which had the advantage of simplicity: he would marry Delphine, have the great pleasure of giving his mother-in-law an apartment and, in addition, would have her crossed off the list of emigrés. Why not indeed? Beurnonville was rich—for Delphine, not a negligible consideration—and he was on the right path, having just been named ambassador to Berlin;

12. By way of comparison, note that Delphine was to buy the château de Fervaques a few years later for 400,000 francs.

besides, he was very taken with her. The young woman, aware of what Bluebeard (as she called him) could bring her, seemed to hesitate only for the sake of form. She informed her mother, who simply urged her to await her return and not rush into anything. Curiously, it was her younger brother, Elzéar, who put an end to the plan.

Elzéar was a strange person, both vague and brutal. He was always frail and always unwell: his sister asked him in 1797—when her little brother was after all twenty-three—whether he had grown and whether the signs of a beard had appeared. Yet this fragile young man was the only member of the family to hold passionate, unyielding political opinions. It was as if he had spent the years of exile, the years of family upheaval, without ever having reflected on the meaning or the means of survival in revolutionary times. Delphine's adaptability and his mother's realistic common sense only exacerbated Elzéar's reactionary ideas. He exploded with rage at the mere mention of what he called "such a degrading and monstrous coupling"[13] and considered ignominious his mother's return in such circumstances. Despite the certainty that this marriage would have provided Astolphe with much needed support, it did not take place, perhaps because of Elzéar's objurgations, perhaps because Beurnonville's having been divorced constituted an even greater obstacle. Delphine must sometimes have regretted the outcome. Under

13. Maugras, *Delphine de Sabran*, op. cit., p. 360.

the Restoration, Beurnonville was made a marquis, a peer and marshal of France, and he crowned his career by marrying the comte de Durfort's daughter.

However, in 1800, the family was at last reunited. Astolphe had written to his grandmother: "My dear Grand-mé, Come back so that I can kiss you, for I really want to, but I beg you, do not dally; we will come to meet you so as to see you sooner: I beg you to ask my grandfather on my behalf for permission to call him *tu*, so that I do not have the discomfort of asking him myself. You will go to the theatre with me which will give me great pleasure. I have a good deal of fun but I will have even more when you are here; Mama will give you her bedroom. I still have your ring; in the summer we will go to the country and you will take your morning walks with me: I will play the piano to entertain you, I draw and I am learning to dance. Farewell Grand-mé, I love you a great deal, give my regards to my grandfather! I love him very much."[14] According to his mother, in fact, he danced quite well at thirteen. At Plombières, where the Custines and the Beauharnais met again, for all her twenty years, Joséphine's daughter, Hortense, was happy to lead the quadrille with him.[15]

---

14. Ibid., p. 367.

15. Joint letter from Delphine and Astolphe to Mme de Boufflers, 15 July 1803, Collection Thierry Bodin.

The Boufflers were completely ruined. There remained only the chevalier's reputation. Bonaparte, who wanted to preside over a light-hearted, brilliant court, welcomed him, asked him to write some songs and made him administrator of the Mazarine library. He was allowed to make use of his membership in the old Académie Française to join the Institut. He was rebuilding his life. Mme de Boufflers spent all her time with her daughter, who went out less than she had under the Directory, not because she despised the new society—her old best friend, the comtesse de La Rochefoucauld, was one of the most influential women at the new court—but by choice. Delphine was shy and was as afraid of *salons* as she was of the dark, animals and robbers. Mother and daughter frequently saw Mme de Staël and the princesse de Vaudémont, the queen of owls, who went to bed when the sun rose and received what remained of the most elegant society in a room where dozens of dogs of every breed were milling. Thus ties dating from before the Revolution were revived. A more recent friendship, which became very important for Astolphe, developed between Delphine and Sophie Gay. Sophie was an enterprising, adaptable woman who, in that little group, represented modernity. The fondness she showed for Astolphe, to whom she remained faithful for the next fifty years, earned her Delphine's affection.

Born in 1776, the daughter of an employee responsible for the financial affairs of Monsieur, the future Louis XVIII, Sophie was married at the age of fifteen to a very rich stockbroker twenty years older than herself, whom she left under the Directory for a much younger lover, Jean Sigismond Gay, another financier. Thanks to the protection of the head of Napoleon's household, Marshal Duroc, he would have a career in the imperial administration. As for Sophie, she invented an entirely new profession for herself, that of literary agent. She went regularly to England to buy ballads, plays and novels which she sold in Paris. By the time she met the Custines, she was already well launched. Known for her many love affairs, she nevertheless raised her two daughters, Delphine and Isaure, and her stepdaughter, Eliza, with the greatest care. Her husband earned so much money that it became quite clear that he was happily confusing his own finances with those of the nation. When he was dismissed in 1810, Sophie set to work, writing novels, making adaptations for the Opéra-Comique, composing songs, and even succeeding in having a play put on at the Comédie-Française, all without giving up her activities as literary agent. It was she who encouraged Marceline Desbordes-Valmore, the great lyrical poet, to write. "Yes, my dear friend, a few more elegies, a few little stories and we will have a charming volume from you. We will sell it for as much as possible."[16] The warmth of this new friend gave Delphine back her confidence. So much enthusiasm and resourcefulness amused her.

16. Francis Ambrière, *Le Siècle des Valmore; Marceline Desbordes-Valmore et les siens*, 2 vols. (Le Seuil, 1987), I, p. 319.

88

Mme de Boufflers and her daughter were rarely seen at the Tuileries, even though invitations from Joséphine were not refused in those days. But Astolphe came first. They read to him and painted and the child spent long hours in his mother's studio. She continued the fight for the return of her property. In 1802, Delphine and her sister-in-law were granted restitution of their hereditary assets and they put the hotel de Sarrebourg and the china factory in Niderviller up for sale. The château where Astolphe was born and where he had spent so many summers was demolished. There he had tasted for the first time "the inexpressible joy which the sight of the fields and all the scenes of the natural world gave [him]" and where he had felt "the heartache . . . the profound horror" which gripped him on returning to the prison that was Paris. But he did occasionally return to Lorraine because the good Nanette had retired to "this village without beauty which has nothing of the countryside but dung and manure."[17] Astolphe came to see her regularly in that part of the country where his family had once enjoyed 600,000 francs of income, of which now only 1,800 remained. But on the advice of her old friend from the bad times, Chaumont-Quitry, Delphine bought in her and her son's name, the château and the large estate of Fervaques in Normandy. She bought the property, with an income of 8,691 francs, for more than 400,000 francs from the duc de Montmorency-Laval and his sister, the duchessse de Luynes. Be-

17. *Lettres à Varnhagen*, op. cit., p. 343.

hind this favorable transaction, consummated just in time, can be discerned both the hand of Fouché and Bonaparte's goodwill, for, in March 1804, the summary execution of the duc d'Enghien* on government orders was to mark Delphine's final break with power. She was never to return to court. Fouché remained a close friend but she definitively broke all ties with Joséphine.

For nearly twenty years Fervaques was to be a haven for both mother and son, a home, an indispensable retreat. "Our region is pretty and rural even in the winter . . . it is restful and calm, which is not usual in France . . . Picture a valley only five minutes across, not deep enough to resemble mountainous country, and yet different enough from the plain to have a character of its own. Not many trees in the bottom of the valley, meadows reaching to the foot of the hillside, then ploughed fields and a few bunches of trees, but above all there are orchards like forests which hide the houses they surround, and magnificent hedges bordering all the lanes. In the midst of this little green universe, picture a large château, too low for its length . . . but set off by very pointed slate roofs and architecture of the time of Henri IV which lacks neither a certain nobility nor solidity

---

*The duke of Enghien (1772–1804) was abducted from the duchy of Baden and judged hastily by a military court on the presumption that he was plotting against Bonaparte. He was shot on 21 March 1804 without having had a chance to defend himself.

. . . all this without a shadow of luxury, but solid and severe without being sad."[18]

Fervaques provided the setting; the principal actor of these years was François-René de Chateaubriand, known as the *Génie*, about whom Astolphe was to write, "Of all my countrymen, [he is] the one whom I most like to see and who, in my earliest youth, had the greatest influence over me. I am no doubt one of the worst of his creations, for he worked on me without thinking . . . the memory of him is intermingled with the first light of my thought."[19]

This seems to touch on the most unusual aspect of Astolphe's relationship with his mother. The child had long since been used to the presence of men around her and it is impossible to imagine him insensitive to the ups and downs of her different liaisons. It is equally difficult to suppose that he never heard or guessed at the tenor of discussions between Mme de Boufflers and Delphine about her love affairs, her chances of marriage, the behaviour of this or that lover. But it is clear that he never felt threatened in her affection, that the conviction that he was more important to her than anyone else was firmly implanted in his soul. But how would he react to Chateaubriand? Chateaubriand, who was made of quite different stuff from her political friends, her South American generals, the Médors of the world.

18. Ibid., pp. 76 and 103.
19. *Lettres à La Grange*, op. cit., p. 72.

In 1803, the prodigious success of *Le Génie du christianisme* brought Chateaubriand fame and influence. Bonaparte wanted his services and made him secretary at the embassy in Rome. Despite the fact that his head was too big for his body, Chateaubriand had not the slightest difficulty in seducing women. The arrival on the scene of this man who could have been a formidable rival for a sensitive, spoilt, delicate thirteen-year-old like Astolphe remained a dazzling memory, and long after Delphine's charms had lost their power over the great man, Chateaubriand conserved a true, deep and active friendship with Astolphe. Never tempted to play the part of husband, he always expressed a paternal concern for the young Custine.

Many a love story begins with the man's passionate advances, followed, after the first signs of victory, by a reversal wherein the man is irritated by the woman's demands; in the best instances, a faithful friendship then develops. Delphine and René were part of this tradition, but their case is exceptional, not only because of the speed with which the idyll evolved, but above all because, thanks to Chateaubriand's letters, it can be closely followed. In 1803, the idea of leaving his beautiful friend *kills* him, he lives only in the hope of seeing her again, waiting for a note from her puts him in such a state that he roams round all the streets of Paris without knowing where he's going. After a visit the following year, 1804, he tells her that he misses "Fervaques, the carp, [her], Chênedollé and even Mme Auguste," but, she points out with vexation, "not the slightest word for my grotto and the little summer house adorned by two superb myrtles. It seems to me that that should not be so quickly forgotten; I have forgotten nothing," she concludes, "not even that you do not like long letters."[20] Finally, in 1806, after a visit from the *Génie* to Fervaques, Delphine wrote to Chateaubriand's close friend, Chênedollé, who had become her confidant: "Everything was perfect for two weeks, consequently everything is over."[21] Chateaubriand was leaving for Jerusalem and had arranged to meet Natalie de Noailles in Seville on his way back.

But this intimacy with Chateaubriand had a considerable influence on Astolphe as it did, of course, on Delphine. First, it brought them gaiety and fantasy. "No one was more childish than he," Astolphe was to write.[22] Without its making any difference to his relations with the beautiful Custine, Chateaubriand had resumed conjugal life with his wife in the rue de Miromesnil, on the corner of the rue Verte, so Delphine moved in order to be closer to him. With her entourage of Astolphe, Berstoecher, old Nanette, who still couldn't speak French, and Trim the terrier, who bit, killed birds and ate provisions for journeys,[23] Delphine settled opposite in the present rue Penthièvre, the then rue Verte, so called because it ran down to the

20. Bardoux, *Madame de Custine*, op. cit., p. 158.
21. Ibid., p. 173.
22. Marquis de Luppé, *Astolphe de Custine* (Editions du Rocher, 1957), p. 30.
23. Chateaubriand, *Mémoires d'outre-tombe*, op. cit., I, p. 472.

large Tivoli and Monceau gardens where Delphine and René used to walk their dogs. When they left for the country, Chateaubriand came down into the street to supervise the departure of the tribe, later announcing his arrival in exquisite letters: "I will make an effort to run a bit all over Paris, and then I will go a little further. It will be like a fairy story: he travelled very far, very far (children love the word 'far' to be stressed), and he arrived at Fervaques. There lived a fairy who had no common sense. They called her Princess Without-Hope, because she always thought after two days of silence that her friends were dead or that they had left for China and she would never see them again."[24]

Occasionally he was serious, even cross, which surely only goes to show how important the Custines—both mother and son—were to him. His reply to Delphine's humorous description of Astolphe's first communion with seventy-two little country children is proof of it. "Do you know that I am not the least interested in your communion? I think you had it given to your son too soon. I would bet that he does not know a word of the principles of his religion. The little girls in white were filthy, the *curé* is a brute, all that is clear. All this is good only when children have been instructed wisely and at length, when they are made to take their first communion, not because of custom, but because of religion. You have your son take

24. Chateaubriand, *Correspondance générale*, 5 vols. (Gallimard, 1986), I, p. 326.

communion although he does not observe the Friday rule, and perhaps doesn't even go to mass on Sundays . . ."[25]

Delphine, delighted to return, if not to the habits of the Ancien Régime, at least to a feeling for its proprieties, didn't appear too concerned by these remonstrances. She installed in her household an unusual steward, a certain abbé Gibelin, who had been attached to the family for many years. Having been ruined by the Revolution, he consoled himself by marrying. He happily accepted Delphine's proposal and, accompanied by his lawful wife and his little dogs, arrived to supervise the renovations. In the language of the Custines, he became the *Gibi*; but Chateaubriand preferred his full surname and liked to imagine him continuing the fight to the death of the last Guelf. What was a château without a real abbé? The one at Fervaques, as described by Astolphe, had already grown old in his grandmother's house. Which is to say that he was a leftover from the eighteenth century "ossified morally as well as physically. He is like a matchstick seen under a microscope." Astolphe observed him cruelly.

"When I remember listening to him," he wrote later, "of all the illustrious people of his time, the friends of his youth: Diderot, d'Alembert, Marmontel, etc. . . . I am reminded of a table cleared after a banquet, and a gnawed bone to be thrown to the dog as the

25. Ibid., p. 328.

room is tidied . . . he is not the least bit wicked, but he is frightening. One doesn't know whether to be more surprised by the slightness of his outward movements, or by his profound innner immobility. Most of the truths of the soul are alien to him, and the ideas which he understands by chance are crystallised in his mind as soon as they enter it. He seems to have lived on the edge of life and I always think of him as a piece of household furniture, condemned by some sorcerer to be a man for eighty years. His is the soul of a château, a bedroom, an armchair, but not of a human body . . . He is the Prince Trautsmansdorff of Fervaques."[26]

Another important character, and genuinely of his own century this time, was the gardener found by Mme de Boufflers. "Impossible to be more active, more intelligent, or to have a greater taste for stealing. I watch him: until now it has not been really possible, there are no fruits, no vegetables and almost no flowers . . . as life goes on, one ends up admiring only rogues, for they are the only ones who are active, who have ideas. The others, with their scruples and their honesty, make way for the rascals and fall asleep over their clean consciences."[27] Then there were the neighbours. There were those like Mme des Boulets, nicknamed *my migraine*, whose conversation lacked substance; others like Chaumont-Quitry, who sulked and was difficult (because he had never recovered from the Revolution);

26. *Lettres à Varnhagen*, op. cit., p. 107.
27. Maugras, *Delphine de Sabran*, op. cit., p. 395.

then there were those, like Mme de Cauvigny, so charming that they made time fly.

Mme de Boufflers, who remained in Paris, was sent on a great variety of errands: a seal for Berstoecher's birthday, "simple, in good taste, not mean, well made, of good gold, neither too small, nor too big either, with the handle absolutely in ebony, and above all not costing more than sixty francs."[28] Or she was sent to find six window panes for the little cottage, but different coloured ones "so that through one, there seems to be a storm, through another fine weather, another moonlight, another rain; and the others, I don't know what!"[29]

Chateaubriand came but, once his passion had abated, he prudently brought his friend, Chênedollé, who, although never in love with Delphine—he loved Chateaubriand's sister, Lucile—offered her friendship and affection. Chateaubriand remained part of Delphine's life until 1806, seeing her both at Fervaques and in Paris. At Fervaques in June 1806 he wrote Veléda's song from *Les Martyrs*. In the evenings, he read passages from it out loud. Astolphe was familiar enough with him to comment on the text, and Chateaubriand so open "that he worked for hours to change what a child had criticised," but his departure for Greece marked the end of the affair. "The *Génie* leaves in two days," Delphine wrote to Chênedollé on

28. Ibid., p. 398.
29. Ibid.

97

24 June 1806, "he is leaving in order to fulfill all his wishes and to destroy all mine . . . you know how sad I was last year, consider then how I will feel this year."[30] He left and on his return there was no longer any question of love, but a lively friendship remained.

When *Les Martyrs* came out, Chateaubriand was faced with the problems of censorship. He was asked to make corrections and cuts. Delphine became involved—that is to say, she approached Fouché —a most successful intervention to judge by a note of the author's: "It is total success for the book! No censorship, great praise, honour, flattery. Everything is perfect! Our great man, a divine man. Till to-morrow, my dear!"[31] Fouché a great man, and that from Chateaubri-and's pen? What won't writers pay to be published? In truth, three months later "our great man" had become "your great friend," for it seems that he hadn't succeeded in muzzling the censorship quite as completely as he had promised.[32]

30. Bardoux, op. cit., p. 172.

31. Chateaubriand, *Correspondance*, op. cit., II, p. 38.

32. Ibid., II, p. 40. According to Mme de Chastenay, whose lover, Réal, was high-ranking in the police, "when the question of publication arose, Fouché sent for M. de Chateaubriand, and addressing him in the superior tone that he never affected without often justifying it, he told him that he would not in any way cen-sor this work, which the public was already devouring in advance; he wanted to leave the matter in his hands only, but he begged not to be compromised, warning him meanwhile that the publication would be seized if the Emperor found any-

A Circle of Friends

As for Astolphe, he quite rightly continued to count on Chateaubriand's friendship, to write to him directly and to receive lengthy replies. If Chateaubriand took long to answer, Astolphe was surprised and angry. Such was his trust that he showed him his poems without fear of judgement, for he said, ". . . he is too good to me to make me waste years because of a lie, instead of wounding me for an instant, and sparing me lengthy disgust by the truth."

In 1806, at the time of the break between Delphine and René, Astolphe was sixteen. "He is so tall that all houses are too low for him."[33] He was a very strong horseman and physically resembled his grandfather, the general. "Until I was twenty-three," he wrote, "I was inconceivably strong. I had a temperament of iron, one which braved anything, and yet I was often ailing." He was in fact so often ill, being paralysed by appalling headaches and subject to fevers which laid him low, that without his mother's having to ask her friends for help, he was excused from military service on medical grounds. Psychologically he was more complicated, as might be expected from his solitary education.

Astolphe was never sent to school or to the *lycée*. He never had

---

thing in it to offend him"; *Mémoires de Mme de Chastenay, 1771–1815* (Alphonse Roserot, Plon, 1896), II, p. 78.

33. Maugras, *Delphine de Sabran*, op. cit., p. 440.

any friends his own age, and himself reached the conclusion that "this type of education [is] more favourable to the mind than to the character."[34] In fact, both his knowledge of languages and literature and his intellectual curiosity were unusual: evenings at Fervaques and in Paris were devoted to reading aloud and to long discussions. He thus acquired the ability and a taste for learning whatever he found interesting. "The serious cultivation of the mind is, for a man of the world, living in our century, the first condition for an honest heart"[35]—but he was also aware of a weakness that resulted from the lack of outside discipline.

"There is no strength without perseverance, and since perseverance is not natural to free men, this social virtue can only be obtained through obedience . . . Hence the inconstancy of isolated minds; they always remain a little savage and they pay the price of their dangerous insubordination through their indecision. He who has never known how to yield can never know how to will."[36] Besides, he was more inclined to melancholy than good cheer and appears to have had neither his mother's energy nor her perseverance—"she would have been happier with a son whose character was less concentrated, and above all one who was more ambitious

34. Alphonse de Custine, *Le Monde comme il est*, 2 vols. (Renduel, 1835), I, p. 67.
35. *Lettres à La Grange*, op. cit., p. 88.
36. *Le Monde comme il est*, op. cit., pp. 67–68.

. . . she is one of Corneille's women, not Racine's."[37] Although Astolphe tried to eradicate "the first impressions [Chateaubriand] had made [on him], the vividness of which he feared,"[38] the *Génie*'s influence reinforced his innate sadness. Many years later, he would write that "the chagrin of youth, at an age when happiness is a man's due, is a secret all the better kept for the fact that it is an inexplicable mystery, even to the sufferer."[39] Thus he retained a fundamental unease, probably hereditary, which manifested itself in his retreat from life. Delphine and her mother were frightened by it. They recognised the symptoms which they had already seen in Elzéar. It must be said that Delphine's refusal to participate in the social life of the Empire was not of a nature to encourage ambition in her son. Brilliant careers in the army and in the new administration were there for the taking, but only for those who had rallied unequivocally around Napoleon. This was not the case with the Custines.

There were no serious consequences for people like Delphine who stayed away from the court. So long as they didn't behave like Mme de Staël, for instance, they could live quite peacefully in their isolated fashion; but what may have had no effect on women satisfied with a small circle of friends and an intense intellectual life had a serious effect on a boy who saw himself as somehow condemned to in-

37. *Lettres à La Grange*, op. cit., p. 83.
38. Ibid., p. 123.
39. *La Russie en 1839*, op. cit., I, p. 26.

activity. It is hardly surprising that Astolphe announced, in his disarray: "Nothing equals the richness of my soul when I am only dreaming; but whenever I want to *achieve* whatsoever it may be, if only to express my thought, nothing equals its poverty."[40] Delphine, growing more and more anxious, watched him and made the decision to leave for Germany and Italy with him as soon as he was twenty-one.

40. *Lettres à La Grange*, op. cit., p. 40.

5

Italy

I was sated . . . with the first happiness of my life: the fulfilment of a wish which had been mine for ten years, that of seeing the Alps. This desire of mine had become a sickness, a frenzy, and no bird escaping from its cage takes possession of nature with such drunken pleasure as I felt on entering Switzerland. I knew in advance all the valleys, all the peaks and it was my great pleasure to name them to the guides."[1] Delphine must have been pleased by Astolphe's enthusiasm, for she was too clear-headed a person not to be concerned about her son's development. Their political situation was certainly hardly favorable to the establishment of a career, but

1. *Lettres à La Grange*, op. cit., p. 65.

that didn't explain the attacks of nerves, the migraines or Astolphe's terrible tendencies to the blackest of moods and the darkest of thoughts. "He is the most unhappy being in the world, and by his turn of mind and his character, he condemns me to a life of eternal tears; but let that be between ourselves," she wrote to her mother, "let us never give others the consolation of knowing us to be unhappy."[2] Delphine still had the pride she had shown when her apartment was searched. The journey was suggested to her by a new friend, David Koreff, the *Génie*'s surprising successor. He too was something of a genius, but of a vastly different sort.

David Koreff, a Silesian Jew, was the Custines' first Jewish friend. He had taken the opportunity of coming to Berlin during the short period when Jewish salons gave intellectual tone to a Prussian society yawning with boredom, stuck as it was between dismal *Biergesellschaften*—beer evenings—and the court of Frederick-William III and Queen Louise populated by automatons. Koreff was not only a doctor like his father, but a philosopher and writer too, who was the soul of the *thés poétiques* where many slightly eccentric characters gathered. There were men such as Varnhagen, another doctor, drawn like Koreff to literature, or Chamisso, a French emigré and director of the Berlin Botanical Gardens. With his short legs, flaming hair, bristling eyebrows, thick lips and "outrageously aquiline nose," Koreff, according to Varnhagen, had something of Mr.

2. Maugras, *Delphine de Sabran*, op. cit., p. 439.

Punch.[3] His bold intellect of a Jewish unbeliever, the scope of his research—under the Restoration he became interested in magnetism—and, above all, his energy, conviction and enthusiasm made him a much sought after doctor. With the fortune he inherited on the death of his father in 1805, he was able to settle in Paris, where he became famous. Talleyrand said of him: "That devil of a Koreff, he is a well of science, he knows everything, even a little about medicine."

Thanks to a recommendation from Cuvier, he was given permission to practise medicine in Paris, where his success was all the more dazzling because he didn't always charge, since respect for his profession generally prevented him from putting a commercial value on it. The German colony swore by so disinterested a scientist. Under the Restoration, he was to become the official doctor to the Austrian ambassador, Count Apponyi, and subsequently doctor to the whole diplomatic corps and the best Parisian society. This allowed him to choose patients to his liking and to care for them as he pleased and when he pleased—which of course increased his authority over them. Stendhal went to him, Merimée called him to his father's bedside, Mme de Staël insisted that he was the wittiest German she had ever met;[4] Mme de Boufflers was completely in thrall to him and on

3. Marietta Martin, *Une aventure intellectuelle sous la Restauration et la monarchie de Juillet* (Paris, Champion, 1925), p. 3.

4. Ibid., p. 13.

his advice luxuriated for three quarters of an hour ("Not a minute longer"!) in baths enriched with boiled herbs. He charmed and amused women and, what was more important in Delphine's case, he reassured them. It also helped that the social status of doctors had changed under the Empire; they were no longer superior servants. They were in society, sought after and to be seen in the best circles. The career of Napoleon's doctor, Corvisart, is an example of this. Corvisart became a baron and an academician.

Despite his own withdrawal, Chateaubriand was annoyed by Koreff's ascendency, and he expressed his irritation in "letters of black gloom,"[5] but Delphine didn't yield. When Koreff suggested taking Astolphe abroad to get him out of his melancholy, she asked him to accompany them. He accepted his turn to be transfixed by Delphine's attractions; now over forty, she remained "one of those ravishing creatures which heaven gives to the world in a moment of munificence," wrote her old friend, Laure d'Abrantès, author of memoirs of the time. And charm was what she needed to lead her little gang across the Alps. The gang consisted of Koreff; the faithful Berstoecher, whose jealousy no one suspected although, thirty years later, Custine remembered his "fits of rage which had no point, no cause and no effect";[6] Astolphe, who did nothing to hide

5. Maugras, *Delphine de Sabran*, op. cit., p. 437.
6. Letter to Sophie Gay, 14 October 1840.

his antipathy for the doctor; and finally, Jenny, the lady's maid forever dying of fright.

This initial trip through Germany and Italy—which lasted for three years—was to be of tremendous importance to Astolphe. For one thing, he wrote an account of it which was to be his first literary work; and during those three years he at last tasted independence, on a short trip to Calabria, and more importantly in 1814, while staying with the comte d'Artois, the youngest brother of Louis XVI and the future Charles X. But shortly after this attempt at emancipation, he was shattered by a great physical and moral crisis which may have been provoked by the vacuity of the prince's entourage, but was more surely due to a hopeless passion for a young German. On his return to France with his mother, he took refuge at Fervaques. He felt there "the kind of happiness one feels on entering port after a long and dangerous sea voyage . . . aged more than had I spent a lifetime at home. I have returned laden with the spoils of experience and stripped of the riches of ignorance."[7]

When they set out in August 1811, Paris was echoing to tales of the baptism of Napoleon's son. They all piled into Delphine's berlin, a real house on wheels, every innumerable pocket of which was stuffed with provisions, books and maps, and which was big enough for Delphine to be able to lie down in the back while the men occu-

7. *Lettres à La Grange*, op. cit., 20 July 1818.

pied the front seat. From the start Astolphe showed his irritation. He was a bad travelling companion who didn't hide his disappointment at the monotony of the road which led across eastern France to Basel, their first stop. Was it the doctor's youth—he was only eight years older than Astolphe—his obvious intimacy with Delphine, or the control that *Ko*, as she called him, tried to exercise over Astolphe which gave rise to this ill humour? Or perhaps Astolphe sensed that the doctor had guessed at the nature of the violent instincts which so troubled him, and dreaded "the unbelieving Jew's mordant wit."[8]

Astolphe's obvious lack of interest in young women compared with the ease of his relations with their elders, his bursts of passionate enthusiasm that soon fell flat, a sort of contained rage that found expression in terrible migraines, were clues to anyone aware of such things. In Berlin, they were aware of such things; they knew how to decode the clues. Astolphe liked people to be interested in him, but consciousness of Koreff's inquisitorial look turned on him all day didn't flatter. It exasperated him. Seemingly for the first time the son took sides against one of his mother's lovers. The relationship between mother and son was naturally so frank that this rift caused them to quarrel openly. Delphine, attentive as she was to her son's well-being, would not allow herself to be manipulated. She needed Koreff and she knew it: "He reassures my imagination," she said

8. Letter to Sophie Gay, 14 October 1840.

prettily to her mother,[9] besides which she didn't deceive herself about the cause of her son's sulkiness. "The sheltered life we have led has not made him able to live with human beings and know how to cede to the will of others, for he is too used to everything around him yielding to his."[10] One part of her knew that the spoilt, inflexible child who was so disagreeable in his "way of life" needed to be pushed out of the nest and subjected to outside discipline. (Delphine, Astolphe himself, all their friends and biographers have noticeably continued to refer to the young man as a child or an adolescent after the age of twenty; and that in an age when men earned their stripes young.) At the same time, her anxiety and her affection for him were such that she couldn't let go of her great big son even when climbing for the first time in Switzerland, although she suffered from vertigo during these hikes.

On Wildkirchen there was "a hermitage placed like a bird's nest in a sort of recess halfway up a three hundred to four hundred foot wall of rock . . . The poorest fencing would be a luxury to the goatherds in these parts . . . I admit that I trembled to see my mother follow me up such a path, but she wants neither to leave me, nor to prevent me from going on any excursion."[11] Mme Gide inevitably

9. Maugras, *Delphine de Sabran*, op. cit., p. 436.

10. Annamaria Rubino Campani, *Lettere inedite di Delphine de Sabran a Auguste-Louis Millin* (Palermo, Grafotip, 1978), p. 19.

11. Astolphe de Custine, *Mémoires et Voyages* (Paris, François Bourin, 1992), pp. 16–17.

comes to mind; another of those "darling mothers" who, unable to steel herself to allow the single object of her solicitude to leave with a pack on his back, followed him—at a distance, of course—on a trip round Brittany. Mme Proust, too, who insisted that her "little one," aged twenty-four and on holiday in Evian, should write every day to tell her the exact time of his getting up and going to bed.

But Delphine had a sense of the ridiculous and, probably influenced by Koreff and Berstoecher, she made up her mind to allow her son to play at climbing on his own. In so doing, she made it possible for him to show his affection for her in all its sensitivity. When he wasn't laid low by headaches or bouts of depression, which he called his moments of apathy, Astolphe was very athletic, courageous, tough and enthusiastic. His first trip without Mama was to cross the Mer de Glace. He was drawn increasingly to the challenges of the wild and to dangerous mountains, but without ever forgetting the anxiety of his mother waiting at the inn. One day when he had promised to return by nine o'clock, he was running late, and refused to sleep in the refuge as the guides advised. "To travel alone at night on a path that the mountain people themselves called dangerous was to risk my life; not to return to my mother before eleven o'clock in the evening was to risk hers."[12] Fortunately Delphine had been misled about the time—a subterfuge made possible by early nightfall—and the crisis was avoided.

12. Ibid., p. 33.

Italy

Once Astolphe's initial ill-humour was over, the first months went well. Enormous physical exertion, the beginnings of independence from his mother and some kind of relief at having left French society behind produced in him a semi-mystic, semi-poetic drunkenness: "Poetry is everywhere, but above all in solitude; and what solitude is more complete than that of the traveller? Society's customs are lost for him; only God and nature remain. A journey, like isolation, is poetic. In society one must choose, compare, consult, reflect on how to behave, travelling one has only to feel . . . to let oneself go . . ."[13]

Mother and son inevitably visited Coppet, Mme de Staël's château in Switzerland, but they didn't stay long although Delphine was on excellent terms with her. At a time when conscription threatened Astolphe, she wanted to avoid annoying the master who had exiled Mme de Staël and always kept her and her entourage under close surveillance.

Good humour among the travellers was established. After having practically smashed his head open—he had a tendency during those years literally to hit his head against the wall—Astolphe acknowledged the intelligent way Koreff looked after him and forgot his grievances. The fact is that he was harder on himself than on others. He showed great loyalty to others and knew, as in this particular

13. Astolphe de Custine, *L'Espagne sous Ferdinand VII* (François Bourin, 1991), p. 143.

case, how to overcome his prejudices with good grace. Besides, they were on their way to Italy. "Italy, on leaving Switzerland, is Racine after Corneille."[14] No doubt. Nevertheless they made up their minds with understandable caution to leave their precious berlin in Switzerland and to take a hired carriage—a large barouche—to cross the Alps. And rightly so, for no elegiac Racine awaited them on the other side. Arriving in a loathsome shelter for travellers, Koreff claimed to recognise the smell of an operating theatre, which immediately made Delphine imagine that there were bodies in the cellar. On one road, the best part of which was in reality a riverbed worn away by floods, a stagecoach bumped into them, broke the front of the carriage and continued on its way. Their coachman dashed out, caught up with the huge stagecoach on an uphill slope and confronted the postilion. They came to blows, pulled each other's hair, and worse still, the poor coachman came back to the carriage with blood all over his face, having lost the end of his nose. He finished the journey with a false nose and a white linen mask which made him look like a ghost.[15]

Because of a lack of letters—Delphine's to her mother having been lost—the only way to retrace the Italian journey is by turning to Custine's own account, based on notes taken at the time and compiled on his return at Koreff's advice. They were published many

14. *Mémoires*, op. cit., p. 36.
15. Maugras, *Delphine de Sabran*, op. cit., pp. 442–443.

years later, in 1830. This account consists of memories presented in the form of letters, a formula to which Custine always remained faithful since it allowed him greater freedom and diversity by virtue of the letters being addressed to different correspondents. He was always averse to the simple account which left no room for the disorder of reality, "the contradictions, the contrasts, the lack of consequence which constitute real life."[16]

More important still was his conception of what an account of a journey should be.

It is not enough to show the land as it appears to everyone's eyes, a man must be seen in the perceptible world, a living individual, passionately involved, a man who registers the nature of things through the impressions he has of them; but the more immediate the reactions of his soul, the readier, the greater in number, the quicker they are forgotten; and so in order to capture this fleeting life of travel, it must be described as it goes along. In this way, a new genre can be created, a journey, the interest of which is born from the description of things, just as it is born from the characters in a play or a novel; in order to attain this end, the precise collection of facts and characters, which is to say the traveller's diary, must become the traveller's unique theme; all the rest can be filled in; the landscape of the journey, painted by the one who has seen it, with all the images these things have left

16. *Mémoires*, op. cit., p. 143.

*reflected in his soul, belongs only to the individual. Additional
knowledge, literature, science, history, belong to everyone; what
a man has done, what he has seen and felt belongs to him alone,
only he can express it!*

*This kind of journey should be called an individual journey;
such is the genre which I conceive and which I would like to make
others conceive.*[17]

In other words, the account became a kind of confession for anyone
who knew how to read it. But although he was a great admirer of
Rousseau, Custine never wrote openly about himself. He certainly
discoursed about poetry, his state of mind and his tastes, but there
is nothing in his account about particular events, like the spanking
administered by Mlle de Lambercier, Mme de Waren's seduction, or
the monk's attack. That is all left to the reader's imagination.

Astolphe had more freedom than he had ever had before. By virtue
of being abroad, he avoided the constraints imposed on those young
men who had chosen a civil or military career under the Empire. His
time, which he used to spend studying, reading and walking, had
always been his own, and now, confronted by the Lago Maggiore,
where "the sounds, the colours and the scents are all in proportion,
in harmony, where everything charms and troubles the soul," he declared disarmingly, "The days seem too short even to do nothing in

17. *L'Espagne*, op. cit., p. 16.

them."[18] He had discovered tranquil tourism. In France, where the martial arts were admired above all others, Raphaels were valued as the equivalent of regimental colours. Victorious armies brought back paintings and statues as trophies, so that the Louvre had become "a prison for paintings [whereas] in Italy . . . every town has its painting, every painting its sanctuary; whole days are spent in studying the works of one master."[19] The party travelled slowly down towards Rome which had taken on an almost mythical quality for them. They were haunted by memories of what Chateaubriand had written, but everyday life in the exotic world of Rome was so rough that it was impossible to succumb entirely to the idea inspired by the name and the dust of "this queen who no longer rules over anything but shadows."[20]

Finding lodgings involved Astolphe in what he regarded as shockingly vulgar discussions. He had "always feared to involve himself in the most necessary things of life."[21] But, as Delphine was exhausted by the long journey and remained lying in the barouche waiting for her son to find rooms, he was obliged to confront innumerable porters, innkeepers, translators and the authorities. Before finding an apartment, they settled temporarily in "the worst rooms

18. *Mémoires*, op. cit., p. 50.
19. Ibid., p. 57.
20. Ibid., p. 64.
21. Ibid., p. 65.

in the worst inn." Travellers who, in those days, used to stay for several weeks in a town rented either two rooms or a whole apartment. A good room could be had for 20 to 30 francs,[22] a three-room apartment for 100 francs.[23] Once foreigners were organised, life for them was easy, with numerous restaurants and the cafés that doubled as convenient reading rooms where French and English newspapers were available.

Nevertheless, Rome had a twofold effect on Astolphe. There he rediscovered his own world and, at the same time, withdrew from it. In 1811, Rome was the seat of the prefecture for the department of the Tiber, within the command of General comte de Miollis, governor of the Roman states. It was a provincial town, "subject to the same authority as Angers or Le Mans." The prefect, M. de Tournon, gave balls and played the double role of French ambassador and Roman senator. The comte de Miollis, as governor of the Roman states, represented the Emperor and therefore took precedence in the city; he was an old acquaintance of the Custines. A "Frenchman of the old school,"[24] he had fought for the first time with General de Custine in America. He was the best man in the world, but, as Mme Récamier[25] unjustly claimed, he thought Mme de Staël's novel *Corinne*

22. By way of comparison, Victor Hugo, as a penniless young man, spent 20 francs a month on food.

23. Maurice Andrieux, *Les Français à Rome* (Fayard, 1968), p. 356.

24. Norvins, op. cit., III, p. 316.

25. Françoise Wagener, *Madame Récamier* (Paris, Lattès, 1986), p. 237.

Italy

was a town in Italy. The general loved the arts, artists and women. He delighted in reading Virgil aloud to his guests, among whom might be found Canova, Rude, the sculptor of the *Marseillaise*, or Pradier, who made the statues of Lille and Strasbourg on the place de la Concorde, the Victories on Napoleon's tomb and the *Renommées de l'Arc de triomphe*. In the Aldobrandini Palace where he lived, Miollis had—with some good advice from Ingres—built a collection which included Caravaggio, Tintoretto, Holbein and Philippe de Champaigne. Ingres himself, taking advantage of the deconsecration by the French of so many churches, had established his studio in the church of S. Trinità dei Monti.

Naturally Delphine also knew the director general of police, the chevalier Norvins, who came from a good, old family of magistrates and whom everyone in French aristocratic society had known when in school at Plessis and Harcourt. He was a man of great sensitivity, who wept with emotion at sung mass, but had remembered to bring an excellent chef with him from Paris. She soon made friends with the prefect, M. de Tournon, a pretty young man of about thirty. Having apparently fallen in love with Rome, he gave wonderful parties in the old Farnese gardens. Finally there was Marshal Daru, in charge of finance, whose brother was Minister of War. He loved gambling, good living and beautiful women, all of which he brought together at his superb receptions at the Quirinale. Delphine was invited as soon as she arrived.

Designated the second city of the Empire, Rome had become

a meeting place for the aristocracy of Europe. Delphine easily adapted to this society despite Astolphe's complaints. "A prefect in Rome! That I should dance in his house, I think I am dreaming! . . . That I should come here to pay court to people whom I do not wish to see in my own country, what inconsistency!"[26] Neither was Delphine's acquaintanceship limited to French people. She met Canova, who was living with his half-brother, the abbé, only a step away from the via del Babuino and they were equally enchanted with one another. Canova, then at the peak of his fame, recited verses in Venetian dialect to her, told her of his plans and gave her a ring whose fate he envied because she wore it on her finger. Astolphe, who watched his mother as closely as she watched him, said to her, "Do you know that with your romantic imagination, you would be capable of marrying Canova!" "Don't challenge me," she replied. "If he hadn't become marquis d'Ischia, I would be tempted." The fact that Canova had a reputation with young unmarried women for not pressing his suit didn't seem to bother her. His having accepted a Napoleonic title did. Two years later he was taking Mme Récamier for walks and sending her passionate letters.

Astolphe was not satisfied with hanging around the ballrooms and chaperoning his mother, but was very taken by the popular life of the city. The carnival season was about to begin, with "the noisy delight, the delirium of a naturally taciturn people who [are trans-

26. *Mémoires*, op. cit., p. 71.

formed] into a senseless herd." During Napoleon's occupation, carnivals became more brilliant and noisier than ever, because, unlike the balls, they were not French festivities and people could participate without compromising their political stand. Besides, the Romans, caught up in the fever of the celebration, were quite willing to have the French take part. So Astolphe happily lost himself "amongst these people who had turned into animals, gods, giants, children . . . these men metamorphosised into women . . . [this] furious herd of people dressed in shifts and wearing nightcaps, who one would think had escaped from a lunatic asylum." He walked "in the middle of the street pell-mell with porters, horses, harlots, princes and grand ladies," moved by "the harmony of a whole nation meeting in the street, with no end in view, other than that of each man's natural pleasure in adding to his own joy by the joy of others," touched by the absence of "social distinctions of money or birth . . . the equality of pleasure equalised everything."[27]

Clearly the *ragazzi* were able to complete his happiness. Not that the literary expression he gave to his pleasure was particularly joyful. If he had had to rewrite Dante's *Inferno*, he would have depicted "a moral hell in which the guilty would feel all the consequences of their crimes without being able to repent. They would be horrified by vice but would not want to change . . . [those] who allow themselves to be led astray by earthly love will always love the same ob-

27. Ibid., pp. 80–81.

jects but will know in advance that happiness cannot be attained by following the path [they] choose but that they do not wish not to choose . . . They are disgusted by the creatures who captivate them, but from these same creatures [they] expect the happiness [which they] did not know how to seek in its right place . . . This is the hell of voluptuous people."[28] This serves also as Custine's self-portrait—torn between the natural, joyful pleasure he has discovered and the interdictions of his religion, having apparently decided to suffer the torments of guilt rather than renounce his leanings. Social mores, however harsh they might be, would never weigh so heavily with Astolphe as the awareness of sin. Hence his torment and his freedom.

So the journey continued. At the end of April, the Custines bade their Roman friends farewell and, travelling a little every day, which for Astolphe meant on foot, went down to Naples. Infected by the city's frenetic atmosphere where the main street—the via Toledo—"gives the impression of a popular uprising," Astolphe forgot his habitual melancholy. He was fascinated by the sight of the cabriolets which seemed small for one man alone, carrying "ten people hanging, hooked up, clinging like monkeys to different parts" of the carriages that charged through the crowd without ever slowing down or hurting anyone. "It represents the revolt of madness against civilization and this permanent revolt is what consti-

28. Ibid., p. 61.

tutes Naples." In the official world of Rome he had rediscovered social obligations which he loathed. In Naples, his untamed side revelled in its natural surroundings, hence his delight. "You have a spirit of freedom and a need for independence which are impossible to preserve in the midst of society . . . your disdainful manner towards the indifferent has become stronger than your will. You are in permanent revolt against life in society," his companion on an expedition to Calabria was to tell him.[29] Certainly he thought differently than most of his kind, never accepting the values of the times without close examination. In Naples he realized that he needed to break away from his times and his country. And so he left to seek adventure.

To his great delight, his mother agreed to allow him to explore Calabria under the protection of Louis Millin, a Parisian naturalist and archeologist. Delphine had such trust in Millin that, unusual for her, she talked to him with surprising frankness about Astolphe and his whims: "He fears boredom and constraint, which is surely a great failing and I blame him very much . . . I have swayed him less on this point than would have been the case in the last century . . . but where does one get the strength to bother about the little things in life? All one's forces have been spent on bearing the big ones."[30]

29. Ibid., p. 141.
30. *Lettere inedite di Delphine de Sabran*, op. cit., p. 19.

They were joined by a third traveller. He was a German painter called Franz Ludwig Catel, who seduced Astolphe by his talent, his modesty and his even temper. To cross Calabria in 1812 was not to go looking for works of art or well-known, much-praised sites. That part of Italy has never been a great centre for tourism. The first few pages of Carlo Levi's *Christ Stopped at Eboli*, written as a result of his exile in the south, are convincing enough. " 'We are not Christians,' the inhabitants say, 'Christ stopped at Eboli . . . Christ never came, just as the Romans who built big roads and never went into the mountains or the forests never came, nor the Greeks who flourished by the sea at Metapontum and Sibari.' "

What was Astolphe looking for in this abandoned area? Certainly not scientific knowledge of the flora and fauna. He cruelly mocked his companion, Millin, for never leaving his books, his herbarium, his drawings or his jumble of papers. Poor Millin, who was able only to make notes but ever incapable of turning them into a book.[31] Astolphe experienced great joy at the extreme wildness of the natural world, so free and so powerful that "having revolted against man's conquests, [nature seems to mock] civilization, not by setting obstacles against it like the Alps, but by embellishment as in a painting." He felt, too, a drunken pleasure at finding himself in a society so violent and so archaic that he seemed to have returned to the Middle Ages. He was carried away by happiness: "We spent a night at

31. *Mémoires*, op. cit., p. 169.

Amantea . . . The war [waged by brigands] has left this town with several factions which perpetuate themselves; fathers, brothers, sons, all hate each other, devour each other and betray each other! Almost with the ardour of the Middle Ages; perhaps it is exactly the same and only the veneer of time is missing to our eyes! The new governor of the place has, however, re-established some order in this unfortunate city [by giving balls several times a week and inviting the leaders of the different factions]. It is well worth while to be born a Calabrian, to eschew this century's civilization, and to quarrel with pigs over a diet of raw onions, so as to be able to lay down your arms at the first sound of a violin."[32]

The entire journey was not spent in a state of feverish admiration worthy of René, the famous Romantic hero. But in what he wrote then, Custine seems capable for the first time of going straight from a description of the sky and the sunrise to one of Millin's servant, Jocrisse. Jocrisse was "lame, one-eyed, or at least squinting, slow at not finishing . . . dirty enough to leave a stain on filth,"[33] and irritated his master—Millin wore silk stockings to ride a donkey—with his mistakes in grammar.

They travelled by donkey or mule with guides whom, "pistol in hand," they had to force to advance because, once they had left the coast, the muleteers no longer knew the way; and they travelled by

32. Ibid., p. 145.
33. Ibid., p. 109.

night to avoid the heat. In order to find lodgings on arrival in a village, they had to find the mayor and present their letters of recommendation. So, "at nine o'clock at night," the poor things "were obliged to cross a dark, dirty, hilly village with exhausted mules and men who talk like slaves and act like enemies"[34] and finally collapsed on beds that were so disgusting they couldn't undress. They had to force themselves to eat, often with pigs pushing at the door, off plates encrusted with dirt that couldn't be wiped because it was impossible to know whether the "cloth dirties the crockery or the crockery dirties the cloth,"[35] that being a question they didn't wish to see answered. In palaces whose walls were covered with magnificent paintings, where four-poster beds were hung with damask, poultry lived in the bedrooms and the unfortunate Astolphe was particularly angry with one rooster whose crowing and aggression got on his nerves. Such inconveniences would have been easier to bear if one hadn't come to the country out of curiosity, he declared. Perhaps.

As soon as he was overwhelmed by the unexpected beauty of the countryside—imagination is essential to visual appreciation—and he felt his curiosity and sensibilities aroused, he would forget his discouragement and regain his enthusiasm. Then he said, "I feel myself go mad; I no longer sleep, nor eat, nor think; I contemplate

34. Ibid., p. 142.
35. Ibid., p. 119.

and I go into ecstasies! The least that can happen is that I may remain an imbecile."[36]

Astolphe's romanticism may have allowed him to be carried away by beauty and the exotic, but the politician in him kept his eyes open, and he was pained by what he saw of a people renowned for their pride whose resignation to authority had come to verge on degradation. Since Napoleon had chased out the Bourbons in 1806, authority meant France through the intermediary of Murat who was made king of Naples in 1808. In the Calabrian language, the word *brigand* was used to describe partisans of the conquered enemy. Thus he was told that eight thousand brigands had captured such a town and five thousand brigands had escaped through a certain pass, and, confronted by such nonsense, Custine protested violently: "Soldiers are not bandits! Call them rebels, if you like, but these rebels only fight the new government out of loyalty to the old . . . if they were to win, they would call you brigands too."[37]

In such narrowness of thought and deed he recognised one of the most pernicious results of injustice dispensed by the governments of usurpers, "whose obliging prime minister is deceit." The Calabrians' docility was made evident by their easy acceptance of conscription, something that was close to Astolphe's heart, so eager was he to avoid it himself. If certain young men little "taken with the

36. Ibid., p. 157.
37. Ibid., p. 144.

need ... to seek death and glory in Poland"[38] ran away, the commanding officer soon made them come back by sentencing their fathers to a flogging and by making their parish priests lodge and feed four soldiers. Could this be the best way of bringing civilisation to countries long neglected by indolent rulers? Already, at an early age, Custine was a clear-eyed observer.

Despite his physical resilience, he was eventually laid low by an attack of malaria. In those days a dying man was said to be "crossing Calabria." The fever certainly overwhelmed Astolphe, who felt his head swelling monstrously and a relentless exhaustion overcome him, as if to make him surrender to a murderous sleep. He felt himself to be literally dying. "Death is no more than a letting-go. It would have cost me less to die of thirst and fatigue than to make an effort of the will to retain my soul in my exhausted body."[39] But he recovered and, nourished by lemons and chocolate, regained enough strength to rejoin Delphine in Naples.

It would be an exaggeration to say that, as a result of this trip and his separation from his mother, Astolphe grew up. He did return from his wanderings with a better understanding of his sexuality. On the way home, he was bowled over by the beauty, the nobility, and the "antique simplicity"[40] of the face of an innkeeper's son. He

---

38. Ibid., p. 161.
39. Ibid., p. 195.
40. *Lettres à La Grange*, op. cit., p. 97.

didn't sleep that night, and the next day tried to calm himself by running behind his mother's carriage, shedding floods of tears and writing love poems. Koreff snubbed him by telling him his poetry was worthless. Perhaps he was afraid that Astolphe might seduce a young shepherd. It was pointless to fight the young man's predilection. Many of the letters in the book he would later publish were addressed to *the friend I will have*. A few months later he was to find this rather special friend, but although he neither detached himself from Delphine nor appeared to concentrate more on the future, it was generally acknowledged that he was capable of living alone and even, as we shall see, of throwing himself into the political upheaval of the first Restoration.

6

Astolphe's Beginnings

By 1813, the Russian campaign had ended in disaster and Napoleon's armies were no longer overwhelmingly powerful, but the government's hold over the people was proving to be stronger than ever. Delphine suddenly heard of her brother's arrest. The harmless Elzéar had been so witty and so imprudent in his correspondence with Mme de Staël that the imperial police locked him up in the fortress of Vincennes. Horrified, Mme de Boufflers turned to Delphine for help. Delphine abandoned Astolphe in Switzerland, put to use her old imperial friends including Queen Hortense, of whom Napoleon remained fond despite his divorce from her mother, and Marshal Oudinot,[1] and managed to have

---

1. Letter from Custine to Jules Janin, September 1846, Collection Thierry Bodin.

her brother released. She also took advantage of her stay in France, to find a replacement for Astolphe in the army. Such was the need for soldiers that men who had been discharged as unfit to serve for reasons of health were called back and young Custine would be unable to avoid conscription indefinitely. But towards the end of the Empire, it was difficult to find volunteers for less than 4000 francs, which was more than a tenth of Delphine's yearly income. Besides, there were very few men available, recruitment having more or less emptied the countryside. She managed nonetheless to discover a soldier who was prepared to re-engage. Having thus accomplished her mission, she returned to Switzerland just as the defeat of Leipzig, in October 1813, opened the French frontiers to the Allies.

For the partisans of restoration there was renewed hope, and Delphine judged the moment right for Astolphe to be sent into action. He had just recovered from one of his bouts of depression during which he "preserved enough intelligence only to think himself stupid." This depression coincided with his meeting in Geneva of Wilhelm Hesse, his "dear Wilhelm," a quite insignificant young German of whom he became enamoured. At the beginning of 1814, however, he agreed to leave him, but not without solemnly promising to return. So Astolphe's public life began with his joining the comte d'Artois's faithful at Basel where, with a certain degree of caution, they were preparing to re-enter France.

The future Charles X had obtained the permission of the English government to return to the continent in January 1814. He disembarked at Scheveningen, near The Hague, and from there went with several of his gentlemen to Basel, where he established what he wanted to be a court in the hotel du Sauvage. The circle consisted of Jules de Polignac, the comte d'Escars, an aide-de-camp, ex-officer in the Austrian service, and a priest, the abbé Latil. A man as unsure of his own mind as Astolphe must have been surprised by the comte d'Artois's entourage. He thought he was entering "the real world, the world of action," only to find himself amongst people who altered their plans every quarter of an hour, who didn't know where they were heading and who, by shilly-shallying and back-tracking, ended up marching without ever advancing. The Allies, having little confidence in the abilities of the Bourbons, didn't openly support the prince. "It is eight days since I left you, and I am eight leagues from you," Astolphe announced ironically to his mother. Then he discovered the enormous difficulty of understanding events when participating oneself in the action. "Nothing is more extraordinary than one's ignorance of everything as one follows an army . . . We are here as if in a tomb, awaiting news from the living."[2] Nevertheless, this curious apprenticeship was useful to him, first because he gained confidence in his own judgement, and then because, when confronted with the real misfortunes of countries subjected to the

2. *Revue bleue*, October 1907, p. 452.

scourge of war, he "forgot his personal ills"; above all, he observed, reflected and passed judgement. In letters of the period, you can see the boy becoming the man.

He showed no enthusiasm for the princes and their entourage, thus displaying great independence of spirit allied to an unexpected sense of humour. His passionate self-observation didn't prevent him from sometimes laughing at what he saw in the mirror. "You cannot imagine me," he wrote to his mother, "with my sword between my legs, my hat under my arm, in a uniform made by a tailor in Morges ... I have not yet dropped my hat, but I get caught up in my spurs, and then I never have a hand free to do anything."[3] He wanted to grow a moustache, but thought himself not yet military enough to emulate his grandfather, the general. Nevertheless, he began to have a certain bearing. He was even mistaken for a Russian officer. He was appalled by the total absence of conversation and admitted that the officers seemed even more boring than bad. When he was eventually presented to the comte d'Artois, he was amazed at the comte addressing him three times without saying anything and on the third time repeating his first question—such frivolous questions that they could have been asked at Versailles but were pitiful in the present situation. In this desert, he perceived only one man

3. Ibid., p. 486.

who reminded him of Chateaubriand. Alexis de Noailles, with opinions similar to his own, was cheerful and active and showed little respect for authority. Here was a young man of character. Having been given a sub-lieutenant's brevet by the Emperor, he refused to serve, was arrested and sent to prison. He stood his ground. Finally, the Emperor ordered him to leave France "where he had no need for this childish conspirator."[4] So Alexis, an imposing, active man, said to be full of good sense, took himself off to join the comte d'Artois. He immediately got on well with Astolphe and before long the two accomplices were indulging in light-hearted debate with those they had nicknamed the *aristocruches*—aristodunces.

Because he hadn't emigrated, and because of his disinterested position as a witness under the Empire, Astolphe de Custine's judgement was not partisan, and the picture he had of his country was fairly accurate. He was staggered by the discovery of emigrés obstinate enough to dismiss the Revolution and the Empire with extravagant self-assurance and no sign of recognizing political difficulties. He wondered where such people could have been for them still to think that the restored king's first duty would be to return their lands and fortunes. Couldn't they see that the people had had enough, that the peasants were revolting and that the army was ordered to attack them? To re-establish "the *Ancien Régime* pure and

4. *Mémoires de la comtesse de Boigne*, 2 vols. (Mercure de France, 1986), I, p. 195.

simple, the *Ancien Régime* with its abuses," was madness, and the young man didn't hesitate to let his indignation at such criminal folly be known. But how was a debate of the issues to begin? The two sides talked to one another but there was no understanding. Astolphe admitted that his words were Hebrew to the other side, and the old duc de Laval's language was Chinese to him. An inhabitant of Peking would have seemed less alien. At meal times he consoled himself in deep conversation with his friend, Alexis, while the others spoke of horses and dogs and good food.

Intimacy with the comte d'Artois and his partisans did nothing to reassure him about the Bourbons' political future: where would they find clever men to serve them? Certainly not among their own entourage. They ought to have the sense to attract some of the people surrounding Bonaparte. He knew how to pick his men. "Governments," Astolphe added, "can no longer separate themselves from their people without losing all support . . . you see, I have made some progress in a month: which is because I have learnt more than one lesson."[5] He listened stupefied as the prince explained to young men in his entourage that clear views were totally useless to the people and that, because of their ignorance, the Russians were the happiest nation on earth. "We would not exchange our misery for their happiness," Astolphe answered, red in the face.[6] But to be, like him,

5. *Revue bleue*, October 1907, p. 527.
6. Ibid., p. 532.

anti-Bonapartist whilst refusing his unconditional support for the Bourbons was hardly the best recipe for a career, should the king be returned to the Tuileries.

On 9 March 1814, Astolphe reached Montbéliard, and so returned to France, in the wake of the Allied armies. He immediately asked himself the question which was bound to torment any legitimist capable of reflection. Amazed that the Allied armies "are made up of nothing but Cossacks . . . hordes of brigands whose flattened faces and eastern dress recall Tartary," he concluded, "had I been able to imagine that a French prince would need the support of five hundred thousand foreigners to reconquer France, I would not have espoused his cause."[7] He had difficulty in overcoming the discomfort he felt at finding himself a protégé of soldiers invading his own country.

He reached Paris on April 12th—Napoleon had abdicated on the 4th. It had been a painful journey across a country whose indifference frightened him, a journey which gave him the sensation of having gone deaf—"not a cry, not a song, not a word could be heard in streets where one saw men . . . as free as birds which have been put outside after being pinioned."[8] He arrived in the capital, suffocating in clouds of dust raised by Russian horses, "drinking the earth . . .

---

7. Maugras, *Delphine de Sabran*, op. cit., p. 487.

8. The first part of the quotation is taken from the *Revue bleue* of August 1910, letter of 13 April; the second is from the October 1907 number, p. 531.

dust reaching even into the brain,'"[9] to discover the heedlessness of the inhabitants who were more fascinated by the occupying armies than humiliated by defeat.

In the magnificent spring of 1814, all Paris was out and about. Women dressed in Russian hats and feathered shakos copied from the headdresses of the Prussian guard and the uhlans gathered round the Cossacks camping on the Champs-Elysées. It was a bivouac without tents or shelter but with three or four horses tied to every tree. Nothing could make the troopers take a step. To fetch a pitcher of water or a mess tin from twenty metres away, they mounted their horses which they rode standing in a peculiar position because the height of the saddle prevented them from bending their knees. They never allowed men near them but let themselves be inspected closely by the women who were interested in their semi-oriental dress, all blue, and adorned with brilliant brass ornaments and buckles.[10] The Cossacks were no longer seen as conquerors but as objects of curiosity.

In Paris during that strange time in 1814, the political dilemma of whether to be unequivocally engaged or to observe from a distance presented itself to Astolphe not so much as the result of objective

9. Ibid.
10. *Mémoires de la comtesse de Boigne*, op. cit., I, pp. 225–227.

analysis, but as the reality of the contradictions that tore him apart. "My worthlessness weighs on me and bores me. I find myself always the subordinate, yet I have more wits than many of them,"[11] he declared to his mother. The concept he had of his own lack of worth was a complex one. On days when he wanted to play a part in his country's future, he was upset by his lack of experience and specific ability; but on days when he wished to lock himself away in solitude, he was distressed by "the misfortune of not having done enough important things for [him] to be allowed to do nothing at all."[12] He was drifting but it must be said in his defense that the establishment of the new order in the first days of the Restoration wasn't simple. Besides, to his surprise, the resurrection of a whole past, which ought to have delighted him, only irritated him.

He may have been touched by the rediscovery of old family friends returning from abroad—Mathieu de Montmorency, who had never seen him, was so moved by Astolphe's resemblance to his father that he embraced him—but he had little use either for their reactionary attitude or for the vestiges of their eighteenth-century sensibility. He was at first surprised and then exasperated by the emigré frivolity. "When listening to our grandfathers, we might mistake them for our grandchildren."[13] "I would like to have lived

---

11. *Revue bleue*, October 1907, p. 531.
12. *Revue bleue*, August 1910.
13. *Lettres à La Grange*, op. cit., p. 24.

a century earlier, if only so as not to hear the eighteenth century talked about," he wrote to his mother,[14] who was still in Switzerland. He was exasperated by these old people rejoicing in the rediscovery of their ancient gilding, their old-fashioned furniture and their outdated mores, reminding him, as they did, of dusty paintings by Boucher. He was even annoyed by his grandmother, who continued to pay social calls even though she was in mourning for her husband, the chevalier. "How can one be prey at the same time to both indifference and sorrow?" he wondered.[15] Like Mme de Boigne, the witty memorialist, he felt that the importance of events since the Revolution should have made people behave with a certain simplicity and dispelled their exaggerated mawkishness. "How did you manage to remain natural, born into such a world?" he asked his mother.[16] Later he wrote to her, "What a comedy the world is! And how different we are from all those people. Do you know that as *detestable* as I am, I am very like you."[17] The resurrection of his world gave him no sense of belonging. Quite the opposite.

He took refuge in Mme de Staël's salon. She had just returned, delighted to be no longer in the opposition but too curious and too intelligent not to listen to the opinions of others. He talked to the

14. *Revue bleue*, October 1910, p. 295.

15. Ibid., p. 355.

16. Ibid.

17. *Revue bleue*, August 1910, p. 265.

mother, chatted with her pretty red-headed daughter, Albertine, and met Mme de Duras, who had succeeded Delphine in Chateaubriand's attentions, if not in his affection. The more intellectual mothers were particularly pleased with this good-looking young man with a grand name, a sweet nature and a reflective mind, who was one of the most eligible men in France. His bearing, the elegance of his manners and his fine seat on a horse all added to his charm. But did they have any understanding of his detachment? A detachment which led him to claim that he didn't mind being in a salon because "nowhere can the mind rest so completely, because there it cannot even concern itself with ideas . . . it is even better than sleeping since, asleep, one sometimes dreams . . . in society . . . one is happy after the fashion of a chair or a log."[18]

However stimulating the Staël-Duras world might have been, it didn't spur him on enough to persuade him to set out in pursuit of honours. In any case, he understood that he couldn't obtain a position and succeed in it without a real and sustained effort. "One is so easily cast aside in this country that it is necessary to row continually, not merely to advance but even to stay afloat." Besides, he was used neither to being bored, nor to begging favours. "Court would kill me if I had to take part in it as I have been doing since coming here. I am dying of it; it is folly's palace," he declared to Delphine. He had no support other than from his friend, Alexis. Chateaubri-

18. *Mémoires*, op. cit., p. 164.

and, who had just published *De Bonaparte et des Bourbons,* was as yet without influence. Mme de Boigne records the somewhat insulting frivolity with which the Tsar treated Chateaubriand at an audience. Since the arrival of the Allies, the author had been going around in a fancy uniform, dragging behind him an immense Turkish sabre.[19]

Like a spoilt child, Astolphe turned to his mother with whom he could let himself be as "young" as he pleased. He "allowed her to step behind the stage and showed [her] the most secret moving forces of [his] soul,"[20] forces which were paralysed, as it happened, by contradictory aspirations and by fecklessness. On the one hand, he wanted to drop everything and return to his "delicious" Switzerland to be with her and his dear Wilhelm, "the private friend, the intimate of the house," and, on the other hand, he realised full well that such a flight would dishonour him. "It's easy to choose between boredom and unhappiness, but one hesitates between boredom and public opprobrium and ends up, no doubt, choosing boredom."[21] But he needed his mother's presence; it was indispensable to him. He insisted that she come despite the dangers of the roads and despite the fact that it was impossible for him to go and fetch her. He was so downhearted that he wanted to "go to bed until her arrival"; he was

19. *Mémoires de la comtesse de Boigne,* op. cit., I, p. 233.

20. *Mémoires,* op. cit., p. 166.

21. *Revue bleue,* October 1907.

unable to look after himself in the big, wide world without her advice. Besides, only women knew how to ask for favours, and such was his mother's reputation that he was convinced only she could obtain a position for him and finally alleviate his anguish.

Delphine set forth but Astolphe seemed to be in such a bad state of nerves that she decided to take him with Berstoecher to Fervaques just as he was named officer of the Maison Rouge, the most elegant section of the king's household; as a result, he was unable to assume his post. A few weeks of calm and solitude under his mother's wing cured him and eventually Alexis de Noailles, who was attached to Talleyrand, persuaded him to go with him to the Congress of Vienna. The geographical position of the family was thereby turned round: while Delphine remained in France, Astolphe left for Central Europe.

Since he went to Vienna without a mission, as a tourist, this new departure proved to be an expedient that sealed his refusal of a suitable occupation for a young man of his kind. Talleyrand said, on granting Alexis's request, "I do not know how we can employ him but bring him to me; after all, he will always be useful, he can go out in society and communicate his impressions to us." Astolphe felt very strongly, and quite rightly, that he had failed his mother and betrayed her ambitions. He wrote to her from Munich on 30 October 1814: "If I did not know how much I love you, I would be able to guess it from the pain I feel at not being what you wish. Why are my ideas so different from other people? My tastes, my feelings, everything carries me away from where you would like to place me."[22] And a month later, more specifically, "what torments me is the idea that your happiness depends on mine, for that makes it my duty to be happy and I know well that I never will be happy in the way that others are. But forgive, once more, this sad refrain."[23]

Astolphe may well have been mortified but, always looking inward, his constant introspection still did not prevent his looking around and doing so with a surprisingly open mind. Talleyrand both fascinated and frightened him. This man "has cut every wire connecting the soul to the physiognomy; his face is as if it were dead and has no more movement than a paralysed limb. It is enough to make one shudder. I am always tempted on entering his room to take to my heels,"[24] but naturally curiosity got the better of him and he stayed. He was present at Talleyrand's morning toilette when the old monster, quite undressed, used to gargle through the nose by breathing in a whole glass of water, and had his atrophied legs rubbed with vinegar. He was powdered and primped in public with the immodesty of a great nobleman, all the while conducting a cynical conversation, "extract of wit," hardly designed to give a young man the feeling of doing something useful. "What can we hope for from the Congress? They are too afraid to quarrel and too stupid

22. *Revue bleue*, August 1910, p. 226.
23. Ibid., p. 228.
24. Ibid., p. 293.

to agree." Astolphe expressed this to his mother in concluding his description of the splendour of Vienna and the uninterrupted sequence of balls and fêtes. "There is something black behind all this glitter."[25] The something black was the old Prince de Ligne, who made a spectacle of himself at all the fêtes, taller than almost everyone else, his grey head unkempt . . . "like one century watching the passing of another and [recalling] the old, half-broken columns remaining in the Roman countryside, as if to show that at other times there was something else."[26] Or the old Prince Trauttmannsdorff, grand master of the court of Vienna, a horrible, grotesque ghost, nicknamed "Death in Full Dress," chasing after the greatest pomp and all the world had to offer at its most brilliant and intoxicating. The sight of this man, once the greatest libertine in Vienna, so terrified Astolphe that he decided: "If I were Emperor, I would make him stand guard at the door of a place of ill-repute, for the sight of him alone is enough to effect conversions."[27] From Astolphe's letters, it would seem that the only result of Napoleon's defeat was to bring all the old men back to power. Why join this circle of semi-cadavers? In Vienna he found Koreff. He looked after Astolphe, which reassured Delphine, constantly worried about her son's moods. The appearance of Wilhelm, the *brother*, whose arrival gave him "palpi-

25. Maugras, *Delphine de Sabran*, op. cit., p. 479.

26. *Revue bleue*, August 1910, p. 265.

27. Ibid., pp. 388–389 and 426.

tations of happiness," seemed to exacerbate the currents pulling Astolphe in different directions. In society he appeared "sombre, morose, unsociable, hating the world . . . a little eccentric."[28] His mother fretted over him and it pained him to realise that she did: "there is something so frightening in your letter that I cannot re-read it without trembling, and it is I who am the cause of the trouble." Perhaps his caricature of Lord Stuart was designed to put her off the scent, "a harlot dressed as a man, a harlot girl from the Palais-Royal. He has adopted a hussar's uniform, no doubt in order to expose his backside to which, they say, he attaches great value and which he caresses in front of all the women, while taking little steps and waving his handkerchief in the most ridiculous manner."[29] Be that as it may, Delphine jumped at the chance to suggest marriage, an old remedy for tormented and undecided young people.

It wasn't a question, as it would be later, of trying to solve their financial problems. For the time being, she was trying to close a breach she felt opening. It must be said that Astolphe hid nothing and openly analysed his feelings for Wilhelm to his mother. A perfect solution, Delphine whispered, would be to marry Mme de Staël's daughter, Albertine. But he had no wish to marry and he told her straight out: "What you suggest for me concerning Albertine would not make me happy. I do not love her, since I never think

28. Quoted by Luppé, op. cit., p. 55.
29. *Revue bleue*, August 1910, p. 264.

about her when I do not see her."[30] Delphine didn't let such a weak argument discourage her. Discussion of the matter continued and did so until the young lady announced her engagement to Victor de Broglie; it also continued because Astolphe didn't have the heart to outright condemn a plan which he knew would make his mother happy. Besides, he willingly admitted that Mme de Staël's circle, "this family which is not French at all . . . is neither narrow, nor limited, nor ordinary," would suit him perfectly. But how could he be so dishonest as not to say that he wasn't ready for such an engagement? "I am wary of her and of myself. In my present frame of mind it seems to me that to marry would be to seal the wounds of my heart before healing them."[31]

Torn between his passion for Wilhelm and the desire to please his mother, he suffered another nervous collapse, again brought about by a bump on the head. "I would like to have a case made for my head, a bonnet lined with wire, a cushion, iron-plated and varnished—I know not what. If I were king I would summon my whole council to design a head-shield."[32] Naturally he gave up his "duties" with Tallyrand and, in his mother's absence, it was Koreff who treated him and calmed him and made him stay in his room to avoid unnecessary agitation. He was taken up by a family of German in-

---

30. Ibid.
31. Ibid., p. 386.
32. Maugras, *Delphine de Sabran*, op. cit., p. 484.

tellectuals, the Schlossers, and "in the midst of this disjointed existence in Vienna they did [him] untold good. This saved [his] mind and [his] heart which were going off in different directions. How frightful a bachelor's existence is. Bachelors are the canker of civilisation."[33] Christian Schlosser had lived for a long time in Italy. He moved in a circle of German Protestants converted to Catholicism, also frequented by Custine when he was in Rome. Schlosser, to whom Astolphe was always profoundly grateful, helped him improve his German. The Schlossers—Christian had two brothers, one a historian, and the other a close friend of Goethe whose affairs he looked after—introduced Astolphe to the city's literary salons and notably to Dorothea von Schlegel.[34]

Only a few months earlier, he had begged his mother to leave Germany and join him in France; now he wanted her to run from Paris to be at his side but, in March 1815, Napoleon set sail from Elba and Delphine, before embarking on the journey, went to Fouché for advice. He thought she shouldn't leave Paris at a time of crisis—she would risk having the future of her property put in question. He was convinced that Napoleon would be defeated immediately and that Paris would remain calm. "He has returned from Elba madder than he was when he went there and he cannot last three months," the

33. *Revue bleue*, October 1910, pp. 484–485.

34. Francine-Dominique Liechtenham, *Astolphe de Custine, voyageur et philosophe*, doctoral thesis presented at the University of Basel, 1988, pp. 23–24.

new royal Minister of Police estimated. Delphine did well to listen and, in fact, three months later, defeat at Waterloo ended the adventure.

Meanwhile, even before the Allied victory was announced, Astolphe had left Vienna. Alexis de Noailles, who continued to keep an eye on him, advised that he was going with Talleyrand to join Louis XVIII at Gand, and offered Astolphe a seat in their carriage. Although he was still unwell, Astolphe accepted happily because he saw the possibility of getting closer to the divine Wilhelm who had left Vienna for Darmstadt. It is amusing to imagine him travelling in the open landau, with a vesicatory round his neck, a poultice on his head and a parasol in hand to protect himself from the sun which he could no longer bear, sustaining himself with coffee and "talking" to his companions "in the most agreeable way in the world." He left them at Frankfurt, claiming quite reasonably that he couldn't travel like that all the way to Belgium. In fact, he was resigning from public life.

He had made what in 1814 had seemed an impossible choice between boredom and general opprobrium and he wouldn't go back on his decision. There would no longer be any question of joining the musketeers or hanging around the Foreign Ministry. A year of exile and study, in fact a year of happiness, in Frankfurt between 1815 and 1816 was, in a way, to define his future. He wanted to study, and that was what he was doing. Koreff, who knew him well, encouraged him to work, advising him to write "on the spirit of the times, the causes of the revolution, the excesses of republicanism."[35] He offered to help him in ascertaining facts, hardly Astolphe's strong point, and hoped that studies would develop Astolphe's talent. "He says above all that I must calm down, be tranquil, no longer think, speak, or write about myself and start courageously on a new life,"[36] he explained to his mother.

In reality, the idea of being a writer appealed to Astolphe and not just because he had cut himself off from any other career. "You speak of my talent for writing and thus you do me a really good turn," he wrote to a German woman friend, "for that is the direction in which I, too, am turning. I felt deeply that I was not made to govern others, or to live a life in which outward action and apparent movement take up most of a man's strength and his time . . . I need truth and love and this makes me afraid to separate myself from my kind and yet lack of action does cut me off from them. It seems to me that the only way of escaping from this false position is by participating in the general movement through writing, by throwing one's works into the torrent from whence one retrieves oneself . . . what pleases me most in the world, to tell the truth, is the writer's way of life . . ."[37]

Being a modest and sensible man, he was aware of his ignorance

35. *Revue bleue*, October 1910, p. 326.
36. Ibid., p. 327.
37. *Lettres à Varnhagen*, op. cit., p. 146.

and wanted to educate himself before starting to write. In a Parisian salon his culture would have left nothing to be desired but he was a child of imperial France, self-sufficient in her glory and her grandeur, subjected as much to a blockade of ideas as of goods. Intellectual exchange and the expression of ideas were not current under Napoleon. The imperial government found anything from abroad suspect. In the exile order sent to Mme de Staël after the publication of *De L'Allemagne*, the Minister of Police specified: "We have not yet been reduced to looking for models amongst the people you admire. Your last work is not French."[38] Under the Empire, it was forbidden to admire German literature.

Meanwhile, French literary genius seemed to have abandoned its native land: Chateaubriand, Mme de Staël and Joseph de Maistre all lived abroad more than in France during those years. In the climate of intolerance, literary inspiration in France was drying up; but in Germany, the country which attracted Custine more than any other, the Romantic school was flourishing, based on national aspirations and a revolt of Christian sentiment against the formal, rigid perfection of the strict rules of classicism. Whereas in France it was fashionable to despise the Middle Ages, the troubadours, knights and unrestricted artists who expressed their imaginations freely, in Germany they were admired. The great German philosophers, Kant, Leibniz, Fichte, played with the new ideas and stimulated

38. Mme de Staël, *Oeuvres complètes* (Paris, 1820), Préface, p. 7.

people's intelligence. Custine discovered there the intoxication of being immersed in a ferment of new thought. Albertine's engagement to Victor de Broglie put an end to the question of his own marriage.

After a year, and to the great delight of her son who was depressed by their long separation, Delphine announced her arrival. Thanks to Fouché, she had money and a valid passport. Horrified in retrospect at the idea that his mother had stayed in Paris throughout the Hundred Days, Astolphe's imagination ran wild when he thought about her. "I see you there in front of me, and after such a long absence you seem like a ghost; for several months, I have concentrated on pushing your image away because it was killing me and it came back with your letter."[39] Delphine prepared to set out, pleased, despite the exorbitant cost of the journey. In the first place, she was overjoyed at seeing Astolphe. Also, despite Berstoecher's sweet and faithful attentions—he was going with her—she hadn't forgotten Koreff. Finally, her great friend, the princesse de Vaudémont, with her merry-go-round of followers, joined the party. The baron Humboldt who never left her side and the princesse de Stolberg, "a naturally boring person, but one who lacks neither good sense nor wit," were able to smooth the path for her arrival in Frankfurt.

She settled in the little apartment found for her by Astolphe, which fortunately got all the sun, since Delphine felt the cold and

39. Maugras, *Delphine de Sabran*, op. cit., p. 498.

wood was expensive. There were lodgings for Berstoecher on the same landing; Astolphe retained his student lodgings only a short walk away. This little uprooted corner of Paris was to become enchanted by Romantic Germany personified, as it was for them, by a new friend, Rahel von Varnhagen. Delphine met her at a salon and on returning to find Astolphe, she told him that she had talked to a person made to charm him. "She will have to please me a good deal to make me forget what pains me." "She will make you forget everything, I tell you."[40]

"Everything one said to Mme de Varnhagen," Astolphe wrote, "was in the nature of a confession, whether willingly or not."[41] She listened, understood everything and immediately became confidante to both mother and son. "I was irrevocably tied to her without being in love." Rahel, who was his mother's exact contemporary, was twenty years older than Astolphe. "This attachment, which is as strong as it is disinterested, is quite simply the perfection of human relations . . . to her I owed the renaissance of thought which had been suffocated by sorrow."[42] Who was this Rahel von Varnhagen, one of the most original people in Prussian society? She was the daughter of a jeweller who had made money, Jewish and quite

40. Astolphe de Custine, *Revue de Paris*, November 1837, p. 215.
41. Ibid., p. 216.
42. Ibid.

unhappy about it. She was lively, nimble, intelligent, a *jolie laide* with dark eyes, for whom it was difficult to find a husband, and poor to boot, since after her father's death she lived off a small income from her brothers. Yet she was to hold an unparalleled position in Berlin society and to play a part in one of the most curious episodes of German cultural history.

At the end of the eighteenth century, aristocratic circles in Berlin were stifling. "The court," Rahel joked, "wept a great deal at the deaths of all sorts of princes and princelings whom no one knew," any more than they did in fact, "so much so that amongst ourselves the court nobility was generally referred to by the nickname of *weepers.*" Life was no less dull among the conventional bourgeoisie with their "intellectual unions," their closed circles which barred women and where the exclusion of Jews—which went without saying—was never mentioned. Then three young Jewesses, Henrietta Lemos, a doctor's daughter of Portuguese origin, Dorothea Mendelssohn and Rahel Levine introduced a new type of salon whose success resulted from the fact that it couldn't be assigned a rank in the society of the day. Impossible to categorise, these salons became a neutral ground where no conclusions could be drawn from the mixed company.

Their mentor, Moses Mendelssohn, was one of the first Jewish thinkers to revolt against the narrowness of traditional intellectual life in the ghetto and to participate in the discussion of modern ideas. He had been elevated by Frederick II of Prussia to the status of a specially protected Jew. From the tiny circle of enlightened men who congregated around him, the young women discovered that everything could be called into question, that differences of opinion enlivened a gathering and that without literature there remained only boredom and sadness. Taking advantage of the few years following the Revolution during which the old hatred of Jews had died down, and before the birth of modern anti-Semitism,[43] they freed themselves from the old patriarchal conventions and brought about a symbiosis between their culture and the German tradition.

Henrietta Lemos married a pupil of Kant, Marcus Herz, and the young couple became hosts to an academic circle frequented by the most intellectual of the *jeunesse dorée*. Mme Herz's reputation was such that the Tsarina wanted to entrust her with the education of the Tsarevitch, providing she converted. She refused. Dorothea Mendelssohn was married to a literary critic, Friedrich von Schlegel, and together they founded both a review and a Romantic circle. Without the support of a husband, the youngest of these women, Rahel, took to receiving with extraordinary freedom in an attic over a cup of tea. Her tolerance bordered on lack of discrimination, or so the jealous said. Her uncompromising lack of prejudice earned her the friendship of the Humboldt brothers, refugees from their family *Schloss* known as Castle Boring, of Metternich's adviser, Gentz, and

43. Hannah Arendt, *Rahel Varnhagen, la vie d'une juive allemande à l'époque du romantisme* (Tierce, 1980), p. 138.

of Prince Louis-Ferdinand of Prussia. The presence of the famous writers Mme de Genlis and Mme de Staël, regular visits from the prince de Ligne and, above all, Goethe's loyalty added incomparable style to her receptions. She knew how to create an intimate atmosphere, she could listen better than anyone, and was delighted to have her salon described as a republic of the mind. Despite her success, it hurt her to feel that because of her Jewish origins, she was excluded from traditional German society. It was this ambivalence which later drew her and Custine together and allowed her to understand him better than anyone else could.

She often talked of the Jews as "of a nation torn apart, neglected, and more than all that, rightly despised."[44] Her love affairs came to nothing because of social prejudice; and finally, after Napoleon's victorious entry into Berlin in 1806, she suffered from the sudden brutal avoidance of Jewish salons. Henceforth one had to be German and pure German. Rahel discovered solitude. "Sitting at my tea table there is only me, with my dictionaries. I have never been so alone."[45] She was saved by a young man's passion. Augustus Varnhagen von Ense was a friend of Koreff. Coming from a poor background, Varnhagen was secretary and then confidant to the King of Prussia's prime minister, Chancellor von Hardenberg, a man of lib-

---

44. Verena von der Heyder-Rynsch, *Salons européens; les beaux moments d'une culture féminine disparue* (Gallimard, 1993).

45. Arendt, op. cit., p. 153.

eral opinion. He was responsible for the emancipation of the Jews in Prussia. When he was made diplomatic councillor, Varnhagen asked for and was granted Rahel's hand. She was fifteen years his senior.

By the time of her meeting with the Custines, Rahel had converted to Catholicism and was married to a diplomat. She had followed him to Frankfurt, and her salon was less spontaneous and more political than the one in the attic. Heine, who mocked the rigidity of Berlin's right-thinking salons in the 1820s, frequented Rahel's so assiduously that it was said he would have liked to wear a dog's collar bearing the inscription, "I belong to Frau Varnhagen."

Astolphe had never met anyone like Rahel: her conversation was open, quite free of prejudice or constraint and she had a rare gift for sympathy. She shared with Astolphe a taste for painful introspection. "My eternal disguises . . . my self-knowledge gnaws at me," she said one day.[46] They definitely spoke the same language, and Astolphe felt all the closer to her because he realized how much she had suffered. "I can only become attached to those who suffer, or at least who have suffered a great deal."[47] They skipped the usual conventional stage demanded of social relations. The tone of their letters, written in French by him and in German by her, was set by the infor-

46. Ibid., p. 31.
47. Ibid., p. 34.

mality of: "If you sign *Astolphe*, I will sign *Rahel*." She listened to him, analysed him and he marvelled at her insight. His confidence in his friend's opinion was such that he said he was expecting Rahel "to give him some news of himself,"[48] and in his letters which, he pointed out, were written for her alone, he opened up. Before long, he imposed the handsome Wilhelm on the Varnhagen household— Wilhelm who didn't appear to respond to his ardour with quite the hoped-for intensity. "He seemed quite insignificant to us," Varnhagen noted, "but Custine, a man of energy and resolution in all his undertakings, spoke with passion of this friend whose intimacy caused such a commotion in his heart and soul that he experienced satisfaction and pleasure, examples such as we only find in antiquity."[49]

For the first time in his life, Astolphe felt he was accepted as he was with such warmth and kindness that he felt he had a second family. Indeed, he was so loved and appreciated that he was introduced to Goethe—ultimate rite of initiation. Aware of the honour bestowed on him, Astolphe described the visit to Delphine who had gone to take the waters. "Nothing is more difficult than to approach this extraordinary man and to interest him. He was kind to me; I could approach him wherever I might meet him, that is all, but it is a great deal. Besides, what do you suppose he could see in me, I am

48. *Lettres à Varnhagen*, op. cit., p. 36.
49. Ibid., Introduction, p. xv.

like a turbulent lake, one does not know what it reflects ... You would have done better than I with him for he is extremely fond of pretty women and of the unaffected ..."[50] Having dashed all hopes of a career, Astolphe might well have suffered a setback during this period. It could have been a period of anguish in which he was troubled by the proximity of Wilhelm who grew colder every day. But instead he found peace, thanks to Rahel. She succeeded in showing him that it was possible to overcome the contradictions struggling within. "There is so much room inside a man," why not accept one's inconsistencies?

The Custines couldn't remain in Germany forever. They had to return to France to watch over their fortune and the date was set for September 1816. Astolphe prepared himself to confront public opinion. "I have friends and relations who do not understand that having been unemployed for two years, I am in no hurry. I will find others who will understand that I desire quite the opposite ..."[51]

50. Maugras, *Delphine de Sabran*, op. cit., p. 502.
51. *Lettres à Varnhagen*, op. cit., p. 49.

7

The Marriage Question

On their return to France the question of Astolphe's employment was not even raised. The Custines spent a few days in Paris before settling at Fervaques, the revenue from which would now be their main income. Delphine didn't pester her son, either because she was marshalling her forces to persuade him to make an advantageous marriage or because, realising only too well how much his shying away from the active life weighed on him, she was loath to burden him with reproaches and advice. It was impossible to be steeped in *René* without being struck by the fate assigned to "young men who, given to useless daydreaming, *criminally* desist from their duty towards society." To read what Astolphe wrote is to realise that he was aware of the disadvantages of his withdrawal from society and that he foresaw the difficulties of having authority with a family-in-law. "The real point of existence is only revealed to man by living in society; it is by playing a part in public life that he becomes something for everyone, that his right to exist is recognised and that his affections can be reciprocated . . . to refuse to serve one's country is not only to deprive oneself of a public career, but it is also to renounce what makes the charm of an inner life, for oneself and for one's nearest: a man needs to have exercised influence, acquired respect, if he is to live peacefully by his own hearth."[1]

In place of a public life and at his mother's request, he assumed a landowner's duties. In fact, they divided the work; he took responsibility for the estate, she for the house and the garden which she looked after with an enthusiasm that he gently mocked. She had the idea of planting their friends. "We have given names to a number of trees," Astolphe explained to Rahel, "and you are by a little waterfall in a green meadow, between Koreff and Count Flemming. I call the grove the sentimental metempsychosis."[2] The running of Fervaques wasn't easy because, after an absence of six years, abuse had become endemic and, as he wrote to his grandmother, "It is necessary to play the master in order to pull out all the weeds." He managed very well for someone who, until then, "had lived look-

1. *Aloys*, op. cit., p. 33.
2. *Lettres à Varnhagen*, op. cit., p. 105.

ing out of a window,"[3] and he took great pleasure in feeling that he was doing his duty towards his mother and, by taking on real responsibility, redeeming his psychological dependence on her. "I had never found myself interacting directly with men, and this experience served me prodigiously in my knowledge of myself."[4] Running his mother's establishment, being in charge of her household and her affairs also meant that a simple, straightforward adult relationship could develop between them. Delphine's attitude was quite different from either Mme Proust's or Mme Gide's, both of whom were also confronted with their sons' refusal to take employment.

These bourgeois ladies, each with a larger, more secure fortune than the marquise, adopted the policy of holding the purse strings: no job—no money. A large part of their correspondence reads like a cook's accounts. At the age of twenty-eight, Marcel wrote to Mme Proust from Evian, ". . . if the boy who brings me my coffee in the morning leaves before closing time, what should I give him? I forgot to tell you that I still have no sponges. Ought I to buy some?" André Gide would send his mother with increasing exasperation more details of his expenses than would be expected of a child today: "I must after all live and you will end by making me eat scraps for

3. Maugras, *Delphine de Sabran*, op. cit., p. 534.
4. *Lettres à Varnhagen*, op. cit., p. 211.

fear of eating too much."[5] In both cases money was a constant irritant. The real difficulties confronting these young men, kept in a state of childish dependence, remained behind a screen.

The Custine style was quite different. What was the point of quarrelling? They didn't have enough money and were loath to incur debt. It was pointless to discuss the matter at length. In their conversations and their letters, they turned to other things. Only literature and the state of their souls really interested them. Delphine was in the deepest depression: Koreff no longer wrote to her. She confided in Astolphe before, with surprising frankness, asking Rahel to intervene, which Rahel did successfully. As she always craved male attention, a letter from Koreff was enough to bring the light back into Delphine's life. "One is no longer young such a long time before becoming old," she wrote, as if excusing herself.[6] The house was peaceful once more and the calm of the countryside contagious despite a new friendship which created subtle complications for both mother and son.

During a visit to Paris, Astolphe had met Edouard de La Grange, a young officer who had started his career under Napoleon and for whom he developed a passion. The young man never suspected either Astolphe's feelings or his leanings, despite a remarkable correspondence in which Astolphe continuously made advances that

5. Jean Delay, *La Jeunesse d'André Gide*, 2. vols. (Gallimard, 1956), II, p. 395.
6. *Lettres à Varnhagen*, op. cit., p. 127.

only went so far and confidences that would have been risky, had La Grange been capable of interpreting them. La Grange was more interested in Delphine. He had discovered with delight the pleasure of being with a woman to whom he could confide openly. "I feel more at ease with her than with my real mother," he wrote in his diary.[7] She endlessly lectured the dissatisfied young man who, having thrown himself into society looking for distraction, found only a void, and if she restricted herself to the part of a sermonizing mother, it was with the charm and flirtatiousness of a woman on the verge of a romantic friendship.[8]

Times were too hard for affairs of the heart to take precedence. Delphine hated the Norman peasants, annoying, crafty, evasive and underhand, because "they used all their intelligence to appear stupid."[9] Astolphe, who went about his estate with his eyes wide open, was less peremptory. In the winter of 1817 peasants were literally dying of hunger in the fields. It was hardly possible to exact rent from people who had nothing. They had been without bread for several months and were reduced to mixing bran with whey. Ready money was needed. Once again the subject of Astolphe's marriage became important. It was not that the Custines were really in need, with

7. La Grange's journal of 10 January 1820, quoted by Olivier de Luppé, university thesis, "Marquis de La Grange, Journal inédit," 1988 (Paris IV, Sorbonne).

8. Unpublished letters from Delphine de Custine to the marquis de La Grange, Luppé Archives.

9. *Lettres à Varnhagen*, op. cit., p. 179.

30,000 francs of revenue at their disposal, but they were poorer than most of the people they saw. Those were the people they knew and if they wanted to make friends in other circles they would not be "understood."[10] Nearly twenty years earlier, Delphine had had to forgo marriage to her rich general. Under the Directory people from her background were ruined and the gap between herself and her suitor was rather too wide to be bridged with comfort, but under the Restoration fortunes had been rebuilt and there were many well-born, well-endowed aspirants to Astolphe's title and bed. The choice was his, quite simply because the middle-aged women who arranged marriages were all charmed by this tall young man with a veiled, ironic expression, who was gentle, witty, shy and always exquisitely well-mannered. No wonder they thought he would make a perfect husband.

Delphine was equally convinced although she knew of her son's predilections. She discussed the matter guardedly with her mother, not because she wanted advice but because she was frank and passed no moral judgements on her family. For her, sexual transgression was not the greatest sin and she had no doubts about his ability to father a child. "Astolphe," she wrote to her mother, "has just returned from a little journey. It had nothing to do with chasing a beautiful young woman." She pinpointed the problem but did not

10. Ibid., p. 288.

consider it an obstacle to marriage. "He wants to be independent, and real freedom can only be acquired with a fortune."[11] Delphine may have dreamed her dreams but she was not without the solid good sense of a Norman peasant. Apart from being attracted by a handsome dowry, how might Astolphe have viewed the matter? He was by now well disposed to the idea for somewhat complicated reasons. Knowing the degree to which the Church condemned them, he still satisfied his desires on trips to Paris and excursions in the countryside where his valets flushed out the game. "I failed in my vocation," he has his double say in *Aloys*, "piety made itself felt in my soul, like a taste, another leaning, but it did not become a code applicable to every aspect of my life."[12] And, in a letter to Edouard de La Grange, "I have a need for goodness and truth, my soul makes an effort to drag itself out of the abyss of sensuality and although I do not succeed, the sincere desire and the hope I have of doing better are enough for me to deserve a tender pity which is all I ask of my friends that I might love them."[13]

For him marriage was not an attempt to put everything in order and live a conventional life. He didn't intend to give up his habits with marriage, as Gide did, but, rather like Oscar Wilde, he sought

11. Maugras, *Delphine de Sabran*, op. cit., p. 536.

12. *Aloys*, op. cit., p. 37.

13. Letter to La Grange, 13 August 1819, in Luppé, op. cit., p. 82.

it as a kind of protection. The very presence of a wife would prevent him from acting imprudently, and it can be inferred from his letters to La Grange that Custine liked taking a risk, sometimes too great a risk. A little marquise de Custine would be like a pretty prop in a warm and respectable setting. "Today, at twenty-eight, I feel the need for something fixed and positive; but it is like a stick when one can no longer walk on one's own," he wrote to La Grange. Astolphe liked family life, he said so repeatedly, he liked the feminine atmosphere to which Delphine had accustomed him. Besides, he was unable to live alone. "I depend on others to a degree which I would be unable to express."[14] The desire for a son must also have entered into his calculations. He couldn't with impunity be the last in line of a great family. "I do not know if I will be a good husband, but I think I am sure that I will be a good father. I sense the need of such feelings."[15] Delphine thought about it too, looking over all the candidates and turning a great number down flat. Mademoiselle de Hautefort because she had a bad figure ". . . and the hump! And what if she had no children, we would be in a real fix."[16]

The Custines decided to leave their beloved Fervaques in January 1818 and embark on a campaign: "We have to absolutely find a woman this winter, and *a rich woman*, for without that we might

14. *Lettres à La Grange*, op. cit., letters of 14 and 30 June 1818, pp. 11 and 14.
15. *Lettres à Varnhagen*, op. cit., p. 210.
16. Maugras, *Delphine de Sabran*, op. cit., p. 536.

as well stay where we are."[17] Among the possibilities, Custine preferred Clara de Duras, who liked literature, intelligent men and conversation. But more than young Clara, he liked her mother, the duchesse. He found himself in the same situation he had been in a few years earlier when he was half courting Albertine de Staël because he felt so at ease in her mother's salon. The duchesse looked favourably on this delicate, cultivated, attentive suitor.

Never having been happily in love, Mme de Duras concentrated on her daughters' happiness. The career of her father, Admiral de Kersaint, had been similar to General de Custine's. After joining the Revolution and hailing the birth of the Republic, he was guillotined. Claire de Kersaint spent the years of the Terror in Martinique from whence, through her mother, she inherited a fortune large enough to tempt the duc de Duras on her return to France. Unfortunately, the marriage didn't please Louis XVIII who wouldn't allow the daughter of a member of the Convention to be admitted to the presence of his daughter-in-law, the duchesse d'Angoulême, the surviving child of Louis XVI. As a result of this insult, the young woman developed an independence of spirit which did her credit and made it possible for her to build her own unusual salon. "In many ways a kind of neutral terrain because of the generous and altogether literary mind of she who was its moving spirit, great inequalities of fortune and opinion gathered there, with people of

17. Ibid.

very different rank and talent."[18] It is clear why Custine, so shocked by the intransigence of the reactionaries, felt at ease there.

According to her friend, Mme de Boigne, Mme de Duras "tolerated all opinions without judging them condescendingly from an attitude of partiality. She was even open to those generous ideas which did not too greatly compromise her position as a grand lady, a position she enjoyed all the more for having awaited it so long . . . In the extravagant world of the Restoration she kept to her own set."[19] Having become aware of her intellectual superiority over her husband, she was tactless enough to let him feel it and so lost all hope of marital happiness. "She has all the intelligence needed to govern; she is totally lacking in that needed to advise. Consider if those are conditions for happiness in a woman,"[20] Custine observed.

She developed a passion for Chateaubriand who never allowed her to become more than a sister, assigning her a position "quite apart where she reigned without trouble and unrivalled," and, it might be added, without the pleasures known to his other Muses. There remained her daughters. To the despair of her mother, the elder daughter, the prince de Talmont's widow, married next the comte de La Rochejaquelin, the most extreme of reactionaries. She

18. Duchesse de Duras, *Olivier ou le Secret* (Corti, 1971), introduction by Denise Virieux, p. 32; quotation from Villemain (*Souvenirs contemporains d'histoire et de littérature*, vol. I, pp. 465–471).

19. *Mémoires de la comtesse de Boigne*, op. cit., I, pp. 348–349 and 362.

20. *Lettres à La Grange*, op. cit., p. 68.

then concentrated all her energies on the younger one. Astolphe, who talked to her with such pleasure, whose political and literary opinions coincided with hers and whose witticisms people quoted, seemed to be the ideal son-in-law and she encouraged him. He succumbed to flattery, spent every evening with the Duras and when spring came, the duc accepted his suit. But, on the eve of signing the marriage contract, scandal broke! Astolphe withdrew from the engagement so suddenly that the insult could not be ignored. To break off in such a way with a young woman he had seen two or three times a day for four months, whose circumstances he knew so well that he was almost one of the family, seemed like the act of a lunatic. What were his reasons?

He explained himself badly. He already knew before the break that the Duras' financial position was no longer what it had been; he was not unaware that the duchesse wanted to keep her daughter by her side, whereas Astolphe considered it his duty to settle with his mother. Had he thought over his decision, such obstacles should have prevented his engagement; in fact, they failed to shed any light on the affair. Hindsight might blame his homosexuality if he had not married someone else shortly afterwards. The lack of real attraction to the young women presented to him was the natural result of his proclivities but that was hardly the point. The need to love his wife had been an obvious element in his hesitation over Albertine de Staël, yet the subject of love was no longer raised in 1818.

A rumour spread, which La Grange echoed. "Courchamps tells

me that M. de Duras won't give his daughter to M. de Custine because he was told he was impotent."[21] The vile Courchamps, son of a modest shipowner from Saint-Servan, who pretended to be a count, was a plagiarist and secret homosexual. His invention wouldn't be worthy of attention, since Astolphe had a son quite naturally as soon as he married, if it hadn't been picked up and used in various novels that appeared shortly afterwards. The broken engagement put a lot of scribblers to work, inspiring four novels.

In 1822, the duchesse de Duras wrote and read aloud in Parisian salons an epistolary novel, *Olivier ou le Secret*, the story of a young man who, for reasons never quite explained, proved incapable of responding to the love of his cousin. Four years later an anonymous *Olivier* appeared. Was it by the duchesse? It was not. The author was a man of letters and Marceline Desbordes-Valmore's lover, Hyacinthe de Latouche, who may have met Astolphe in Rome where he had spent several years with the French administration. He was delighted by the confusion between him and the duchesse and was careful not to correct it. The novel was also about a young man who wanted to fall in love but couldn't, although he was unable to explain why. Then there was *Armance*, Stendhal's first novel, also published anonymously. Its subject was once again a marriage that couldn't take place for reasons unclear on the first reading.

21. La Grange's journal of 9 August 1818.

The Marriage Question

The Christian name chosen by the first two writers was a clue, at least for anyone familiar with the works of Saint Augustine who had juxtaposed some reflections on impotence and an allegory about an olive tree. Initially Stendhal, too, had chosen the name Olivier for his hero, because "this name alone is an *exposure*, an exposure without indecency. If I were to put Edmond or Paul, many people would never guess at the *babilanisme*."*[22] Then he changed his mind and Olivier became Octave. This roman à clef, published without a key to unlock its secrets, was considered incomprehensible and had no success. In his 1921 preface, André Gide wrote that "the plot is not played out only between the characters, but above all between writer and reader . . . It might be said the book's real proposition is the inference of impotence and I know of none which demands a subtler collaboration from the reader; to tell the truth, it is only once one knows, and on re-reading, that one understands the full meaning of certain hints where initially no mischief was apparent." Recently, Dominique Fernandez, that most mischievous of readers, gave a totally convincing homosexual interpretation.[23] Is Octave

*A babilan is an impotent man. The word comes from *Babilano Pallavicino*, who was sued for impotence in the seventeenth century.

22. Yves Citton, *Impuissances; défaillances masculines et pouvoir politique de Montaigne à Stendhal* (Aubier, 1994), letter from Stendhal to Mérimée, 23 December 1826, p. 45.

23. Dominique Fernandez, *Le Secret d'Octave*, in Stendhal, *Armance* (P.O.L., 1992), pp. i–xxi.

Astolphe? How could he not be? Stendhal had very few models on which to base a young, inverted aristocrat. Besides, by the time the book appeared, Custine had long since abandoned the uncertainties and disguises of youth. But in order to attempt to comprehend his flight from Clara de Duras, one needs to read between the lines of Astolphe's own book.

In 1829 he published—anonymously, of course—a novella about a hundred pages long called *Aloys*. "For me," he wrote to Rahel, on sending her the text, "it is of first importance not to admit that I am the author because the substance is true; it is an anecdote in which I played the principal part."[24] Aloys-Astolphe retells the story of an engagement which is broken because the young man is too much in love with the mother to be able to live near her as a son-in-law. The truth cannot be so extravagantly simple even in a novel. The homosexuality is not latent as in *Armance*, although Aloys's cry of "Am I then a wild animal, am I sick or frenzied, to be approached only with fear?" echoes Octave's "Am I a monster?" A cry which expresses more likely the turmoil, despair and self-loathing of a homosexual overwhelmed by the violence of society's censure than a lover's bashfulness. Then there is the mother's curious remark about Aloys's handwriting being so small and so delicate that no one would ever think of attributing it to a man; a remark that was all the more meaningful coming, as it did, from the so-called loved one. In

24. *Lettres à Varnhagen*, op. cit., p. 317.

the end, Aloys flies into a rage when he realises the extent of the determination to impose on him a fate from which *his penchants* caused him to recoil. "Penchant" was a code for homosexual tastes. These details are so slight as to be almost hidden; what emerges from the novel is a terror of being tied down.

Aloys runs from the mother even more than from the daughter, who is barely described in the text, whereas the mother, apparently so attractive, is described as grasping her prey: "It is she, she alone who determined my most secret decisions! I have not been free for an instant in my life; she attached herself to me like an infernal spirit. Without my knowledge, she assumed the right to direct my actions, she imposed on me a destiny contrary to my penchants; she cast her invisible net around me, from trap to trap she dragged me into the abyss, a Fury sent before me; and from the cradle to the grave, I will not have taken one step without her having marked it out."[25] This was no excuse invented by the novelist after the event; in a letter to Rahel, the only one of his women friends to congratulate him on not marrying, he confided how he had been *bewitched* during the preceding months, and told her of the *terrible assault* mounted against him after he had let himself be persuaded by a woman he loved a lot that he loved her daughter even more and wanted to marry her. He allowed himself, out of weakness, to be pushed into asking her father for her hand in order to benefit from the mother's kindnesses

25. *Aloys*, op. cit., p. 98.

and from the pleasure of being with her that would ensue from such an arrangement. Later he admitted to being pushed, "by another kind of weakness that showed me how, having proceeded as I had done, it was impossible for me to take the action required to disengage myself."[26]

How did he eventually find the courage to make the break, thus provoking public censure for his inexplicable behaviour? By prayer, he suggested. It seems unlikely that a few novenas would have sufficed to make him bold enough to brave society. I am inclined to believe that this man of a violence as cold as ice experienced suddenly a passionate desire for independence, a profound revulsion at having his hand forced. Astolphe's gentleness, his ease of manner and accommodating ways belied his determination. "An iron bar wrapped in cotton"—this description of Aloys by his doctor applies perfectly to Astolphe. Ever ready to be carried away by his imagination and with a possibly exaggerated awareness of his ability to suffer—it must never be forgotten that he was after all a Romantic—he was overcome by panic at the idea of living forever under the eye of Mme de Duras.

The tender sympathy which he hoped for from his friends was not a speciality of the Duras family. He knew that he couldn't do without the freedom, the shadowy areas in which to lead his private life as he intended, and that he also needed warmth, understanding and

---

26. *Lettres à Varnhagen*, op. cit., pp. 252–253.

a circle whose disdain for the world and its judgements was real. He summed up such a need by announcing, "I need independence and intimacy."[27] The atmosphere Delphine had created around him had become indispensable. After this incursion into "unyielding, narrow reality,"[28] he hurried back to her, sufficiently unshaken to joke and regret that Alfred de Chastellux, who had replaced him as Mlle Clara's suitor, was not more clever. "For my part, I would have liked her to marry someone much better than I, for it would have been the only way of truly winning round Mme de D., for whom I have always had a weakness, and who will never forgive me that her son-in-law is an inch shorter than I."[29]

Delphine was able not only to comfort him but also to put a stop to any malicious stories by at last finding, with the help of her neighbour, *la Migraine*, the ideal bride. She was, needless to say, rich, from an excellent Norman family, very young, gentle, sweet natured and—the ultimate perfection—an orphan. Léontine de Saint-Simon de Courtomer had everything that was required. The marriage took place on 15 May 1821. Delphine adopted her daughter-in-law with the spontaneous kindness natural to her. Towards his wife, Astolphe displayed "a regime of moderation in imagina-

27. Letter to Sophie Gay, August 1826, quoted by J.-F. Tarn, *Le Marquis de Custine* (Fayard, 1985), p. 70.

28. *Aloys*, op. cit., p. 98.

29. *Lettres à La Grange*, op. cit., 29 July 1819, p. 117.

tion and in love."[30] How could he express more delicately that he didn't pretend to be in love with her? But marriage suited him and he respected Léontine. To be sure, the quality of her mind didn't necessarily make for "a brilliant, easy conversational life" but "one attaches more importance to the behaviour of the woman who shares one's life than to her conversation," he remarked to La Grange.[31]

Family life was peaceful. Chateaubriand came to visit; they read Rousseau out loud; the young wife was expecting a baby. Astolphe believed her to be happy, which happiness, he wrote—as ever to La Grange—was essential to his own because the last thing he wanted was to hurt her, and God knows that a less naïve wife might have been upset by a husband who, in the most natural possible way, introduced his new lover into the family circle. This was Edward Sainte-Barbe, an Englishman Astolphe had met at some "little mysteries" celebrated in Paris during his rapid, furtive trips. He was penniless and had survived in Paris thanks to dubious protections. No questions were asked. Sainte-Barbe was courteous, discreet and perfectly presentable. Astolphe installed him at Fervaques and, more surprisingly still, the two men left for England as soon as Léontine had given birth. Astolphe de Custine and Edward Sainte-Barbe were never to leave each other.

30. Ibid., p. 130.
31. Ibid.

The Marriage Question

Was Léontine the person to be most admired in this arrangement, with her discreet smile and constant good humour as proof of marital bliss to all visitors at Fervaques? Or was it Delphine, who, understanding her son's game as clearly as she must have, drew a veil over her home life? She had seen so much. At the age of fifty, she had been through too much and was too astute to rock the delicate balance thanks to which Astolphe appeared to have found happiness. She must have realised that to deprive Astolphe of physical satisfaction would have meant catastrophe. Perhaps the prospect of the cloister with which he had always threatened her during his depressions seemed much worse. And wasn't Astolphe like her? She had always known how to manage her love affairs without neglecting her child, her brother or her mother; her bold imagination had momentarily drawn her to the brink of incest. Why shouldn't he be able to manage his peculiar *ménage à trois*, particularly since she was there to protect little Léontine with her affection? And what to think of Chateaubriand's benevolent indulgence? The only one to disapprove was Mme de Boufflers who had more principles than her daughter. But Astolphe never recognised her as having the least moral authority. "No one in the world has less influence over any of us," he told Rahel[32] with unusual frankness. In her, he confided the circumstances of his happiness. "I have an intimate friend . . . who has taught me English. I have a beautiful son, my mother who has be-

32. *Lettres à Varnhagen*, op. cit., p. 287.

come his, is mad about him and we are all leaving for Normandy where we will spend six months."[33] He wasn't to stay there long, for as soon as little Enguerrand was baptised, he embarked for England with his friend, Sainte-Barbe, in July 1822, fully aware that this escapade constituted a "bad deed."[34] Chateaubriand's presence there, as ambassador to London, was probably enough justification in Delphine's eyes. As for Léontine, she was busy playing mother.

Chateaubriand, always quick to abandon his pretty mistresses, showed unusual loyalty to their children. In the *Mémoires d'outre-tombe*, he mentions only four visitors during his time in London, among them Astolphe and Natalie de Noailles's daughter, "just as pleasing, witty and gracious as if she were still wandering at fourteen in the beautiful Méréville gardens."[35] She was travelling with her husband, whereas the young marquis was inseparable from the amiable Edward of whose charming character he boasted to anyone prepared to listen. Chateaubriand was, of course, wise enough not to put them up at the embassy but far from being offended by the situation, he busied himself even before their arrival with all the necessary details to make Astolphe's stay in England a pleasant one.

"On arrival, Astolphe must go to Grillon's in Albermarle Street, or Brunet's in Leicester Square, from whence he will come to me;

---

33. Ibid., pp. 311–312.
34. Letter to La Grange, 18 October, quoted by Luppé, op. cit., p. 92.
35. Chateaubriand, *Mémoires d'outre-tombe*, op. cit., II, p. 83.

we will find him lodgings in my neighbourhood and he will lunch and dine at the embassy. If he stayed at the inn, he would be ruined . . . ,"[36] he wrote to Delphine. A few days later, on 26 July 1822, he sent a further note: "I have received at this moment a note from Astolphe, dated from Dover. He announces himself for this evening or tomorrow. I have reserved lodgings for him near me. Do not concern yourself for his person. I hold myself responsible to you, body for body . . . your big boy will not be lost."[37] He carried his kindness even further. Convinced that Astolphe would be too busy to write regularly to his mother, he took it upon himself to send her news of him: "As it is possible that in the midst of all the pleasures of Scotland, Astolphe will be unable to write, I wish to put an end to your anxiety. He arrived in Edinburgh in good health; he is going deep into the mountains from whence he will return to London via Glasgow. Sleep in peace; not the least harm can come to him."[38]

This unusual kindness from Chateaubriand, who was ordinarily so high-handed with his lovers, is explained by the tremendous interest he took in Astolphe, an interest fuelled by curiosity over the young man's evasions and subterfuges. Chateaubriand was not a man to delight in love's fulfillment, either in his books, in which denial always triumphs over the gratification of desire, or in life. He

36. Chateaubriand, *Correspondance*, op. cit., V, p. 178.
37. Ibid., V, p. 214.
38. Ibid., V, p. 265.

had not experienced the joys of marriage, nor did he allow them to René who, on arriving amongst the Natchez, is obliged to take a wife in order to conform to Indian mores, but the union isn't consummated, nor does he live with her. As for himself, he rapidly abandoned the most passionate women to find happiness with the century's iciest beauty. (If Mme Récamier ever yielded to him, she seems not to have wanted to repeat the experience.) He was both fascinated and charmed by Astolphe's complexity, especially as he recognised in this young man, unable to integrate himself into the society of his time, many of the characteristics he had attributed to René. Astolphe's unusually intelligent and clear-sighted views, being those of a man of the new generation, couldn't fail to open unexpected horizons for Chateaubriand, who was enjoying himself far too much in England with political games and memories of his own youth to recognise the innovations of the new age.

For his part, Custine observed and took stock of England's incomparable advances over the Continent. His *Voyage en Angleterre* achieved none of the success or renown of *La Russie en 1839*, yet in it he showed astonishing insight. Writing nearly twenty years before Dickens, he was the first to discern the consequences of the Industrial Revolution. For once, the young aesthete was less curious about natural beauty than about the work of man, having understood that therein lay the country's importance. Nowhere in the ambassador's correspondence can be found a hint of the commercial and industrial transformation which was creating modern England, while Custine immediately grasped that the functioning of the richest country in the world was to be observed in its ports, factories and mills. "London," he remarked upon arrival, "has established on the banks of the Thames a sort of colony destined to supply the world. This accumulation of buildings, extraordinary in their diversity and size, can be called neither a city nor a village; it consists of a line of innumerable commercial establishments, shops, workshops, ingenious machines of extraordinary power; these warehouses are built so close to the water that they can be filled and emptied without the use of transport, by the aid of revolving cranes; after all the port is two leagues long, and so crowded with vessels that at this place the Thames resembles a flooded forest ... These double, these triple rows of ships frighten the imagination with the idea of unlimited power."[39]

This prodigious commercial boom was explained more by the price of English goods than by their quality. Machines and the steam engine were put to use for the greatest glory and the greatest profit of English manufacturing. Fascinated and horrified, Custine visited a factory making household utensils. He examined in detail an astonishing, extremely complicated machine making part of a button which was sewn on clothing and marvelled at the ease with which iron could be worked cold with scissors powered by a steam engine. The metal "seemed no more than soft wax ... One sees very big

39. *Mémoires*, op. cit., p. 223.

bars, very thick sheets of iron, cut, bent, shaped with something of an enchanted ease; and it is these miraculous yards which have produced the first ship made entirely of iron ever to sail upon the seas."[40]

In Newcastle, he went down a mine. "Going through this dark country, made forever anxious by the sudden passing of horses, stricken with fear of the rank air," he walked for an hour through galleries that were too low to stand up in, until, "with profound pity," he saw half-naked men digging for coal. He also went to one of the biggest cotton mills where two hundred and fifty looms— "consequently five hundred artificial hands"—passed the shuttle backwards and forwards with almost magical precision.

The social consequences of such an evolution didn't escape him: in the first place, the aim of these manufacturers was not to satisfy existing demands, but to create new ones; in their greed, they were attempting "to awaken in men of all classes in every country, unknown tastes and desires." The dictatorship of fashion and frivolity, normally only exercised over the leisured classes, would conquer new territory and give rise to an indispensable "spirit of hostility to anything lasting," because industrialists only grow rich by change. He foresaw the days of consumerism when a garment would be discarded after one season. He realised that, far from improving the

40. Ibid., p. 257.

worker's lot, use of machines made his work much more punishing. "When I entered a workshop, the more workers there were, the keener I felt to leave. One tires quickly of admiring the marvellous results of the single action that every man is bound to repeat imperturbably for the whole of his life; and it fills one with indignation to hear the word prosperity applied to that pitiless wealth which condemns one half of the nation to be brutalised, in order to maintain the corruption of the other . . . Today, our helots are obliged to desire their own misfortune: that is the only advantage to be gained from perfecting administration in modern states."[41]

Custine really didn't like England. He felt "a personal enmity"[42] towards the country. Could this antipathy have arisen only from the ills inherent in an industrial society, from the uniform monotony of the streets, the detestable climate, the coal dust you inhaled, the crushing fog and endless meals? Or did it come from the ridiculous balls where "you seemed to be witnessing some treatment for a sickness of the mind in a magnificent mental hospital," as you watched "haughtily ill-clad figures jumping with icy seriousness, and drunk with pleasure in imperturbable silence"?[43] No doubt, but there was something else besides.

41. Ibid., pp. 292–293.
42. Letter to Sophie Gay, quoted by Luppé, op. cit., p. 117.
43. *Mémoires*, op. cit., p. 273.

A Taste for Freedom

In July 1822, a terrible scandal shook the kingdom, a scandal that was spread over all the newspapers and details of which were bandied about every drawing-room. The bishop of Clogher had been found with a soldier. His high birth and relationship to a peer of the realm were of no help. Caught in flagrante delicto in a public house, he was taken to a police station in ecclesiatical dress, followed by a threatening crowd. Five hundred pounds bought him temporary freedom of which he took advantage to escape to Scotland where he earned a living as a butler in a castle until he was recognised by one of the guests.[44] Custine was appalled by the way the press dwelt on the circumstances of the scandal, leaving no detail to the imagination, and his perception of the advantages of English freedom was affected by it. What was freedom in a country where "an entirely free press threatens the individual's every action: a ball, a walk, a conversation and a great deal more as well, *some offence against morality*, against received opinion . . . will be published the following day in numerous newspapers throughout the kingdom . . . Misdemeanours, *the strangeness of which should itself ensure secrecy*, are described and published with no regard for pure and refined souls"?[45] Custine came to the conclusion that public freedom, as guaranteed by the press, was certainly not worth the resulting domestic enslave-

44. H. Montgomery Hyde, *The Love That Dared Not Speak Its Name* (Little Brown, 1970), pp. 83–84.
45. *Mémoires*, op. cit., p. 213.

ment. What good was it to be free of political chains only to be "voluntarily shackled . . . [by] the pedantic efforts of an entire nation to regulate men's private lives"?[46]

Custine came home to his own way of life and put more value than ever on "the sweet ease of character, the lively imagination, the true *freedom* of spirit of the gay people of France."[47]

46. Ibid., p. 245.
47. Ibid., pp. 245–246.

8

Freedom

Astolphe returned home, "happy to rediscover [his] lair and without being punished for [his] wanderings by any bad news on [his] return,"[1] and to bury himself once again in the quiet life of Fervaques where, under the fond eyes of Delphine and Léontine, he read, worked and conversed with Sainte-Barbe, of course, with Koreff and his old friend Schlosser from Frankfurt, who was "a stranger to everything but Greek and philosophy." Delphine, thinking ahead, began to pester Chateaubriand to ask the king to make Astolphe a peer.[2] "I have told you a hundred times,"

---

1. Letter to La Grange in Luppé, op. cit., p. 92.
2. The peers who sat in the Luxembourg Palace were personally appointed by

he replied in the usual tone he adopted with Delphine, "and I repeat, I think that Astolphe's real career lies in the peerage. It is now impossible that he will have to wait very long. The peerage is a stepping stone to everything, have a little patience . . ."[3]

Astolphe was worried. During the winter, the family had returned to Paris where his young wife, suffering from the early effects of a pregnancy, fell ill. Throughout the spring of 1823 she was confined to bed with pneumonia. Nothing Koreff could do worked. She wasted away. Her youth, her resignation and her good humour moved Custine to write to La Grange that he lived and thought only of her[4]—and God knows, he had never made a show of conjugal love. She weakened so quickly that it was impossible to return to Fervaques, and, hoping that a change of air would help, the family, including Sainte-Barbe who never left Astolphe and who cared for Léontine "like a brother," all went to Saint-Germain-en-Laye where Mme de Boufflers had bought a house. There was nothing to be done. After a terrible struggle, on 17 July 1823, aged twenty, poor little Léontine died.

Custine, who was more appalled by "the horrible convulsions"[5]

---

the king and could hand the office down to their sons. Legislative power was shared between them and the Chamber of Deputies.

3. Maugras, *Delphine de Sabran*, op. cit., p. 557.

4. *Lettres à La Grange*, op. cit., p. 147.

5. Ibid., p. 151.

of death than by the misfortune of the separation, tenderly cosseted his mother; he estimated rightly how irreparable the loss was for her and knew that despite looking after her grandson, she would have difficulty picking up the threads of everyday life. Chateaubriand, too, was aware of her loss: "Astolphe is young, he will console himself; but you?"[6] he wrote immediately. Astolphe needed only a few months before his zest for life was quite restored. "Little by little ideas fade . . . sweet ones regain their colour . . . Love of life cannot be extinguished with one stroke in a heart as eager for happiness as mine."[7]

Despite his distracted manner, he was concerned about his career and having satisfied himself that Chateaubriand's efforts on his behalf were useless, he turned to Mme de Montcalm; since the death of the duc de Richelieu, who was her brother and Louis XVIII's former prime minister, her influence had been greatly reduced, making it more difficult for her to help in his quest for a peerage.[8] In the government circles of 1824, the name Custine was barely known, although Astolphe's reputation as a husband was so excellent that it was high on the list of every aristocratic mother with a daughter

6. Letter from Chateaubriand to Delphine, 8 July 1823, quoted by Bardoux, op. cit., p. 380.

7. *Lettres à La Grange*, op. cit., p. 152.

8. E. de Lévis-Mirepoix, *Correspondance de la marquise de Montcalm* (Editions du Grand Siècle, 1949), p. 218.

to marry. Delphine's presence in his lodgings—at that time a furnished apartment—meant that there need be no question mark over Sainte-Barbe, the permanent companion who lived there too. The princesse de La Trémoille was a grand, authoritarian, disdainful woman, "cruel at the expense of the sheep of the majority,"[9] who used her dropsy as an excuse never to rise for anyone and whose wit and effrontery livened up an extremist salon. She had made friends with Astolphe and wanted to marry him to the young Marie de Flavigny, the future Marie d'Agoult, a difficult beauty who refused all suitors. Another possibility was General Sébastiani's daughter.

All these ladies were charmed by Astolphe's affability, his conversation, taste and the somewhat convoluted politesse he expressed in long, leisurely letters. Like Proust he adored the extreme refinements of manners. Neither he nor his mother liked society life but they both knew how to receive with elegance. They introduced people of their world to artists like Gérard or Mme Vigée-Lebrun, a friend of long standing who had painted a pretty picture of Mme de Sabran, or to the well-known singer, la Malibran. They delighted in encouraging new talent and the young Delphine Gay, known as the Muse and daughter of their friend, Sophie, made her début in their salon. She could successfully reduce the company to tears with her

9. Jacques Vier, *La Comtesse d'Agoult et son temps* (Armand Colin, 1955), I, p. 96.

readings from Chateaubriand.[10] Astolphe's polite reserve belied the energy he devoted to his nocturnal activities.

On returning to Paris, Astolphe, satisfied neither with the familiar attentions of the handsome Edward nor with the usual visits to "strange salons" and heedless of prudence, sought stronger satisfactions further afield, thus causing a scandal which was to echo throughout Paris and revolutionise his life.

What exactly happened on 28 October 1824? According to the newspapers, M. the marquis de C. went to Saint-Denis to see the inside of the church where Louis XVIII's funeral had taken place a few days earlier. Having sent his carriage away despite the pouring rain, he walked to Epinay and was attacked by hooligans who left him for dead by the roadside. He was brought home half naked and covered with bruises and, reluctantly, lodged a complaint. He needed to make credible the only honourable and plausible version of the facts. He did so in vain since some non-commissioned officers from a cavalry regiment stationed at Saint-Denis unexpectedly presented themselves to the examining magistrate. They stated that the marquis had arranged a rendez-vous with one of their comrades, as a result of which they had decided to give him the punishment he deserved. Custine dropped his complaint, of course, but was obliged to face the consternation of society.

10. Vier, op. cit., I, p. 78.

The world he frequented did not take morality lightly. The ladies of the aristocracy turned unanimously against the poor man, "angrily as if they had been personally betrayed." These women, considering themselves to have been deceived, were furious. Their indignation was a measure of their former respect. From her chaise-longue where she lay, her thin, little deformed body wrapped in shawls and blankets, Mme de Montcalm charitably advised Astolphe to go and get himself killed in the army. It is easy to imagine Mme de Duras's comments as she finally understood the inexplicable; the comtesse de Saint-Aulaire congratulated herself that the marriage that she had suggested with Fanny Sébastiani had not taken place. (How could she have guessed that her protégée would then marry the duc de Choiseul-Praslin who, desperate to marry his children's governess, was to kill his unfortunate wife by hitting her with a candlestick?) Mme Swetchine, a studiedly sanctimonious Russian, was surprised by the way Astolphe bore his well-deserved shame: "I cannot understand how a man can live amongst people who think they have the right to heap scorn upon him: in comparison a desert or a Trappist monastery should seem like paradise."[11]

Mme Swetchine had little understanding of Astolphe's inner strength; she could only see the cotton wool wrapped around the in-

11. Mme Swetchine to La Grange, letter of 30 July 1825, quoted by Bardoux, op. cit., p. 27.

ner steel and furthermore showed herself incapable of imagining the remarkable solidarity of the small circle surrounding him. Astolphe was not alone. He had his mother, impervious to social scandal, helped by his uncle Elzéar; and his grandmother who, despite her dismay, which was apparent to everyone, would not have dreamed of abandoning her daughter in adversity and so stood by her grandson. Nor was he without the support of the faithful Berstoecher. Besides, his first cousin, Scipion de Dreux-Brézé, Léontine's sister and her husband, Alfred de Maussion, the princesse de Vaudémont and Chateaubriand were all prepared to shake hands with him. Later the duchesse d'Abrantès offered hers. From a distance, Rahel provided the constant comfort of a loyal friend. Unmoved, Sainte-Barbe remained at his side. His friends, who knew and accepted his proclivities, did not condemn him because his behaviour had been made public. Chateaubriand's and Mme Récamier's understanding in these matters didn't extend to Custine alone. Their best friend, Adrien de Montmorency-Laval, had confided in them that he found himself in a wild, lonely place near Rome with a little seventeen-year-old secretary: "I am taking him with me, this sort of child, who is, besides, so reasonable, amiable, sensible, interesting, that he may study, and I would ask you to offer him the friendship offered him by a friend, my blood relation [Mathieu de Montmorency]," and Adrien finished his letter by reminding Mme Récamier that she "knew all the affections, all the miseries, all the wounds, the weaknesses and secrets of [his] heart."[12] Let it be said that in these circles no one mocked the group of "tender young men"[13] whom Lamennais* seemed unable to do without. At Mme Récamier's salon in the Abbaye-aux-Bois, passion was understood and not judged.

The break with the dowagers, which in any case was not definitive, was no catastrophe for Astolphe; he simply didn't acknowledge their moral or social authority. His caste had suffered an earthquake of such strength that he felt no obligation to subscribe to its rules of behaviour. This gave him a freedom he was to use and define in one of his novels: ". . . The relaxation of all rules, the absence of tradition, universal indifference, the abolition of etiquette to the point of disdain for convention, the absence of any moral tie whose last consequence means the loss of manners and of elegant ways of thinking . . . all these political misfortunes became favourable circumstances for someone whose life had to be rebuilt."[14]

He had sufficient intellectual and emotional resources to be able to live away from society, for a time, at least, without suffering. By refusing a career and, more especially at the time, by his remarkable

*Robert de Lamennais (1782–1854) was a democratic-minded priest who favored the separation of church and state. He was condemned by the Vatican.

12. Françoise Wagener, *Madame Récamier* (Paris, Lattès, 1986), pp. 391 and 457.

13. Henri Guillemin, *Introduction aux oeuvres de Lamennais* (Geneva, Editions du Milieu du Monde), p. 8.

14. Astolphe de Custine, *Ethel*, 2 vols. (Paris, Ladvocat, 1839), I, p. 310.

break with Clara de Duras, he had already braved public opinion with impunity. Most important, the scandal, which seems to have been neither a source of grievance nor of suffering, did nothing to alter the relationship between mother and son.

They simply decided to leave as quickly as possible for Fervaques, followed by their usual friends. One would wish to say that they rested there a while, but their peace was shattered by the illness and then, in January 1826, the death of Astolphe's son, little Enguerrand. This time the blow was too much for Delphine: the child was gay, attractive and a hope for the future. Exhausted by cancer of the stomach which Koreff had diagnosed but could do nothing about, she no longer had the strength to recover. Astolphe and Berstoecher persuaded her to go to the Alps. She agreed to leave for Bex in Switzerland, drawn there by Chateaubriand's presence in Lausanne. She smiled on him a last time "with her pale lips and beautiful teeth."[15] But on 13 July she suddenly collapsed. Chateaubriand rushed to keep vigil over the one who "had wished him well . . . whiter than the Parcae, dressed in black, shrivelled by death, her head adorned just with her silken hair."[16] But he didn't accompany Astolphe when he brought his mother's coffin back to France to take its place in the church, whose slated tower could be glimpsed from the windows of Fervaques, and where his wife and son already lay beneath two

---

15. Chateaubriand, *Mémoires d'outre-tombe*, op. cit., I, p. 472.
16. Ibid.

marble stones engraved with a simple cross, their names and dates. Mme de Boufflers survived her daughter by only a few months. Berstoecher, *the friend*, left the house. There remained only Sainte-Barbe, known as *the slave*, a gentle submissive slave as was only right and proper.

[My] fate was determined on the day in which my mother's ended. However sensitive, understanding and loyal she was, Delphine weighed on Astolphe, because he loved her, was aware of her fragility and wanted her to be happy. "My mother made so many sacrifices for me that I certainly owe it to her, too, to renounce some plans to which no sacred duty obliges me; one can live with less than I would want if I were alone in the world."[17] To a certain extent he was alone in the world; he could now and would in the future live as he wished, rejoicing as he did in a twofold liberty, based first on a disdain of society and second on money. From the multiple inheritances of his wife, his son and his mother, Astolphe was rich. His freedom was complete, allowing him to organise his life as he pleased.

He lived openly with Sainte-Barbe and if Edward worked partly as his secretary it was because he had no other talents. Astolphe tried to establish them on a footing of social equality and to force Edward on his friends. One evening, when the young Englishman was suf-

17. *Lettres à Varnhagen*, op. cit., p. 268.

fering from an attack of rheumatism, Custine cancelled dining with Victor Hugo, saying that he was loath to leave his sick friend alone. Sainte-Barbe was certainly not a lackey or some kind of seedy underling; he was a man of the world, a little younger than Astolphe and from a very respectable family. His father, a descendant of one of William the Conqueror's companions at the Battle of Hastings, was a Justice of the Peace in the county of Hampshire. Such details were important to Custine, wounded by the nonsense circulating about Sainte-Barbe. "I know full well," he wrote to Sophie Gay,[18] "that a man's birth proves nothing about his character. However, it makes it more difficult to sink to certain depths." He was unable to prevent the sneers with which Sainte-Barbe was often greeted. Even Stendhal admitted to being somewhat perturbed by the young Englishman's "quite truly Petronian" manners and his clasping handshake. The situation had only a precedent unique in French society of the time. Two other men, about whom more will be said later, were known to live as a couple in Parisian society. What was extraordinary about the Custine–Sainte-Barbe household was its having been established after a sordid, brutal, Pasolini-style incident. The incredible aspect of the situation was that Custine was liberated precisely by the horror of his adventure. One cannot fail to be struck by the fact that nearly a century later Proust would touch on that particular act of aggression without being able to look it in the face.

18. Quoted by Luppé, op. cit., p. 118.

Freedom

One day a man who is one of the best known in the faubourg Saint-Germain, as Balzac would have said, but who in an early somewhat distressing phase displayed bizarre tastes, asked my uncle to [his] bachelor apartment. He had barely arrived when he began to make a declaration, not to the women, but to my uncle Palamède. My uncle, pretending not to understand, made an excuse to fetch his two friends, returned with them, took hold of the culprit, stripped him, beat him until he bled and in a temperature of 10 degrees below zero, kicked him outside where he was found half dead so that an enquiry was instigated by the law, which the poor fellow had all the trouble in the world persuading them to drop.[19]

The changes Proust makes are interesting. He turns the soldiers into society men and, more particularly, he draws a veil over the real significance of the incident. In the novel, Saint-Loup relates the story to the narrator to show that his uncle Charlus loved women. Thus he denatured the liberating incident which transformed Custine's life. For Custine was to prove that having been found out, far from putting an end to his conditional freedom, brought in its wake real freedom such as Proust never knew because he was unable to reveal his true nature to his parents; he was always forced to save appearances both in his life and in his work. It wasn't by chance that

---

19. Marcel Proust, *A la recherche du temps perdu, A l'ombre des jeunes filles en fleurs* (Bouquins), I, p. 615.

195

the narrator never yielded to the tide of homosexuality that courses through *A la recherche*. Throughout his life Proust reacted violently to the slightest hint at his leanings and even went so far as to fight a duel to defend his reputation.[20]

The difference between Proust's careful attention to form and Custine's free, bold attitude could derive from the origins of the two men. The young, half-Jewish bourgeois, born into a strictly conventional family, refusing to face the world head on, could hardly be expected to behave in the same way as the heir to an ancient name, brought up by an unusually open-minded, doting mother, and availing himself with the ease of a great nobleman's scorn for plebeians. Times had changed. There was less tolerance of misbehaviour towards the end of the century than there had been in its first three decades. Moreover, the scientific edifice constructed around the subject of homosexuality from the 1870s onwards, labelling it an hereditary defect, an instability bordering on insanity, made it more difficult to admit to unorthodox tastes.

In the nineteenth century, homosexuals wanting to explain the injustice of the treatment to which they were subjected always referred to their golden age in Athens. Let us also look back. Homosexuality didn't exist as a category in the ancient world. There were

20. Jeanine Huas, *Homosexualité au temps de Proust* (Danclau, 1992), p. 14.

words in Latin and Greek for every position, every act, every imaginable fantasy, but the conviction that a normal man might take his pleasure equally from a boy or a woman was so deep-rooted that there was no need to define a man who desired another man. The difference between being attracted to one sex or the other, which seems fundamental to us, was of no interest to the Greeks. Their morality concentrated on the difference between the active and passive partner in these matters. The Greeks were not obsessed with forbidding or codifying every aspect of sexual behaviour, but they did have certain principles: a Charlus, for instance, the prototype man/woman, allowing himself to be humiliated by someone like Morel, would have forfeited his rights in Athens. Proust was wrong when he wrote that "no one was abnormal when homosexuality was the norm";[21] merely a different category was classed as abnormal. For the Greeks, an adult man could only play the dominant role. A passive complaisant man was regarded as abnormal, an object of derision and thus excluded from political life.

Rome altered nothing although such activities seemed less noble there than they had in Greece. That the love object might be a boy destined to become a citizen was peculiar to Greece. In Rome, there was a tendency to protect young Romans. There were enough slaves and foreigners to satisfy every taste and the sons of good families

21. Proust, op. cit., *Sodome et Gomorrhe*, p. 511.

could be spared the awkward passage from object to subject. Since they didn't concern the citizens, the most curious practises were indulged in Rome without question.

Such pastimes were somewhat restricted by the barbarian invasions and the disappearance of the great cities, but they were soon revived under the Church which ignored them completely. Significantly, in 1051, Pope Leo IX refused to defrock priests who indulged in homosexual love. Fifty years later, Urban II refused point blank when the bishop of Chartres asked him to oppose the choice of the bishop of Orléans because of the nature of his relationship with his colleague in Tours.[22] Homosexuality was not regarded as a mortal sin until the fourteenth century.

Then came the Crusades, the rise of absolute power, a huge drive towards uniformity in Europe, accompanied by an exaggerated desire for codes of law and rules. Religious and social intolerance took root. By about 1300, Jews, heretics or "sodomites" were not accepted and homosexuality, which until then had been admitted without any difficulty, was suddenly punishable by death: an ignominious burning at the stake. All the subtleties of the ancient world were abolished. The murder of Edward II, the last English king to be openly homosexual, and the annihilation of the Order of Tem-

22. John Boswell, *Christianity, Social Tolerance and Homosexuality, Gay People in Western Europe from the Beginning of the Christian Era to the Fourteenth Century* (The University of Chicago Press, 1980), p. 207.

plars because of accusations of sodomy, caused the most intrepid to tremble if only for a moment and humbler men to dissemble. Such persecutions were the exception, resulting from political expediency rather than a desire to improve morals. Society wasn't ready for so brutal a volte-face.

Far from disappearing, homosexuals—at least those protected by their birth, fortune and position—flaunted themselves. The French court was famous for its *mignons* and poets under the Valois, its princes, dukes and marshals under Louis XIV and Louis XV's broad-cuffed chevaliers who fancied both women and men. In the upper classes, homosexuals were all married—a taste for boys didn't mean the family line could be sacrificed—and, besides, exclusivity in sexual matters was unknown. Not only did they advertise their predilections without the slightest embarrassment, but these men, whose activities should have led them straight to the stake, enjoyed a surprising political and artistic influence.

In this respect, the rules of conduct at Versailles under Louis XIV are revealing. At the end of his reign, Louis XIV, "full of a just and singular horror"[23] for the Italian vice, maintained in public a rigidly pious stand. He had his bastard son, the duc de Vermandois, whipped when he discovered his taste for male orgies, and yet he surrounded himself with the most blatant enthusiasts of these same

23. Saint-Simon, *Mémoires* (Edition du Tricentenaire, 1975), vol. 7, tome XIII, p. 282.

orgies; if their talents were indispensable, he gave them the best jobs, especially in the army. There clearly existed a sharp divergence between custom and the law. Despite the revulsion of an absolute monarch like Louis XIV for their practises, homosexuals played an essential role at his court.

Versailles wasn't Athens; relationships between men were not common or encouraged but, as in Greece, an attraction between men represented only one aspect of personality. Saint-Simon never used the word sodomite. He used the word *taste*—"His taste was not for women"—and a man is hardly defined by a taste. At the court many different kinds of men were attracted to men and any generalisation would have been pointless. There was the king's brother, Monsieur, all the more feminine for being prevented from exercising his natural talent at the head of the army: "a small, pot-bellied man, walking as though on stilts because his shoes were so high-heeled, always adorned like a woman, covered in rings and bracelets, with precious stones everywhere, a long wig spread out in front, all black and powdered, with ribbons wherever he could put them, bathed in every sort of perfume, cleanliness itself."[24] He was accused of making himself up imperceptibly, having "the manners of a woman rather than a man . . . liking neither horses, nor hunting . . . enjoying only gambling, holding court, eating well, dancing

24. Ibid., vol. 4, tome VIII, p. 349.

and dressing."[25] He enjoyed everything that women enjoyed, including children of which he had seven and to whom he proved an excellent, affectionate and attentive father. The king used the chevalier de Lorraine, who was always glued to Monsieur "and ruled him absolutely,"[26] when he needed to persuade his brother about something.

Besides the effeminate ones, there were the large, virile chiefs of the king's armies. The maréchal d'Huxelles "looked exactly like one of those great brutal butchers, lazy, voluptuous to excess in every kind of way . . . in his choice of company, in the Greek debaucheries which he took no trouble to hide and where he picked up young officers whom he domesticated along with some very good-looking valets, and all without concealing it from the army or in Strasbourg."[27] Then there was the duc de Vendôme about whom rhymes were written to the effect that he pleasured the army, the court, the old timer—indeed the whole militia[28]—and who "knew how to take advantage of the greatest of vices . . . being most foully immersed in them, and in so public a fashion that he made no more

25. *Correspondance de Madame*, in Saint-Simon, op. cit., vol. 4, tome VIII, p. 630.

26. Ibid., vol. 6, tome XI, p. 74.

27. Ibid., vol. 6, tome XI, pp. 41–42.

28. La Fontaine, dedication in *Philémon et Baucis*. To the delight of poets, "Vendôme" was naturally crying out to be rhymed with Sodom.

of it than of the merest intrigue . . . This scandal followed him all his life at court, at Anet and in the army. His valets and his officers always satisfied this horrible taste."[29] Then there were those like Langlée. "He was a nobody of a man," introduced early into the best society by his mother, the Queen Mother's Lady of the Chamber. "He was particularly drawn to Monsieur by their shared tastes, but with no dependency, always keeping the King in his sights . . . so he was there on every journey, was there on every outing, attended every Court festivity . . . He had made himself the master of fashion, of festivities and of taste, to such a degree that no one, not even the princes and princesses of the blood, did anything without his supervision: no baptism was arranged, no house bought without his advice in decorating and furnishing."[30] In 1707, he was asked to prepare a layette and furnishings for the young queen of Spain. So, not only were Greek ways much in evidence and accepted at court, but because of them an influential political and artistic network developed among the initiated.

Exasperated by the civil and religious contempt in which they were held, homosexuals became increasingly provocative in the following century. They were accepted but—paradoxically—always against a background of savage repression: without protection from the highest in the land, they were at the mercy of implacable author-

29. Saint-Simon, op. cit., vol. 7, tome XIII, pp. 281–283.
30. Ibid., vol. 4, tome VII, pp. 73–74.

ity. Jean-Baptiste Nattier, older brother of the official court painter of Louis XV, was a very talented artist and a member of the Royal Academy of Painting. In 1726, at the age of forty-eight, he was implicated in the Deschauffours affair. Deschauffours was accused of kidnapping little boys for the pleasure of a few grandees. Nattier was sent to the Bastille and, together with Deschauffours, condemned to be burnt at the stake. He only escaped this horrifying death by cutting his throat with a glazier's knife.[31]

Helped by the ex-prostitutes who acted as agent provocateurs, the police hounded the "infamous," locked them up and sometimes put them to death. The last man to don the sulphur shirt and be burnt alive, in October 1783, was a former Capuchin monk convicted of having stabbed a young man he had invited to see him who had resisted his advances. Yet in spite of these threats nothing changed; homosexuality thrived and spread. In 1725 the Paris police held files on twenty thousand men because of their morals, a figure that had nearly doubled by the eve of the Revolution.[32]

In the new civil code of 1791, there was no penalty for sodomy between consenting adults, although in the wards and public commit-

31. J. de Nolhac, *Jean-Marc Nattier, peintre de la cour de Louis XV* (Paris, Goupil, 1905), pp. 26–27.

32. *Mémoires de Canler*, former head of department at the police headquarters, 1797–1865 (Mercure de France, 1986), chap. 65.

tees, homosexuality was perceived as a privilege of the aristocracy and the Church. For the first time since 533 A.D., homosexuality was decriminalised and neither Napoleon nor his successors would ever again raise the question of this basic freedom. Jews and homosexuals, two completely different minorities but both victims of intolerance during the same period, from the Late Empire until the Nazi concentration camps, were granted civil liberties in France at the same time.

That Napoleon didn't see fit to reintroduce a policy of repression is symptomatic of the fact that for him the problem didn't exist. Whereas he had very definite and harsh opinions on the need to control women, he was indifferent to the morals of men, which was clear from his attitude to his arch-chancellor, Cambacérès, who chased young men at the Palais-Royal. One day when Cambacérès arrived late at the council, excusing himself on the grounds of a prolonged visit from a lady, Napoleon retorted sharply, "Next time tell her to pick up her stick and her hat and leave." After centuries of drama and passion and sometimes bloody ostracism, homosexuality no longer meant that you belonged to a minority, both persecuted and powerful. It is hardly surprising that it wasn't the subject of novels at the beginning of the century.

When the subject was touched on in the literature of the time, it was so disguised as to be difficult to identify, as in *Armance*. Only the notes to the manuscript of *Lucien Leuwen* reveal that Lord Link has the bearing of a groom although his "magnificent horse which appears not to touch the ground" arouses the enthusiasm of Lucien. Link is a "sardonic character, a bishop of Clogher,[33] deftly leading women by the nose because they have no greater effect on him than a seven-year-old child," but, the author stresses, *this must remain unspoken.* Stendhal aligns himself with George Sand on this. On that famous October night, she seems to have heard Custine's cries from her house at Epinay but refused to mention the incident. "I cannot and do not wish to recount it," she was to say more than thirty years later,[34] adding that the "insane or unhealthy deviation" which was part of the Ancients' ideal friendship seemed to her "characterised by perversity and degradation."[35]

Balzac chose another, equally discreet, path. Without the slightest equivocation, he described the lesbian love of Séraphita or Paquita, the girl with the golden eyes, a castrato in *Sarrazine*, impotence in *Dona Massilia* and the disturbing love of a man for his panther and the ravages of syphilis in *Le Lys dans la vallée*. However, he left male homosexuality in the shadows. The clues remain difficult to decipher, and most of us fail to do so at the first reading. *Père Goriot*

---

33. Stendhal always uses this expression to designate a homosexual man. It refers to the above-mentioned scandal of the bishop, in 1822, when Astolphe was in England; Stendhal, *Romans* (Gallimard, Bibliothèque de la Pléiade, 1956), vol. I, p. 1534.

34. George Sand, *Histoire de ma vie* (Gallimard, Bibliothèque de la Pléiade, 1971), II, p. 47.

35. Ibid., II, p. 125.

opens with a description of the pension Vauquer, "a lodging house for two sexes and others." Balzac doesn't dwell on the strangeness of what he calls *the third sex*, although one of the most formidable characters, the terrible Vautrin, is clearly attracted to men. Vautrin's apparent, but not flagrant, homosexuality is not a perversion or a pathological or hereditary weakness and is accompanied by no anguished sense of difference. He is a thousand miles removed from Octave or Aloys; neither has he anything in common with the Proustian homosexual or with Gide's pederasts.

Like many convicts, Vautrin became homosexual in jail because his companion in chains happened to be a pretty boy. That he remained so on regaining his freedom had more to do with his contempt for and fear of women than an irresistible attraction to boys. The fate of many of his friends and of many men in high positions who had fallen and fallen again because of a woman confirmed him in his unshakeable misogyny: "These people who dictate our destinies . . . a certain sigh breathed by a female turns their intelligence inside out like a glove. They lose their heads for a glance . . . Oh! What strength a man gains when he is freed, as I am, from this childish tyranny . . . Women with their hangman's genius and their talent for torture are and always will be man's downfall."[36]

Vautrin's homosexuality is no more than one characteristic

36. Balzac, *Splendeurs et misères*, *Dernière incarnation de Vautrin* (Gallimard, Folio), p. 639.

among many; Balzac portrays him not so much as one of the third sex but as a study in the conquest and exercise of power. His despair at Rubempré's death hardly disguises the fact that in his lifetime the young man was above all else an instrument Vautrin intended to use. *Le Cousin Pons*, a far less complex novel than *Les Illusions perdues*, is a further and more obvious example of Balzac's refusal to treat the subject in depth. In it, he describes with false innocence a male couple neither of whom has ever had relations with a woman. It is false because Balzac uses expressions which obviously describe the nature of what ties Pons to Schmucke—his "divine Schmucke"[37]—without ever elaborating on their relationship or passing judgement. We are told that Pons "contracted the only marriage which society allowed him, he married a man . . . a musician like himself."[38] This friend, not satisfied with lavishing "caresses . . . on his homing pigeon . . . bringing him back at night . . . taking him by the arm, like a lover with an adored mistress," guides his steps with exquisite tenderness.[39] Back at their lodgings, as both "mother and mistress . . . he kisses his eyes,"[40] and when, despite the greatest loving care, Pons dies Schmucke doesn't throw himself on his knees, but lies down "beside his friend in the bed and [holds] him

37. Balzac, *Le Cousin Pons* (Ollendorff, 1900), p. 295.
38. Ibid., p. 22.
39. Ibid., pp. 74–75.
40. Ibid., p. 312.

in a close embrace."[41] He survives less than ten days. Once again, the reader rarely questions the nature of the couple's relationship: the conjugal love evinced by the two old boys is less the subject of the novel than family greed and the passion for collecting.

Why were such bold, enquiring writers silent on the subject of homosexuality? Perhaps the fashion for provocative behaviour disappeared with the libertines and the decadent aristocracy. Yet an uneasy, quite personal fascination remained which was neither explained nor examined in depth. Stendhal tried, in a strange letter, to analyse the overwhelming effect of a Russian officer's beauty on him. "If I had been a woman, he would have inspired in me the most violent passion . . . I felt the nascent stirrings; I was already shy. I dared not look at him as much as I wished . . . Had a woman made such an impression on me, I would have spent the night searching for her home."[42] He did nothing of the kind but an obsession with male beauty is evident in his novels. This obsession can also be found in Balzac who, like Stendhal, suffered because of his ugliness and who, like him, compensated by imagining the most exquisite dandies and dwelling on a delicate ankle or a velvety cheek.

The strict censorship which applied to publishers may be all that prevented the Romantics from pushing their narcissism to the point

41. Ibid., p. 370.

42. Stendhal, *Aux âmes sensibles*, Lettres choisies et presentées par Emmanuel Boudot-Lamotte (Gallimard, 1942), p. 138, unaddressed letter, dated 26 May 1814.

where it became one man's fascination for another. Publishers had
to produce proof of good moral standards to obtain what was a very
expensive licence; they were naturally hesitant to risk losing it by
publishing shocking material. One has to wonder why Custine, so
open in the way he lived, referred to his proclivities in such veiled
terms that they appear stifled in his work. This silence continued
until the end of the century but in two generations a perception of
homosexuality had evolved.

Gide and Proust obviously come to mind as the first modern writers to confront the problem. The young Gide's efforts to avoid im-
purity and, to a greater extent, Proust's tragic tone both bear witness to the homosexual's fate, so awful for so long. As members of
an "accursed race," they were forced to live a lie and defend their
way of life as if against slander. Custine wouldn't have recognised
himself in Proust's "motherless son . . . this friendless friend . . . this
lover for whom there is almost no possibility of the love he hopes
will give [him] the strength to take so many risks and to bear such
loneliness."[43]

Custine's casualness and the daring with which he stressed the
conjugal nature of his relationship with Sainte-Barbe, thus taking
advantage of "a shift in hypocrisy,"[44] are a sure mark of his times—

43. Proust, op. cit., *Sodome et Gomorrhe*, p. 510.

44. Custine, *Les Amitiés littéraires en 1831*, in *Le Livre des Cent et Un* (Paris,
Ladvocat, 1832), vol. V, pp. 103–128.

of the Restoration when one man's love of another had not yet become a sickness and was no longer a crime. For all its catholicism and right-mindedness, the Restoration never tried to reinstitute the Ancien Régime's merciless, useless legislation. Two men "living conjugally" could no longer be hounded; so Custine and Sainte-Barbe may have been less exceptional than might be supposed. In good society—the only society, unfortunately, from which to draw conclusions—Custine was not the only one to live with his friend. Joseph Fiévée and Théodore Leclercq, both better known than the marquis, had shown him the way.

Joseph Fiévée was one of the most distinguished intellects of his time and, according to Sainte-Beuve, "sensible even in passion, steady even in his versatility, an elegant novelist, witty, almost dainty, a clear-sighted publicist, clever, practically a statesman." During the Directory he met Théodore Leclercq in a club. Théodore was a young man from a good Parisian family. The two men liked each other so much that they never wanted to be separated again. They rented an apartment together; their union, interrupted only by death, lasted more than forty years. Sainte-Beuve, who devoted one of his essays to Leclercq, had no difficulty in describing the liaison with equanimity. Leclercq wrote light-hearted, witty proverbs to be read aloud. He could certainly live as he pleased without shocking anyone other than his friends; the same could hardly be said of Fiévée, who had an important position in public life.

Freedom

By making him prefect of the Nièvre in 1813, Napoleon nominated a notorious homosexual to represent him in the province. One might have expected Fiévée to attempt to disguise his way of life, but this was unlikely from a man who declared: "When one has a vice, one must know how to wear it."[45] He settled in the prefecture with Leclercq and made him entertain as the lady of the house—although not a very pretty lady, as Théodore was "horribly scarred by smallpox, nearly blind in one eye and had jerky manners."[46] Nevertheless, the new prefect was accepted without any fuss. The best families received the couple. Even nowadays an overtly homosexual prefect would not be welcomed quite so easily.

Under the Restoration, Marie d'Agoult's father, the comte de Flavigny, a man of impeccable lineage, often invited the two men to his château in the Vendée where they were much appreciated by all the family. On returning to Paris, the comtesse organized a little theatre in her mother-in-law's salon which she entrusted to Théodore and from then on the two couples were never apart. As Marie pointed out, "the prudery of *comme il faut* women"[47] was alien to her grandmother.

Marie took after her grandmother. For the sake of love, she aban-

45. Jean Tulard, *Joseph Fiévée* (Fayard, 1985), p. 8.
46. Marie d'Agoult, *Mémoires, Souvenirs, Journaux* (Mercure de France, 1990), I, p. 117.
47. Ibid., I, p. 118.

doned a way of life based on traditional morality, causing a scandal like the one surrounding Custine. It was an equally grave offence to have a rendez-vous with a soldier as to leave a child and a titled husband and run away with Franz Liszt—a promising musician, his great works as yet unwritten—and bear him a child. Like Astolphe de Custine, Marie d'Agoult bravely confronted the outcry and rebuilt her life.

There was another world, a more exciting, more amusing, more varied world than that of the Faubourg Saint-Germain; a new society was opening up to artists and writers. It lay across the Seine on the Right Bank.

FIGURE I The execution of Astolphe's grandfather,
General de Custine. "I do not know how I shall behave when
the end comes: one can never be sure of oneself before one
faces it," he admitted, on the eve of his death. In fact, he showed
the greatest courage, as did his son, guillotined five months later.

FIGURE 2 The comtesse de Sabran,
painted by Mme Vigée-Lebrun. Within
the family circle, Astolphe's grandmother
was full of good spirits, tender and a bit
untidy, her hair a tangled mess. She
recovered all her dignity in society.

FIGURE 3 The chevalier de Boufflers was
famous for his wit, the insolence of his
verse, and his success as a lady's man.
He had to wait twenty years before he
finally married the comtesse de Sabran.

FIGURE 4 Sophie Gay, in a lithograph by Lucienne Collière. Sophie was good at everything: books, children and preserves. In 1850, Astolphe sent her a big bouquet of flowers to mark the fiftieth anniversary of their friendship.

FIGURE 5 Anonymous portrait of
Delphine de Custine. Utterly seductive,
the blonde Delphine seemed to have
stepped out of a Greuze painting. She
collected a wide assortment of lovers all
the while remaining her son's best friend.

FIGURE 6 Claire de Kersaint,
duchesse de Duras. She never forgave
Astolphe for refusing the honor of
becoming her son-in-law.

FIGURE 7 Portrait of Chateaubriand
by Girodet. Chateaubriand, always called
the Genius by the Custines, won the
mother's unfailing love and the son's
enduring admiration.

FIGURE 8 Astolphe de Custine. Every mother wanted this elegant, intelligent, modest young man, whose conversation was delightfully brilliant and full of surprises, for her daughter. His unassuming attitude hid a steely determination, and Custine did not let himself be caught. Attracted much more by men than by women, he managed to stick to his own way of life.

FIGURE 9 Rahel von Varnhagen's attic in Berlin, a woodcut by
Erich M. Simon. "Give me some news of myself," wrote Astolphe
to Rahel, his faraway correspondent, who was the most faithful
and the most perspicacious of his friends.

FIGURE 10 The château of Fervaques in Normandy:
"A big building too low in relation to its length . . .
without the slightest luxury, compact and severe and
yet cheerful" was bought by Delphine de Custine
in 1804 and sold after her death in 1826.

FIGURE 11 Saint-Gratien, less than an hour from Paris, was Custine's favorite home. He organised many ravishing parties and wonderful concerts in this Italianate villa.

FIGURE 12 St. Petersburg. "In St. Petersburg, everything has the look of opulence, grandeur and magnificence but, if you judge reality from the appearance of things, you might find yourself exceedingly disappointed." After his return from Russia, Custine published his devastating *La Russie en 1839*, in which he recorded his impressions of the empire.

9

The Writer's Trade

C ustine was not a man in a hurry. After his mother died he took a kind of holiday, he shut up his apartment in the rue d'Anjou and left for Italy with Sainte-Barbe, but was obliged to interrupt his trip to see to the sale of Fervaques. Since Delphine's death the place was too haunted by ghosts of the past. Although the matter was still not settled, he returned to Naples in the winter. His need to escape was understandable.

Astolphe remained unmoved by worldly scandal. In his view "this narrow circle which used so emphatically to be called the *world* has become so small that there are a thousand ways and means of living well outside it."[1] To behave for the sake of society, as one would

---

1. Astolphe de Custine, *Le Monde comme il est*, op. cit., I, p. 46.

have under Louis XV, seemed "pure dupery"[2] to him but he did suffer from the loss of his old friends. Edouard de La Grange and Alexis de Noailles disappeared from his life, never to be replaced. Despite his wit, the favour he found in the best houses, and a very real talent as a writer of fables, Astolphe's uncle, Elzéar, was so bizarre and so egocentric that relations between the two men grew ever more distant.

"Outwardly [Elzéar] was no help to me, and inwardly no consolation under any circumstances . . . [This] child without naïveté, [this] man without courage, this intransigent old man"[3] indulged his every eccentricity. He was said to wash his hands only on days when he read of Pontius Pilate in the Passion. His love of cemeteries was a further peculiarity which led to his crying for a whole week by his parents' graves on the anniversaries of their deaths. After weeping copiously, he made himself tea from a brandy still he had brought with him; at dawn on the eighth day, he gathered together all those who had also come to the cemetery to mourn and invited them to lunch.[4] He dissociated himself from Delphine who had long since ceased to confide in her brother and refused to mourn a sister who "resembled him so little that she did not belong to him." Astolphe was wounded by so pointless an insult.

2. Ibid., I, p. 84.

3. Letter to Sophie Gay, 6 March 1842, quoted by Tarn, op. cit., p. 241.

4. Rodolphe Apponyi, *Vingt-Cing Ans à Paris* (Plon, 1913), II, pp. 402–405.

Custine's only male friendship in adulthood, based on shared political and literary interests and illuminated by their faithful memory of Rahel, was with Varnhagen. After Rahel's death in 1833, the two men drew closer and corresponded regularly. But Varnhagen and Custine practically never saw one another and their relationship was purely intellectual. Custine appears to have been more at ease with women friends. When Delphine's old friends Rahel and the princesse de Vaudémont, who had both remained loyal to Astolphe, died, there remained only one family of intimates: specifically three women since he didn't much like their husbands. In Paris he "spent his whole life" visiting Sophie Gay, her daughter Delphine and her stepdaughter Eliza O'Donnell; and they often joined him abroad.

There were a few other women of whom he was fond, like Mme de Courbonne and the comtesse Merlin. He had a great liking for Louise Bertin, the daughter of the editor of the *Journal des débats*, who was brilliantly clever, sensitive and musical, but unfortunately crippled. With Laure Junot, duchesse d'Abrantès, he had a friendly relationship complicated by the fact that she borrowed large sums of money from him and had got it into her head that she wanted to marry him.

Although older than Astolphe, Laure had no desire to mother him. The fall of the Empire had been a catastrophe for her. Her husband, General Junot, having gone mad, committed suicide in 1813, leaving debts of more than a million. She was obliged to sell her furniture, her jewels and her wine cellar and retire with her two daughters to a small villa at Versailles but she never allowed herself to be defeated by misfortune. She had a passionate, easy-going nature, and still beautiful with bright eyes and black hair, she threw herself into a double literary career. She had an affair with Balzac and then, on his advice, began to write. Of the two careers, the second lasted longer. Her memoirs of the Empire were very successful and she could have earned her living "doing this *job*"—she saw literature as a job like any other—had she been able to break the habit of spending three times what she earned. She always defended Custine energetically but when she persuaded herself that he loved her, he fled.

His real friend through the years was always Sophie Gay; it was said of her that she made everything well: books, children and jam. She acted as his confidante, his information bureau and urged him to act. Her old friendship with Delphine, whom she met in 1800, combined with having known Astolphe since he was a child, gave her certain rights for which he was grateful. Her gossiping and worldliness sometimes led to indiscretions which Custine preferred to ignore, and although she was not his wife, sister or daughter or, he might have added, his mother,[5] thanks to the absolute freedom of their relationship, she offered him what he most needed: "indepen-

5. Letter to Sophie Gay, 31 December 1833, in Luppé, op. cit., p. 162.

dence and friendship."[6] Sophie's daughter was Delphine's namesake, the Muse of Muses—a muse being a young person who wrote and recited in salons. Although she was only a few years younger than he, Astolphe declared a fatherly affection for her which she flirtatiously rejected. "I feel nothing filial for you . . . you are not old enough for me to claim to be so much younger."[7] He had the most straightforward relationship with Eliza O'Donnell. She had "a delicate wit, the more elegant for being unstudied, useless, thrown pointlessly out of the window like the money of the rich . . . not malicious, always sincere and as disinterested in her likes as in her dislikes,"[8] and listened as well as she talked. He always ran to her side after an absence abroad because she could describe a whole year in Paris in an hour.

It would have been impossible not to be at ease with the Gays where "no awkwardness hindered the soaring spirits; where one could be witty, amusing and amused under a cloudless sky . . . The house ran itself; no masters of the house were ever to be seen . . . Besides, what frank gaiety there was . . . [Only] the cursing of the wigmaker living opposite [indicated that] it was time to leave, for in

6. Letter quoted in Luppé, op. cit., p. 112.
7. H. Malo, *La Gloire du vicomte de Launay* (Paris, Emile-Paul, 1925), p. 152.
8. Vandérem, "Letters from Custine to Mme de Courbonne," *Revue de France*, 15 June–1 July 1934, p. 93.

winter he came, well after midnight to drag his wife away from the open window where she would sit and savour the melodies of Garat, Dalvimar and Frédéric."[9] Furthermore, Sophie's advice on literary matters was as sound as Delphine's and Astolphe was "working like a slave" despite the very real difficulties concerning the château and land which were proving impossible to sell. He decided to sell them in lots. Encouraged by Sainte-Barbe, he was working simultaneously in three literary forms: a novel—whose title, *Aloys*, was suggested by Sophie—a travel journal and a poem, *La Cenci*.

After years of haggling, he managed to get enough money from Fervaques to buy a house in the rue de La Rochefoucauld, "ravishing, but horribly expensive,"[10] which needed three years of renovation. Since he always recoiled from returning to Parisian society, he was not the least inconvenienced by the delay, and as soon as the contract was signed in April 1829, he left for Germany. Meanwhile, he had finished and published—albeit anonymously—*Aloys*, his first book. The book had a small *succès de scandale*, enough for two editions to sell out and for it to be distributed in Germany, where Astolphe was quite surprised to find it in the famous Schlesinger bookshop, Unter den Linden. It was then forgotten until 1971. His official début, writing under his own name, came with the publication in 1829 of a long poem, *La Cenci*, which tells the story of a Re-

9. Norvins, op. cit., III, p. 298.
10. Quoted by Luppé, op. cit., p. 121.

naissance Roman, Beatrice Cenci, who was raped by her father and executed for murdering him in revenge. *Mémoires et Voyages* came a year later, published by Vézard.

Custine was not satisfied with simply writing, he wanted to define himself as a writer. As a true nineteenth-century man, he explained to Sophie Gay that "the idea of working only to kill time or to entertain a few friends who take an interest in everything that concerns me plunges me into incurable idleness. But when I hear someone who knows what talent is telling me to work, and when I know that this person does not wish me to appear ridiculous like a writer who knows nothing of his trade but its pretensions, then the word glory reverberates in the depths of my soul and this distant echo makes me capable of everything . . . at least with regard to effort and perseverance."[11]

This was a new attitude. After the trauma of the Revolution and the silence of the arts under the Empire, the Poet was making for himself a huge place in French society. It could no longer be said that "literature does not exactly lend position, but it is a substitute for those who have no other."[12] From now on it became a profession, and a respectable profession in which it was possible to make money, as many women, who yearned for independence, were to discover.

11. *Bulletin du bibliophile*, Paris, p. 478.
12. Paul Bénichou, *Le Sacre de l'écrivain* (José Corti, 1973), p. 39.

A Taste for Freedom

When George Sand left her husband and found herself obliged to work, she chose not to take in sewing, which would have earned her ten *sous* a day at most, or hand-paint ornaments, for which she had considerable talent, but decided instead to write a novel. She gave it to Hyacinthe de Latouche, author of the second *Olivier*, to read but later, judging it to be no good, she never published it. Latouche encouraged her to persevere while warning her that she could never make more than fifteen hundred francs a year from writing. Fifteen hundred francs would be quite enough, she declared, and sat down to write *Indiana*.[13] As we have seen, Laure d'Abrantès published her memoirs to pay her debts. Marie d'Agoult, too, earned her freedom with her pen. Sophie's daughter, Delphine, who married Emile de Girardin, founder of *La Presse*, changed very satisfactorily from Muse to journalist.

Now people could be writers just as they were soldiers, magistrates, clerics or financiers.[14] Custine was the first to realise that everyone, it seemed, wanted to publish something: "Paris is nothing but a great scribblers' workshop. Every city in the world has its own dominant sound . . . the sound of Paris is the sound of a quill scratching on paper."[15] Literary people—the term *intellectual* had

13. Sand, op. cit., II, pp. 150 ff.
14. Bénichou, op. cit., p. 39.
15. *Ethel*, op. cit., I, p. 330.

not yet been coined—were not only more numerous but more independent and more respectable than they had been in the eighteenth century. Under the Restoration, a good publisher who knew how to advertise was more useful than a patron. Literature was seen not only as a breadwinner, but also as a ministry. Novelists, essayists and particularly poets considered that they had a social role to play, whether royalist or liberal, as well as a moral responsibility. Chateaubriand again analysed the situation brilliantly:

> *Different times, different mores; those who preceded us, as inheritors of a long line of peaceful years, could devote themselves to purely academic discussions that were less a proof of talent than of good fortune. But we, the unfortunate survivors of a great shipwreck, we no longer have what is needed to taste so perfect a calm. Our ideas and our minds have taken a different path. Man has replaced the academician in us . . . [This new dignity demands total independence.] Is freedom not the greatest good and man's first requirement. It fires the genius, lifts up the heart and is as necessary to the friend of the muse, as the air he breathes . . . Literature which speaks a universal language, languishes and dies in chains.*[16]

A writer's intellectual freedom is inseparable from his financial freedom. When Custine started writing, the literary world was divided

16. Bénichou, op. cit., p. 155. [Chateaubriand, *O.C.* (Garnier), vol. VI, p. 510.]

more by savage competition than by quarrels between royalists and liberals. It wasn't easy to succeed, especially if you were rich, handsome, witty and recalcitrant.

Custine was well aware that he struck quite a discordant note in literary circles; "I am a Huron from Paris," he wrote to Sophie Gay, "what a peculiar kind of animal."[17] In the first place, he had started his career late—at nearly forty. In a favourable review of *Mémoires et Voyages*, "the best work to have appeared in England,"[18] Stendhal wrote, "His great error is to be afraid of the public." His most successful contemporaries had published their first works at a much younger age. Hugo, ten years younger, had been well known since *Les Odes* appeared in 1820 when he was twenty-eight; Vigny was twenty-five when *Moise* and *Eloa* came out. George Sand was twenty-eight when she wrote *Indiana*. Lamartine, born the same year as Custine, in 1790, was about to be thirty when he had a tremendous success with his *Méditations*. Balzac, too, launched himself as a very young man. Although Stendhal came late to novel writing, he had already gained a certain prestige from some essays published before he was thirty. It was also peculiar to Custine that he played no part in the great literary quarrel of his time between

17. Letter to Sophie Gay, *Bulletin du bibliophile*, op. cit., p. 478.

18. Stendhal, *Correspondance* (Gallimard, Bibliothèque de la Pléiade, 1967), II, p. 171.

Romanticism and Classicism. When he started on his profession in 1830, like it or not Romanticism had won the day.

Marked as he was by tragedy, violence, sublime moments, family ruin, crumbling châteaux and sensitivity to the natural world, Astolphe was the absolute embodiment of Romanticism. Often prey to the feeling of soaring beyond human limitation whence came his inspiration, he wrote to La Grange: "I felt inexplicable stirrings within me, I communicated with a better being, torrents of happiness gushed from my heart; I thus created an ease which was hitherto refused me by everyone, and this power increased my strength, sustained my illusions and caused me to live a fantasy life instead of applying myself to practical duties."[19] Yet this man detested the Romantics. It was an absolute contradiction which he finally admitted when he announced: "I love Romantic poetry, but I hate . . . Romantic men, their intrigue, their exclusivity, their pride, their ill-founded claims to genius, their innovations which are no more than impudent imitation, all that causes me to be disgusted by their circle; this, however, does not prevent our classics from tiring me at the same time."[20]

Custine criticizes Vigny's style with his usual intellectual precision as "not meticulous enough for its lack of fundamental originality. His negligence makes it seem laboured." Walter Scott was "the

19. *Lettres à La Grange*, op. cit., p. 39.
20. *Lettres à Varnhagen*, op. cit., p. 355.

great master of all the bad novelists and small-time historians of the day." "M. de Sainte-Beuve's *pensées* seem to me like given rhymes filled in with set subjects . . . I find these clippings from *René* tedious. M. Lamartine [whom he did, however, credit with the qualities of a colourist] is swamped by the ideas of others."[21] He continues his analysis of Lamartine, "Nothing involuntary, nothing unexpected, never the reverse side of any object or of any argument, never the pleasant side of anything, as if life were not made up of every contradiction! My God, how he always does and feels the right thing! [. . .] No, it is impossible to go so far as to find this *poetico-religiosity*—I will not say amusing, I will not say instructive—but readable."[22] Musset is treated no better: "He is quite content to satisfy himself instead of his public. This self-satisfaction turns doubt into success, such an advantage fully compensates for modesty." Hugo, "this seditious man of letters whose bizarrerie is an acquired varnish,"[23] is the one who annoys him most. "Our great thinkers are set on the path of folly. This evening Victor Hugo offers us a trilogy which surpasses anything before, during or since Homer."[24] In a letter to Sophie Gay, he explains his aesthetics in more measured tones. "I like imprecision in feelings but I want exactitude

21. Letter to Sophie Gay, in Luppé, op. cit., pp. 134–135.
22. Custine to Sophie Gay, quoted by Tarn in *L'Espagne*, op. cit., p. iii.
23. Letter to Sophie Gay, in Luppé, op. cit., p. 137.
24. *Lettres à Varnhagen*, op. cit., p. 445.

of expression ... Whatever one describes, the outline should be drawn with precision. Our little gentlemen fear aridity and imagine they do themselves favours by making their style ambiguous. Writing must be neither dry nor unclear; in fact to please me, it must be neither Hugo nor Sainte-Beuve."[25]

When Custine complained to Sophie Gay and later to Varnhagen of his "intellectual loneliness," it wasn't just talk. He was telling the truth. That didn't prevent him from paying court to Hugo whose support was essential for anyone in Paris wishing to make a career of writing, most especially in the theatre. "I feel at home in my country only when I speak to men like you," he wrote to him in March 1830. Victor Hugo—whom he had once described as an ignorant madman, arrogant and antinational![26] The scandal surrounding *Hernani* had been a very lucrative affair for Hugo, resulting in his having enormous influence in literary circles. Custine, who, by defining himself as a "sauvage de salon" liked to feel that he resembled his mother, proved that he was also the spiritual heir to his grandmother and the chevalier de Boufflers for whom smiles and obeisance were a part of life.

Custine also had the disadvantage, for anyone wishing to be accepted as a serious writer, of being rich. If he had earned his money

25. Luppé, op. cit., p. 140.
26. Ibid., p. 139.

from writing it would have been all right, but to have inherited the title of marquis *and* several hundred thousand francs and to claim to be totally part of literary society was improper. He had made matters worse by announcing that a writer should be less concerned with money than with the diffusion of ideas. "Riches can do so well without honour, that honour, it must be hoped, will eventually be able to do without riches; it is thus that she will gain all her influence: this is what I thank Rousseau for having made me understand."[27] In the preface to *La Femme supérieure*, Balzac replied by congratulating him publicly for ignoring the fate of so many men of letters reduced to living from "the painful produce of their writing case." Stendhal, who had praised *Mémoires et Voyages* so highly, couldn't resist telling the London lawyer Sutton Sharpe that Custine had an income of 60,000 francs before he even mentioned his sexual proclivities. The marquis was never allowed to forget his advantages: "At the time in which I speak, a marquis may decide to become an author and M. de Custine, the writer, is a marquis. Imagine the weight this carries when the title is accompanied by an income of 90,000 francs."[28]

And Custine was hardly discreet. The considerable renovations in the rue de La Rochefoucauld set tongues wagging, besides which he was always only too ready to personally finance his literary under-

27. *L'Espagne*, op. cit., p. 223.
28. Mary-Lafon, quoted by Tarn, op. cit., p. 200.

takings. His poem, *La Cenci*, was greeted with little enthusiasm, unlike *Mémoires et Voyages* which, as he wrote modestly to Rahel, had
"more success than he had hoped."[29] On extremely vague advice
from Stendhal—who skillfully disregarded Custine's efforts because he intended to use the subject himself—Custine decided to
turn the poem into a play. When it was accepted by the Comédie-
Française, *Le Courrier des Théatres* summarised the play in one sentence: "On 25 December we are going to see the young lady who,
having been abused by him, kills her father. That is one way of passing an hour or two."

The Comédie-Française began rehearsals of the play, having insisted that Custine advance the necessary money and pay for the
sets. The theatre then removed the play from its bills on the pretext
of immorality. Custine was obliged to negotiate the repayment of all
his expenses and the right to keep the sets. In order not to quarrel
with the director of the theatre, he did not sue for damages. Victor
Hugo was kept informed of all the details. In 1831, his *Marion de
Lorme* had been performed at the Porte Saint-Martin and *Lucrèce
Borgia* was to follow, so his influence over Harel, who managed the
theatre, was considerable; Custine, who was determined to see *Beatrice Cenci* performed—if not at the Comédie-Française, on another stage—pestered Hugo obsequiously.

Harel, one of the sharpest men of the day, had had an eventful ca-

29. *Lettres à Varnhagen*, op. cit., p. 344.

reer as secretary to Cambacéres, as former sub-prefect of the Aisne and as prefect of the Landes. In 1815 he was exiled. He seemed to be in no hurry to produce the play and, in any case, Hugo's efforts to advance Custine's interests may well have been less than enthusiastic. So Custine languished in extremely unpleasant Paris. Europe had been swept by a cholera epidemic from the Orient which passed through London in February 1832 and reached Paris in the spring. At the height of the scourge, more than a thousand people died a day. In the working-class suburbs, where cholera was thought to be an invention of the bourgeoisie to rid them of the people, there were incidents of violence. The city was becoming very dangerous. Why hang around in such a desolate place? Custine and Sainte-Barbe took refuge in Italy and recovered their strength by taking the waters at Ems; they returned to the capital in the autumn once order was re-established.

Although he hadn't given up hope of *Beatrice Cenci* being performed, if only "among the ruins of Paris,"[30] Custine concentrated above all on furnishing his new houses; they included a huge property at Saint-Gratien on the lac d'Enghien with an old château that he quickly sold and a modern house, set in a superb park, to which he made some additions. He also had his house on the rue de La Rochefoucauld. "From the difficulties I experience, I realise that to

---

30. Letter to Sophie Gay, in Luppé, op. cit., p. 151.

have the money to pay for what one wants means nothing. More patience and intelligence are needed to use it than to keep or acquire it."[31] He had no shortage of friends who, under those circumstances, would have been happy to compete with him in intelligence and patience.

On the professional plain, he showed real perseverance. After the extraordinary success of Alexander Dumas's *La Tour de Nesle* and then of Hugo's *Lucrèce Borgia*, Harel still seemed reluctant to put on the play. Custine wouldn't allow himself to be discouraged; the delicate, shy Astolphe relaunched his assault on Victor Hugo. He began with a flattering article about his most recent play and went on to a direct appeal, reminding him of "his promise to protect *Beatrice Cenci* against I know not what that causes it to be rejected in this theatre." Meanwhile he set Sainte-Barbe to work on Adèle Hugo, who was always on the look-out for help in distributing invitations to advertise her charity sales. He then turned to casting and managed to persuade the first-class actress Marie Dorval that the part of Beatrice was made for her. That was his master stroke.

Marie Dorval, Mlle Mars's only rival, was at the height of her career as an actress and a woman (Vigny wrote of her with passion). According to Marceline Desbordes-Valmore, "Her intelligence is vast, I know nothing more powerful than her tempestuous ravings.

31. Ibid., p. 155.

229

She has a caressing boldness of imagination . . . which makes one tremble before such a genius of despair."[32] Frédérick Lemaître, who had recently had a great success in *Lucrèce Borgia*, was to play opposite her. Delighted by so much brilliance, Harel finally set a date for the performance but, realising that success in the theatre had to be worked at, Custine continued to solicit Hugo. A few days before the opening, he asked Hugo to send him "the great personage of theatrical success," by which he meant the leader of the claque—or hired audience—as well as his theatrical agent, to be a liaison between the writer and the journalists. He discovered what kind of a mob writers, journalists and actors depended upon and decided to deal with the key figure. The ticket seller was a man who resembled Braulard in *Les Illusions perdues*, and "appeared wrapped in a grey felt frock coat, wearing long trousers and red slippers, just like a doctor or a lawyer . . . with an ordinary face, a pair of very sharp grey eyes, the hands of a clapper and a complexion over which orgies had passed, like rain on a roof . . ."[33] Next he relied on Hugo's friendship "for the battle in the audience and in the papers where [Hugo had] some influence." By way of conclusion, "I would," he wrote, "like you to be able to do everything everywhere."[34]

There remained the financial arrangements with Harel which we

32. Ambrière, *Le Siècle des Valmore*, op. cit., I, p. 490.

33. Balzac, *Illusions perdues* (Pléiade), p. 799.

34. Letter from Custine to Victor Hugo, 4 May 1833, Victor Hugo Museum.

know about from Lemaître's *Souvenirs*. Although they were using the old Comédie-Française sets, Harel, "having inquired about the author's financial position," demanded 15,000 francs for the costumes and sets and insisted that Custine pay for the first three performances. When Custine left, Lemaître, who witnessed the scene, is supposed to have said to the "little, stinking, unworthy creature"[35] that was Harel, "Are you letting him go? He still has his watch." Custine paid up. He organised an elegant, friendly audience for the first night. The following two performances went well; Marie Dorval, unanimously praised for her interpretation, and Frédérick Lemaître were both applauded but the reviews were bad.

Was such harshness justified? Was the play really only a sequence of "incoherent and disconnected scenes"? Had Custine produced "an obscure melodrama with incomprehensible, pointless, badly described characters"?[36] Or had Victor Hugo's agent kept too much money for himself instead of distributing it wisely? Hyppolyte Auger recounts in his *Mémoires* how he took Loève-Veimars, the critic of *Le Temps*, to task over his venemous article, to be told frankly in reply, "My dear fellow . . . M. de Custine has the reputation of getting away with any oddity at a price . . . If I had spoken well [of the

35. Barbey d'Aurevilly, *Correspondance générale*, 9 vols. (Les Belles-Lettres, 1983), to Trébutien, 23 August 1833, I, p. 22.
36. Extracts from reviews in *Le National* of 29 May and *Le Constitutionnel* of 26 May, in Tarn, op. cit., pp. 199 and 198.

play], it would have been thought, and perhaps said, that I had received my thousand-franc note. Now since I have not had that advantage, I do not want the odium. That is why I treated the thing badly . . ."[37] *La Revue des Deux Mondes* remarked cruelly, "M. de Custine is one of those rare poets who thinks that the honour of being publicly performed cannot be bought too highly."[38]

The final insult came from Harel, who closed the play after the first three performances for which Custine had paid, even though there was no lack of audience to justify this brutal decision. Such suppression, the *Revue de Paris* pointed out, "was not the way of the theatre, and showed not only a lack of respect for the author but also for the public who grant the management the right to drop a play only when they drop it themselves and they did not seem disposed to give proof of their disdain for Beatrice Cenci so soon." It was more or less common practice to hire the claque, pay the journalists and arrange for a friendly audience but not stifle public opinion. Custine was well able to assess the injustice done him, since he had few illusions as to the loyalty of his friends and acquaintances. Invited audiences resulted in authors being "judged only by rivals; actors jealous of those who were performing, writers whose muse is envy and by journalists with ready-made opinions."[39] He wrote this

---

37. Hyppolyte Auger, *Mémoires* (Paris, 1891), pp. 481–482.
38. *Revue des Deux Mondes*, 30 May 1833.
39. *Lettres à Varnhagen*, op. cit., p. 383.

many years later to his friend Varnhagen; at the time, he suffered the humiliation with dignity, "not wishing to brave the ridicule of pleading for his own work," nor wanting to appear difficult, bitter and vain. Not one of his colleagues defended him.

He gave up the theatre permanently, retired to Saint-Gratien and began writing a novel in which the main character, faced with ruin, his friends' betrayal and the end of a love affair, finally kills himself. The character wasn't guiltless since all his misfortunes sprang from one foolish and wicked act knowingly committed. Custine sounded the depths of gloom, melancholy and guilt but he didn't write day and night.

The aesthete finally moved into his house. The rue de La Rochefoucauld was to be decorated and furnished in grandiose style. Balzac's description of the comte Laginski's house in *La Fausse Maîtresse* was based on Custine's, crammed with works of art, the ceilings painted in the style of the Middle Ages or of Venetian palaces, "a staircase, white as a woman's arm, . . . a display of merchandise to distract the eye as if boredom threatened the most excitable and the most excited society in the world."[40] There was a conservatory, a long gallery in the Italian style, a Renaissance drawing-room, an eighteenth-century *salon*. Modern art was represented by the Romantic painter and great friend of Hugo, Victor Boulanger. Théo-

---

40. Balzac, *La Fausse Maîtresse* (Ollendorff, 1900), p. 350.

phile Gautier, his pretty mistress and a few of their friends posed for the *Triomphe de Pétrarque*, commissioned for 1,200 francs but of which, according to Balzac, "the infamous miser" only paid 1000 écus. The picture was exhibited in the Salon before being delivered to the rue de La Rochefoucauld.

It was no easy task to hang a painting eight metres long in the gallery so the occasion was marked by an elegant preview at which the newly discovered young poet, Théophile Gautier, was invited to read some lines he had written especially.

Receptions, concerts and readings at the rue de La Rochefoucauld competed with the splendour of Saint-Gratien. In preference to the seventeenth-century manor, Custine had chosen to occupy the modern villa built under the Empire for the comte de Luçay. Standing on the Saint-Gratien hills, the house, "a Florentine villa, with a flat roof, furnished in the English style," overlooked the valley and the lac d'Enghien. Enghien, a spa town, whose sulphurous waters were supposedly good for rheumatism, was very fashionable with its hotels, restaurants and open-air cafés.

Custine had no difficulty attracting the most brilliant company. In a typically suburban way, he was always careful to point out how close to the place de la Concorde Saint-Gratien was—only an hour and a half away; less time, he explained to Hugo, than it took him to go from the rue de La Rochefoucauld to the place Royale. Socialites and artists gathered around him and Delphine de Girardin, in an article in *La Presse*, described marvellous meals in the stimulating company of Musset, Balzac, Meyerbeer, Victor Hugo, Lamartine, Berlioz, Stendhal, Heine, Koreff, Mme Vigée-Lebrun, George Sand and Chopin, "dear Chopinet," whose genius Custine immediately recognised.

> *Look: here is a lamp found at Nola, a goblet brought back from Rome, a table made in Florence; this statue comes from Egypt, these vases from China, these carpets from Constantinople; this comes from Athens, that from Syracuse, this from Vienna, that from Madrid and all these charming, practical things have been sent from London! Enter the beautiful salon through the delightful oratory, so reminiscent of the Alhambra, but speak quietly, walk silently, for your arrival will interrupt an aria from* Norma *or from* Orpheus, *an inspiration of Berlioz or Chopin, a sublime ode, an ingenious fable, a profound remark, a piquant tale, in fact, a sound which may be precious for its wit or its harmony but which you will regret having missed.*[41]

There were few writers who could take such material and spiritual luxury with equanimity and few disinterested friends who could resist the rumours of constant scandal surrounding Custine. He called it "the immense workshop of gossip which, after half a century of confusion, had replaced French society." Custine had little respect for the morals of artists in general: "In a nation of writers . . . con-

---

41. *La Presse*, 6 July 1837, "Courrier de Paris," vicomte de Launay (Delphine de Girardin's pen name).

cerned only with looking for subjects . . . envy alone would be real, sincere and vital, the ineradicable leprosy that eats into the souls of artists."[42] That suited everyone since Custine was still held at arm's length by the professional circles which he so badly wanted to belong to, not only by virtue of his wealth and lack of commitment but because of his peculiar sexuality which made him a target, if not a victim.

In fact, the scandal of 1824 had in no way caused him to be ostracised. He was received everywhere and he invited whom he pleased. He still saw his former fiancée, Clara de Rauzun, the duchesse de Duras's daughter. His worldly success was such that it provoked spiteful comment, from Heine for one: "the marquis was only half a man of letters, and thus felt obliged to fill his salon wholly so as not to appear hollow himself." But it was his sexual orientation that seemed to justify every barbed attack. As soon as his back was turned his morals came under fire. Stendhal didn't like *La Cenci* and mocked *"Mme la marquise de Custine"*[43] for her taste. Marie Dorval, who was flattered by Custine taking her to see the great English actress Harriet Smithson, opening in *Lucrèce Borgia*, silenced Vig-

42. *L'Espagne*, op. cit., p. 121.
43. Stendhal wrote in the margin of a copy of *Promenades dans Rome*, "the difference between what seems good taste '*to me*' [in English] and what seems like good taste to Mme la Marquise de Custine."

ny's jealousy by assuring him that she attached no importance to a "gentleman in petticoats."

Antoine Fontaney was a penniless young journalist and a bitter, ambitious man who described himself as a *literary labourer*. He never missed a lunch or dinner at Custine's but he repeated, without the slightest embarrassment, a conversation with Hugo about the marquis's "infamous acquaintanceships." Sainte-Beuve, never too anxious about morality where his friends' wives were concerned, wrote, "[M. de Custine] has such a bad reputation here and one which is so notoriously deserved with regard to his behaviour . . . that he is read and quite appreciated but no one respects him. He almost had to go into hiding. His pretty house in the Montmorency valley was pure Sodom and Gomorrah."[44] Mérimée wrote to the comtesse de Montijo about the latest scandal: [Custine] "has had trouble with people from the village outside Paris because of certain liberties he took with them. They wanted to knock him out and he had to flee as quickly as possible."[45] At least neither Sainte-Beuve nor Mérimée was a friend but there were others like the comtesse Merlin, the pretty Cuban widow of a French general. She was extremely musical and, being regarded by Custine as one of his close

44. Sainte-Beuve, *Correspondance* (Paris, Stock, 1935–1966), V, p. 623.

45. Mérimée, *Correspondance générale* (Le Divan, 1943), letter to the comtesse de Montijo, 22 May 1841, III, p. 55.

friends, was at all his receptions. In her own salon, just as Custine left after talking so lightheartedly and wittily "that an hour seemed like a minute," she wiped her hand and exclaimed, " 'The poor marquis, he is charming, but I cannot touch him. His hand disgusts me.' 'Why?' 'It's limp and sticky.' 'He's a wonderful raconteur. His words are like fireworks.' 'Printed on water,' she went on, 'he has such a sad core! Such black depths!' "[46] Not content with rejecting and betraying her friend, she felt obliged to depict him as practically accursed.

Another of Custine's "friends" and extremely close to the beautiful comtesse was Philarète Chasles, a successful journalist and professor at the Collège de France. His description of the marquis exemplifies the popular conception of Custine as a figure of tragedy and ridicule who, despite a brilliant life, inspired pity in his contemporaries; they felt that everything he did "was influenced by a fatality that diluted all his happiness."[47]

Philarète Chasles saw him as a "real gentleman, his malice swathed in silk and cotton, [with] the barely virile refinements of the world, a strange timidity and a kind of sentiment of personal abasement and mortification, hardly in keeping with his sharp wit and philosophical insight or with the bold remarks that burst from a mixture of painful modesty and melancholy, of mysticism and base

46. Philarète Chasles, *Mémoires*, 2 vols. (Paris, 1876–1877), I, pp. 308 ff.
47. V. Ancelot, *Les Salons de Paris, foyers éteints* (Paris, Tardieu, 1858).

sensuality . . . an extraordinary, unhappy being, problem and proto-type, phenomenon and paradox, driven by, to my mind, the most odious vice, dominated and oppressed by it, swallowed up; wading in it, before the whole of French society, like Fiévée and his friend Leclercq . . ."[48] He goes on to reach some alarming conclusions:

> *My herbarium of cryptograms, my collection of social phenom-ena, my repertoire of monstrous nosology, wouldn't have been complete had my great museum of originals lacked this fervent Catholic, this sensuous mystic, this subtle, poetic and elevated talent—lost in vice; this austere conscience bending under the burden of its guilt; or the sickness and misery of a social pa-riah weeping before a society which was perhaps worth less than he . . .*[49]

This description takes so little account of the real, active Custine, rejoicing in total freedom, with "the most voluptuous literary tem-perament and *the most sensitive mind* of his time,"[50] that it seems as if such witnesses, blinded by their own conception of vice, may have ascribed an exaggerated sense of guilt to their subject. He disturbed people because he did not allow himself to be influenced by their opinions but led his life exactly as he pleased. To pity him was a way of underlining the envy he provoked. Like the comtesse Merlin,

48. Chasles, op. cit.
49. Ibid.
50. Barbey d'Aurevilly, op. cit., letter to Trébutien, 12 March 1856, V, p. 71.

Chasles stayed at length at Saint-Gratien, apparently extremely flattered to be the guest of a "social pariah." Not surprisingly, the opinions Baudelaire held were quite different. Custine, he wrote, "was a genius whose dandyism went so far as to encompass the ideal of negligence. Such gentlemanly good faith, such romantic ardour, such true irony, so absolute and nonchalant a personality are inaccessible to the understanding of the common herd, and this precious writer had all the ill-fortune his talent deserved stacked against him."[51]

51. Charles Baudelaire, *Oeuvres complètes*, 3 vols. (Club Français du Livre, 1966), in *Madame Bovary* and *La Tentation de saint Antoine*, III, p. 523.

10

Custine's Way

Objectively seen in the years around 1835, Custine hardly appeared to be devastated, "bearing public scorn with his head hanging down." He wasn't the first grandee to have taken to debauchery;[1] and, after all, he was convinced that "the century was [ruled] by indifference to everything, except money."[2] He had suffered from practising "the infernal art of deception without lying, or at least of using truth in the service of deception" and had admitted that "the false position in which he was trapped by [his] weakness [had made him] the most impenetrable, dou-

1. *Le Monde comme il est*, op. cit., II, p. 70.
2. Ibid., I, pp. 83–84.

ble man."[3] At last he seemed able to breathe, to live and to do as he pleased. "I am always disposed to align myself with good-humoured people," he insisted, "with youth and with springtime."[4] Varnhagen, who saw Custine whenever he came to Berlin, noted that he was "in good health, content, reasonable: an important personage."[5]

A few years earlier he had needed Victor Hugo to put him in touch with the odious Harel but in 1835 when Hugo, as a candidate for the Académie Française, wished to pay the obligatory visit to Chateaubriand, whom he didn't know, it was Custine who arranged the meeting. Victor Hugo was not elected until 1841 but Chateaubriand gave him his vote. "If the votes were weighed, Hugo would be elected; unfortunately they are counted,"[6] was Delphine de Girardin's conclusion. Barbey d'Aurevilly, who was an unusual man, underlined Custine's prestige. He was an intransigent Catholic, a provocative and formidable polemicist with a great admiration for Custine, of whose considerable influence he was aware. (In discreet homage, he named a character in *La Bague d'Hannibal* Aloys.) Whenever he chose to help a writer, an artist or a musician, Custine could obtain

3. *Aloys*, op. cit., p. 83.

4. *L'Espagne*, op. cit., p. 194, and *Lettres à Mme de Courbonne*, op. cit., p. 66.

5. Quoted by Michel Cadot, *La Russie dans la vie intellectuelle française (1839–1856)* (Fayard, 1967), p. 180.

6. André Maurois, *Olympio ou la Vie de Victor Hugo* (Hachette, 1954), p. 262.

the most flattering and exalted publicity and force "the attention of whatever remains of intelligence in these miserable times."

Custine always came generously and willingly to the help of his acquaintances, with the tact of a man who didn't need to buy his friends' goodwill. He took upon it himself to help Chopin, "the only person whom I allow to come to Saint-Gratien whenever he wants and without warning me,"[7] and who he felt was too shy to complain. "You are ill; and you could become more seriously ill. You have reached the limits of spiritual anguish and physical pain; when the heart's anguish manifests itself in sickness, then we are lost; this is what I want to avoid for you . . . My friendship for you is such that you can allow me to go to the bottom of things. Is it lack of money that keeps you in Paris? If it is, I can lend you some. You will return it later, but first you will rest for three months."[8] He didn't dare advise him to leave George Sand, "the ghoul," whom he detested and whom he held responsible for Chopin's deterioration.

Théophile Gautier touched him endlessly for money and, unlike Sophie Gay and her daughters, rarely paid his debts. He helped them so kindly whenever they needed it that Delphine, requiring yet an-

7. Luppé, op. cit., p. 185.

8. Pierre de Lacretelle, *Souvenirs et portraits* (Monaco, Editions du Rocher, 1956), p. 33.

other loan, wrote to him, "I ask your forgiveness for bothering you again but you seemed so cross when I settled matters two weeks early that I want to console you."[9] His generosity was not limited to money. An example was wicked little Fontaney who had suffered nothing but misfortune; he eloped to England with Gabrielle Dorval, Marie's daughter, and an "ideal beauty," but they had to return soon. Both lovers were in pitiful condition, suffering from the last stages of tuberculosis, penniless and unable to support themselves or to afford medical attention. Custine welcomed them at Saint-Gratien, sent them his doctor and was the only person to take care of them. Gabrielle died first on 15 April 1837; Fontaney stayed on with Custine and died two months later. Most importantly, Custine established himself as a writer and a prolific one at that; his writing was published regularly from 1835 onwards. He was said to work slowly but called himself lazy, yet *Le Monde comme il est* came out in 1835, *L'Espagne sous Ferdinand VII* in 1838 and a third novel, *Ethel*, in 1839.

Aloys is the only one of Custine's novels to have stood the test of time. His last, *Romuald*, published in 1848, is an unusual, disconcerting book which retraces a voyage of initiation and ends in a conversion. *Le Monde comme il est* and *Ethel* are more conventional and both deal with a love affair set against a background of

9. Quoted by Henri Malo, op. cit., p. 149.

contemporary society.[10] The interest of the novels lies in Custine's personal reflections but the weakness is, that for all his imagination, Custine lacks the novelist's fantasy. When not writing about himself, he fails to hold the reader's attention. He doesn't have Balzac's ability to see himself as the comtesse de Mortsauf, Tolstoy's to see himself as Natasha or Proust's to be Mme Verdurin. He hasn't the skill to unify different elements or to make the reader forget the improbability of his romantic plot. Neither hero is exactly like Custine, although they both offend society and are ostracised. In both cases society's rejection results from a deliberate action of the hero's. In *Le Monde comme il est*, Edmond d'Offlize boasts in writing that he can seduce a very rich heiress whose face is so ugly that it would be acceptable "only in the land of frogs." His troubles begin when the young woman hears about the letter. Never mind the real love which she awakens in his heart. Never mind Edmond's finer qualities. Never mind the feelings he arouses in her. How could she ever trust him? And when she does, it is too late.

In *Ethel*, the comte Gaston de Montlhéry, the perfect Parisian dandy, falls madly in love with his wife's sister, a scandal that refuses to die with the legitimate spouse. The book can only be taken se-

---

10. J.-F. Tarn has analysed Custine's novels so thoroughly in *Le Marquis de Custine* that I feel it would be pointless to develop the theme.

riously when Custine appears in the guise of his hero but, unlike Aloys, neither Edmond nor Gaston is at all moving. Custine is much more successful in a short analytical novel where all the characters relate to the narrator.

All the same, *Le Monde comme il est* was a commercial success; the critics were harsh but the book was talked about and read. The contemporary public was delighted by this often brilliant *roman à clef* in which Custine took pleasure in nailing a few enemies. "I have been hunting this kind of beast which is so easy to find and so difficult to kill," he pointed out to Balzac. Several society women could have recognised themselves in his portrait of Mme de Villemagne, "indulgent, gentle and yet not at all insipid thanks to the depths of egoism and savagery which she nurtures with careful love in the only corner of her heart reserved for the truth." And which pretentious young woman was the inspiration for Lady McNally, who, disappointed that her talents as a Latinist were insufficiently admired, took it into her head to learn Chinese?

The book is surprising in its extreme misanthropy and the virulence of its attacks on the conservative Catholic community. Balzac very privately congratulated Custine on it and did not try to prevent his friend and protégé, Jules Sandeau, from publishing a cruel review. "It is not enough, as M. de Custine has done . . . to stand at the window and spit on passers-by . . . M. de Custine is a great nobleman, an artistic man, a man of grace and wit but one without a secretary."[11] The tone of the reviews seemed to count for little; the controversy provoked by the novel was essential.

The publisher, Renduel, was happy with the sales and Custine began to be paid reasonable advances. In 1837, he got 5,000 francs from Ladvocat, 2,000 in cash and 3,000 for publicity with a guaranteed print run of 1,500. Two years later, he sold *Ethel* for 2,000 francs to the same publisher who promised to print 1,000 copies and to reprint *Le Monde*. These figures were comparable to what his contemporaries were earning. Hugo received 2,000 francs for his *Nouvelles Odes*; Balzac 1,135 francs in 1831 for two volumes of *La Peau de Chagrin*,[12] 3,750 francs for *Scènes de la vie privé*, 5,250 francs for *Romans philosophiques*[13] and 20,000 francs from the *Figaro* for the serial rights to *César Birotteau*. The novel sold less well than the previous one, but meanwhile Custine had begun to make his true mark in literature with the appearance of *L'Espagne sous Ferdinand VII*.

His volume of *Mémoires et Voyages* on Italy and Great Britain was the work of a young man. He had revised it over the years before publishing it but it remained a work whose charm and interest lay in its description of a first impression of the world. *L'Espagne* was, by comparison, a work of maturity both in form—Custine is master

11. *Figaro*, 16 February 1835.

12. André Maurois, *Prométhée ou la Vie de Balzac* (Hachette, 1965), p. 177.

13. Ibid., p. 189.

of the epistolary form—and in content. "A man who spent his time thinking while travelling the world would be unable to depict it; one who only wrote would not be interesting . . . ,"[14] he declared straight away, then held to his ambition to create a new genre, the genre of one man's journey. *L'Espagne* is a travel book in which stables are disguised as inns and where corridas, lusty servants, jealous husbands, bandits, fêtes, landscapes and cathedrals abound; but it is also a political reflection on the poor, Catholic, African country that was Spain in 1831. The book served as a vehicle for Custine to develop his own views and personal concerns.

Whereas in *Mémoires et Voyages* the letters addressed to anonymous or imaginary correspondents were more or less reminiscent of a diary, in *L'Espagne* Custine refined and confirmed his technique. He was helped precisely by a problem peculiar to the travelogue: variety. So, "a flexible style alone [can] help a writer to make the unravelled threads of truth bearable . . . Formerly the writer's art consisted in coordinating everything, in tempering everything so as to substitute the beautiful harmony of a book for the exaggerations of an enthusiastic imagination. This time-worn method bores . . . [but then] how can disorder be eschewed? How, when hurrying from surprise to surprise, will you avoid the inconvenience of changing your opinion at every step and dragging your readers along with

14. *L'Espagne*, op. cit., p. 16.

your own uncertainty?"[15] Had he worked for a newspaper, like Théophile Gautier, he would have resorted to the serial form to solve this problem. The use of letters provided an elegant solution, allowing him to vary his tone, to return to a point of interest, to ignore whatever bored him and to indulge in personal digression. Custine takes advantage of this and devotes whole pages to Tocqueville on the occasion of the publication of *De la démocratie en Amérique*; he quotes from ballads or from a biography by Murillo without appearing to interrupt the text. In short, he achieves "variety without confusion." Giving himself wholeheartedly to the task, he writes about what interests him with a pretended ease.

In this book no imaginary friend would do; the letters are addressed to real friends like Sophie Gay, a young Englishwoman called Miss Bowles (who was very close to Sainte-Barbe), Chateaubriand or Mme Récamier and occasionally to future friends, since he did not know Hugo, Lamartine, or Heinrich Heine in 1831 when he went to Spain. That is unimportant. What matters for the reader are the intimacy and the freedom the epistolary form gives Custine; he deftly mixes comic scenes with political thoughts growing out of his observations in a country ruled by traditions very different from his own.

He proved himself capable of humour for the first time, whether

15. Ibid., p. 12.

describing with a light touch the appearance of some yoked oxen, "majestically dressed and coiffed in the style of Louis XIV," covered with white cloths, with sheepskins like wigs on their heads,[16] or depicting a woman grenadier beside him in a stagecoach. A "naturally large and protuberant mouth held in a heart shape thanks to those French, bourgeois grimaces that one remembers but can't describe, her sixty-year-old body, square and nervous, too marked for a handsome corporal."[17] Another woman consists of only "a few bones strung together with nerves" and he entertainingly describes a Spanish woman whose ambition, like every Andalusian woman's, "is to wear shoes so small that no foot could fit in them, even her own . . ." and who, on visiting the English consul, asks permission to remove these instruments of torture. When the time comes for her to leave, she is unable to force her feet back into their prison. The pretty young woman is asked if she would like to borrow some shoes from the young lady of the house, but on seeing the "Northern shoe," she exclaims that for nothing on earth would she cross town with "such a machine on her foot." After renewed efforts—cold water, ice and soap—the "intrepid coquette" was able to return home. He tells too of a visit to a tobacco factory, perhaps Carmen's, in Seville where he was "surprised by the silence reigning in the

16. Ibid., p. 25.
17. Ibid., p. 34.

men's workshops whilst [being stunned] by the tornado of words in the women's. Two thousand Andalusian tongues were clacking involuntarily, as though a spring had been sprung. It was not the least curious piece of machinery in the factory."[18]

He also makes fun of himself. On arriving at his first Spanish inn, he refuses a damp room smelling of a musty cellar and sets up a camp bed in the kitchen; there he savours the frothiest, airiest hot chocolate, better than any Parisian waiter could prepare. The eve of his departure from Seville he gave a superb reception for everyone who had helped make his stay so agreeable, "the great and the humble, gentlemen and labourers." His hotel was transformed into an orange grove. He had cartloads of branches brought in from the country and against this background of greenery he arranged oranges, lemons, citrons and flowers. The party, with songs and dancing and sequidillas and supper washed down with sherry, was so successful that the guests refused to leave, dancing enthusiastically on the patio. Soldiers had to be called in for order to be re-established, albeit temporarily—only a few hours later all his new friends reappeared, some to thank Custine and others, dazzled by his generosity, to beg help for a mother, a small child or even for themselves, "in the name of undying friendship."[19] Custine felt as though he were in Syria,

18. Ibid., p. 292.
19. Ibid., p. 353.

surrounded by a troop of Bedouin. That wasn't the end of it and what followed gives today's reader an insight into another aspect of nineteenth-century travel.

Custine delighted in extravagant spending. On the morning of his departure everything he had ordered from all over town was delivered, "costumes, engravings, comestibles, wine, ham, antiques, pictures."[20] Packers were filling cases and nailing them up, surrounded by the débris from the night before. Crowds of creditors, followed by what Custine referred to as their understudies—parasites whose only job was to double the bills—turned up and Custine realised that he didn't have enough ready money to settle all the accounts. He hurried to see the banker with whom he had dealt on his arrival and, pouring with sweat, agitated by the heat and fearful of missing his boat, he cut through the formalities and asked for the money outright. But he was unable to produce his bill of exchange. He didn't know where he had put it. The banker declared that without a credit order he could have no money. Poor Custine ran back to the inn, ordered his valet to unpack his writing case from the trunk and rifled madly through his papers. He found nothing. In a final effort, he returned, breathless with rage and exhaustion, to his "pitiless Croesus," only to be received with the same rigour and the same refusals.

20. Ibid., p. 354.

Custine's Way

[He] led me to the door, according to the inviolable etiquette of the country. As he took leave of me, he noticed quite a big piece of paper, folded in four and held tightly between the thumb and first two fingers of my left hand. "Are you sure, Monsieur," he said to me, "that you have looked for your bill of exchange everywhere you could hope to find it?" "Huh! What is it to you, Monsieur? I have done nothing but look." "Please allow me," said the solemn Spaniard as he undid my fingers, clenched in anger, "I think I recognise it: here it is . . ." I had been holding it like that in my hand all morning! There was more sense in my hand than in my head. Since I had first gone out, my hand had never stopped holding the paper, two of my fingers and my thumb clamped onto it during all the fruitless searching which my foolish imagination led me to do elsewhere.[21]

A thousand miles from Paris, Custine was gay, scatter-brained and comical.

Custine also loved art. He devoted a whole letter to Louis Boulanger to a study of Murillo, questioning the relationship between genius and society, between an artist's talent and the beliefs, morality and prejudices of the times in which he lived. As is evident from his astonishment at Arab art, he was not always enthusiastic about what he saw. "The particular characteristic of Arab architecture lies

21. Ibid., pp. 358–359.

in the profusion of what is small . . . it is no longer stone, marble, jasper or wood, it is stuff, a palace of overworked draperies, a temple of figured muslin, a brocade prison; it is in fact the masterpiece of a society in which architects might be chosen from among fashion salesmen: for all its brilliance, all its originality, all its perfection of detail, Arab architecture is the art of an effeminate people. I can only compare the decoration of certain rooms, of certain over-festooned porticos, to those cut-out papers in which our confectioners wrap boxes of sugared almonds."[22] And finally *L'Espagne* gave him the chance to stress his political interests. He was not as interested in Spanish politics as in understanding his own country. (In any case, between the time of his journey in 1831 and the book's publication in 1838, the situation in Spain had been changed by the war between the Carlists, who were loyal to Ferdinand VII's brother, Don Carlos, and the partisans of Ferdinand's daughter, who demanded the abolition of the Salic law so that Isabella could come to the throne.) One way for him to refine his ideas was to test them against a foreign society.

At this time in France, "the craze for equality makes [men] tense to the point of rendering them coarse,"[23] whereas in Spain people everywhere are "exquisitely polite [which] instantly puts you at

22. Ibid., p. 253.
23. Ibid., p. 63.

your ease."[24] These manners, "whose basis is perfect equality,"[25] are partly explained by "Catholicism, [which] with its respect for the great social powers, its submission to force . . . disposes men's minds to true politeness which is only the art of rendering effortlessly to everyone his social due,"[26] and partly by the flaws in Spanish law. The administration was too corrupt for everyone to be assured justice; under such conditions moderation was essential to men who could only count on themselves to obtain justice. "In Normandy," he concluded, "it is not so much fear of the knife as fear of the summoner that keeps men from speaking with passion: they keep quiet. In Caen a man lies to avoid a court case; in Seville he suffers in silence because he calculates the risk he runs in making an enemy . . . The Normans are discreet so as to live in peace; the Spanish are polite so as to remain alive."[27]

The study of mores was invaluable to Custine because "mores everywhere are the law's corrective and its substitute . . . regulated by a people's instinct for preservation, within the state, [they] re-establish the balance which has frequently been upset by the legislature."[28] Here he disagrees with the eighteenth-century philosophes

24. Ibid., p. 262.
25. Ibid., p. 261.
26. Ibid.
27. Ibid., p. 207.
28. Ibid., p. 262.

for whom the law was all-powerful. "If the laws are good, mores are good; if the laws are bad, mores are bad," Diderot declared.[29] The better Custine understood the ways in which the Spanish differed from the French, the better he would understand his compatriots. In order to do this, he had to define his own position. "I, who am neither democrat nor royalist, but who am an aristocrat in the widest, and consequently the most liberal, sense of the word, believe that there is and that there will always be more wisdom and enlightenment in the ideas of a few superior men than in the opinions of the masses, and yet I count myself a Christian."[30] He had expounded on this idea even more forcefully in a letter to Rahel where he defined civilisation as "a country where a large number works with its hands to give a small number the time to work with its head."[31] His mistrust of forced equality is echoed in his opposition to Tocqueville on the role of Christianity in the inevitable evolution of humanity towards equality. For Custine, Christianity was less about man's equality than his spirituality.[32]

The relationship between equality and liberty was one of the problems which obsessed him. He refused to believe that liberty and equality were brothers. He had a horror of equality because, if it was

29. Quoted by Albert Lortholary, *Le Mirage russe en France au XVIIIe siècle* (Editions contemporaines, 1951), p. 100.

30. *L'Espagne*, op. cit., p. 316.

31. *Lettres à Varnhagen*, op. cit., p. 361.

32. *L'Espagne*, op. cit., p. 313.

absolute, it could only result in complete tyranny. A trip to Morocco where "the religious discipline which dominates the entire people, makes of the empire an immense school of Muslim superstition whose high priest is the emperor," caused him to think. "Equality is a form of violence condemned by liberty . . . real, unlimited, absolute equality is an attribute of the wild state . . . Liberty, on the other hand, is a blessing of the perfected social state . . . Real liberty can only arise from the scrupulous exercise of the duties of a social man towards others and towards himself, it is the crowning glory of political work . . . It results from the practise of social duty by the greatest number, and is society's conscience just as free-will is the conscience of the individual."[33]

He weighs the complexity of the relationship between liberty and equality carefully, but makes no claim to have reached a satisfactory conclusion.

Today, where government is concerned, I see problems every-where but find a solution nowhere; I don't know a way of harmonising in any lasting fashion the love of liberty which man brings with him from the depths of the forest with the need for and by society of a created order . . . This double need, for order and for liberty without belief, seems to demand contradictory laws; I know of no modern legislature which has formed a superior law whereby these two contradictory forces might be pre-

33. Ibid., pp. 461–462.

*served without destroying themselves. I know of admirable po-
litical codes, but I do not know of a power to maintain or enforce
them. I can only see that freedom pushed to the ultimate, and it
always has that tendency, is an abuse of the right to choose, and
that such an abuse produces a licence capable of excusing even
despotism. I also see that the principle of monarchy, unless it is
mitigated, leads to a tyranny that justifies revolutions.*[34]

Custine develops and refines these ideas in his letters from Russia,
but the seed was planted as early as 1831.

Although Custine may have grown firmer and more confident and
detached, he still suffered from a "spiritual disquiet"; he was still
torn between his love of tranquility and his passions; he still regretted each time—and it happened often—that he fell for a handsome boy, thus hurting Sainte-Barbe, his slave, also known as the
canon. He was more than conscious of the "inevitable sorrow" he
caused. He even admitted to Sophie Gay that he had left Sainte-
Barbe sick in Naples to go to Sicily with a companion he hardly
knew. "My journey to Sicily was complicated by several things, by
pangs of the heart, by apparent and unreal wrongs. I have suffered,
I have caused suffering, and at my age all this harping on destiny
is shameful."[35]

34. Ibid., p. 160.
35. Letter to Sophie Gay, in Luppé, op. cit., p. 166.

But shame never restrained Astolphe. The question even arises as to whether Astolphe ever resisted temptation. This fervent Catholic and devoted friend seems to have overlooked social, religious exigencies and the demands of friendship when his own pleasure was in question; a very obvious contradiction which may have influenced Proust in his creation of the irrepressible Charlus, loving son, inconsolable widower and scrupulous Catholic. Custine was not yet prepared to "sacrifice his sensual life."[36] To wit, an adventure on an eastward-bound corvette placed at his disposal by Metternich.

In 1835 Custine planned to go to Jerusalem, but decided to stop in Vienna where the good offices of Mme d'Abrantès had secured him an interview with Metternich. The two men liked each other; they came from the same background. "Since the old days, which I still remember, I have seen nothing so perfectly amiable, so noble, or so simple as M. de Metternich."[37] Metternich, who was charmed by the conversation and manners of Boufflers's grandson, suggested he accompany two Austrian princes, Frederick Schwarzenberg and Franz Lobkowitz, on an imperial corvette which was leaving Trieste for Smyrna. Custine gladly accepted and the three men had an excellent trip. In a letter of thanks to Metternich, Custine claimed that his travelling companions and the captain of the corvette had all

36. *L'Espagne*, op. cit., p. 217.

37. Letter from Custine to Sophie Gay, 6 June 1835, quoted by J.-R. Derré, *Approches de lumière; mélanges offerts à Jean Fabre* (Klincksieck), p. 137.

looked after him wonderfully. Yet the journey was suddenly interrupted and Custine left the ship in Athens, neither on account of a fever nor because of the new plague raging in the Orient. The Austrian minister in Constantinople reported to the chancellor that "M. de Custine risked a great deal of trouble on board the *Veloce* on account of the obscenities of which he was suspected and which the pen hesitates to describe."[38] Metternich didn't hand the report over to the police and kept it in his personal archives; neither did he mention it to Custine, but continued to be friendly towards him. It is highly unlikely that Metternich's disapproval would have bothered Custine. He had a certain bravado and he would continue to organise his pleasures unashamedly, ready to defy society once more.

It is impossible to understand Custine without permanently bearing in mind the fact that he never took the judgement of the times too seriously. "In Louis XIV's century," he was to write in *La Russie*, "one had a freedom of language dependent on the certainty of being heard only by people who all lived and talked in the same way; there was society, but no public. Today there is a public, but no society . . . Frankness of expression would appear to be in bad taste to people who have not all learned the same French vocabulary. Something of the bourgeois sensibility has passed into the language of the best company in France . . . a nation needs to be respected more than

38. Ibid., p. 140.

an intimate society does . . ."[39] He remained unquestionably on the side of the intimate society.

During 1835, it became apparent in Paris that Custine was now at the head of a *ménage à trois*. A young and extremely attractive Pole, Ignatius Gurowski, had moved into the rue de La Rochefoucauld. "He has an excellent heart, an original mind, is graciously ignorant of everything, and what settles it all, a charming bearing and countenance."[40] Gurowski was both heedless and capricious and blessed with a desire to please which amazed and amused Custine. Nevertheless, Custine wasn't fooled by Gurowski's superficiality, which he excused on grounds of a lack of education. Later, in his letters from Russia, Custine was to say that Slavs "like to be left because they fear they will be understood too well if they are kept close for too long."[41] It can be assumed that he was thinking of his young friend back home.

Poland was fashionable during the July monarchy. After the failure of the 1830 uprising, France welcomed a number of exiles, among them Adam Mickiewicz, nominated to the Collège de France, where he gave a remarkable course on Slav literature which Custine attended. Custine became fascinated by the problem the

39. *La Russie*, op. cit., I, p. 211.
40. *Lettres à Varnhagen*, op. cit., p. 412.
41. *La Russie*, op. cit., II, p. 204.

Polish writer posed. Between Poland and Russia, which "deserved the greatest gratitude from the West for having protected it from the Mongol hordes"?[42] Mickiewicz laid claims for the Polish nobility. Pushkin esteemed that Russia, by virtue of her long martyrdom under Tartar domination, had provided the main bulwark. This was one of the first signs of Custine's interest in Eastern Europe. He began to prepare for his journey to Russia which would take place a few years later.

The Polish nationalists that Custine knew best in Paris were Prince Czartoryski, political leader in exile, and Chopin, "whose elegant, poetic and graceful talent lent a voice and a soul to the instrument least adapted to touch hearts,"[43] and who thrilled the public at the Pleyel by playing the *Grande Polonaise* at his first concert in Paris. Then there were the Gurowskis. Five Gurowski brothers had taken part in the Polish insurrection, two of whom chose to go into exile in France. Their sister, a childhood friend of the Tsarina and reputedly the king of Prussia's natural daughter, stayed at the Russian court with her husband, Baron Fredericks, grand equerry to the Tsar. The eldest brother, Adam,[44] who was deeply involved

---

42. Cadot, *La Russie dans la vie intellectuelle française*, op. cit., p. 190.

43. Letter from Custine to Metternich, 3 January 1837, in Derré, op. cit., p. 143.

44. Adam Gurowski returned to Russian-dominated Poland in 1835 after Nich-

in politics, and the youngest brother, Ignatius, aged eighteen, found themselves penniless on the streets of Paris. As a fine horseman, Ignatius earned his living teaching in a Parisian riding school. Custine may have met him there or at a soirée in society, since this indefatigable dancer was invited everywhere. Whatever the case, in 1835 he was part of what Custine blatantly called "our trio." The trio only broke up when Custine went abroad. Whereas Saint-Barbe always went to Italy with him, Custine preferred to set out alone for his great Russian journey in 1839.

Ignatius was not an easy guest. He ran up debts with the insouciance of a grandee, evinced unusual energy in seducing both men and women and shamelessly used Custine to achieve his ends. Custine must have been amused by all this since he agreed to offer the handsome Pole's hand to Rachel who at the time was dazzling audiences at the Comédie-Française. She, showing great good sense, refused; she preferred that Monsieur Ignatius remain just "a friend." Poor Custine's troubles were not over. Gurowski was convinced that he had been beaten out by a lover of Rachel's, the baron de Vendeuvre, a peer of France, and decided to avenge himself. A duel with the poor baron, who was too old, too cowardly and too shaky, was out

---

olas I had revoked his sentence. He became a functionary of the Empire and a fervent follower of pan-Slavism.

of the question. Ignatius found it more expedient to pummel him. Custine recounted the scene to Varnhagen. The two men chanced to meet in the street.

> *The old lover looked at the young lover in a particular way . . . then, overwhelmed with anger, [Ignatius] punched him in the face, the old man fell and tried to pick himself up; with another punch his teeth (which we are assured were false) were broken, his nose was cut and a deep gash made on his cheek. Blood flowed, passers-by stopped, the wounded man shouted murderer! The incident took place in the rue Tronchet, one of the busiest streets in Paris, at two o'clock in the afternoon . . . Back at home, that is to say my home, [Ignatius decided] to go into hiding at a friend's house . . . On the evening of that very day I had invited a great many people to dine; imagine my discomfort, and, above all, imagine my guests' amazement at not seeing one of the people who lives in my house, especially the one whom my frequent women visitors are unwilling to do without.*[45]

The story continued but changed direction so drastically that Custine—whether with regret or relief—turned from lover into doting uncle. Gurowski was not satisfied with his affair with Rachel. Meanwhile, because of the Carlist agitation, one of the Spanish infantas, Ferdinanda-Isabella, Don Francisco's eldest daughter, took refuge in France where she fell in love with Ignatius. The young

45. *Lettres à Varnhagen*, op. cit., pp. 413–414.

princesse was as ugly as she was ardent and romantic. She had met Ignatius at Enghien. A few riding lessons led to further adventures. When the princesse's father was informed, he had her locked up in the Augustine convent of the Sacré-Coeur from where she escaped by knotting a pair of sheets together and sliding down them into the arms of her lover. The two young people ran off together.

All this happened a few months after the episode in the rue Tronchet. The infanta's great-aunt, Queen Amelia, was not amused. The gendarmerie was alerted and the lovers were found in a hotel room in Namur and taken to Lille where Gurowski was obliged to relinquish his prize. She was brought back to Paris. Her parents refused to take her in, so she took refuge in the Ministry of the Interior where she told her whole story to the First Secretary. Without her "confounded red hair" which made her recognisable, they would never have found her. She then demanded to be examined by a gynecologist, knowing full well that such an examination would convince her parents of the need for a prompt ceremony. Between a suspect Polish nobleman as son-in-law and an unmarried mother as infanta, the parents opted for marriage which was celebrated in Dover on 26 June 1841. "Is it not a fine end to Louis XIV's line, that one of his great-nieces should marry a Pole supported by a man?" Prosper Mérimée wrote to the comtesse de Montijo.[46]

Custine appeared pleased. He joined "the children" in Belgium,

46. Mérimée, op. cit., letter of 22 May 1841, III, p. 55.

admired their little girl, the eldest of what was to be a family of nine, and let it be thought that Ignatius had been the result of a youthful escapade. People may have smiled. Mérimée gloated at the idea: "It is manifestly untrue and were he his father, [Custine] would be no better than the Lot of biblical memory."[47]

The episode with Ignatius, however, marked a turning point in Custine's life. On one hand, he realised how much he and Sainte-Barbe, the tried old couple, would miss the young man's informality and gaiety which had so enlivened their ménage. On the other, he recognised that the kind of life they led in order to keep Ignatius with them didn't entirely suit them. "I was living to amuse people who neither shared my tastes, and who were not my age," he admitted to Sophie Gay.[48] Besides, he had money troubles. To put things right, he decided to sell Saint-Gratien, to rent the rue de La Rochefoucauld and to travel.

The 50,000 francs of income at his disposal were enough for him to rent a decent house on the banks of Lake Annecy, and go to Italy. The trip was filled with concerts, lectures and meetings but he didn't allow himself to be distracted. He was editing notes made during his visit to Russia in 1839. The book which he was to write from them would finally earn him a lasting place amongst the writers of his day.

47. Ibid.
48. Luppé, op. cit., p. 225.

II

The Russian Journey

n June 1839 Custine left Paris for Germany; on 6 July he embarked at Travemünde, near Lübeck, for Russia. It didn't take long to cross the Baltic on the new steamships. On 10 July he reached St. Petersburg, where he stayed for three weeks, and on 3 August he arrived in Moscow. About ten days later he headed north-east on the road to Siberia but followed it for only two hundred kilometres. At Yaroslavl he stopped and headed south; he spent fewer than eight days in Nizhniy-Novgorod and returned via Vladimir to Moscow. He chose not to go on to Kiev, where he could have been received by Mme Hanska, Balzac's "Beautiful Foreigner," and also decided not to go to Poland, preferring to return to St. Petersburg. Rather than make the sea crossing a second time, he went back to Germany via Tilsit and Königsberg. On 1 October he was back in Berlin. His journey had lasted three months and from those three months he produced one of the most celebrated books on Russia, the most explosive and the most unexpected account of his day.

The book was a success twice. It was at once a success in Europe, and was translated into English, German and Swedish as soon as it appeared in 1843. A hundred years later, it reached a wider public. Right in the middle of the Cold War, it was discovered in the United States through a new, somewhat condensed, translation.[1] In France it was rescued from the obscurity into which it had fallen since the end of the nineteenth century by Pierre Nora's abridged edition of 1975.[2] Complete editions appeared in the United States in 1989 and in France in 1990.[3] From whatever angle it is looked at, this book with its unusual history raises as many questions about Custine as it does about Russia.

Since Russia was not much visited by tourists at the time, the first question is the reason for the journey. Romantic travellers, painters and writers, seeking new inspiration and new horizons, regularly left

1. *Journey for Our Time: The Russian Journals of the Marquis de Custine*, translated by Phyllis Penn Kohler with an introduction by Walter Bedell Smith (Henry Regnery Company, 1951).

2. *Lettres de Russie: La Russie en 1839*, preface by Pierre Nora (Folio, 1975).

3. *Empire of the Czar*, preface by Daniel Boorstin and introduction by George Kennan (Doubleday, 1989); *La Russie en 1839*, preface by Hélène Carrère d'Encausse, postscript by Julien-Frédéric Tarn (Solin, 1990).

for the Orient or North Africa when they wanted to immerse themselves in landscapes more exotic than their familiar European ones. Thanks to Chateaubriand, America with its woods and its Indians also played a part in the new French sensibility. America figured in artists' dreams; Russia did not. In the eighteenth century, when young French aristocrats left in large numbers to fight on the American side in their War of Independence, a simple journey to Russia, even at the invitation of Catherine the Great, was often refused.

Despite declaring that "the fine arts would take refuge in Moscow," and for all of Catherine's pressing invitations, Voltaire never felt the need to check in person that science, art and taste in fact reigned in the Tsarist Empire. D'Alembert refused the distinguished and lucrative position of tutor to the Tsarevitch. The mathematician Euler remarked to someone surprised by his silence on his return from St. Petersburg, "I come from a country where, if you speak, you are hanged." That remark weighed much more heavily than the empress's generous offers.[4] Even Diderot waited for more than ten years before accepting Catherine's hospitality although she had rescued him in times of severe financial difficulties, buying his library and, grandly, granting him the use of it, in addition to an annual salary of 1,000 francs. He stayed only a short time in St. Petersburg. On his return, he strongly advised Greuze against going because he hated being ordered around and the empress could

---

4. Albert Lortholary, *Le Mirage russe en France*, op. cit., p. 90.

easily send him any day on a trip to Siberia.[5] Even under the rule of an enlightened sovereign, desirous of maintaining her reputation with the philosophes, and with the very best welcome guaranteed, Russia was frightening. Travellers avoided it.

The many Frenchmen who did go to Russia at the end of the eighteenth century were driven by the precise and horrible fear of the scaffold. Mme Vigée-Lebrun's and the vicomte de Julvécourt's accounts of their time there are coloured by the relief of having escaped the Terror. Mme de Staël, fleeing Napoleon's dislike, crossed Russia in 1812, from Kiev to St. Petersburg, in order to embark for Sweden from Finland. For her, too, the more dangerous France seemed, the more welcoming Russia appeared. Once peace had returned to Europe, few were curious enough to make the journey. So in the nineteenth century Custine was something of a pioneer. Alexandre Dumas and Théophile Gautier were not to go there for another twenty years.

Many motives for the journey have been ascribed to Custine. Taking into account his literary ambitions, some have sensed the hand of Balzac who, after the success of Custine's book on Spain, suggested to him Russia or the North, as it was called at the time. "There are very few modern books that can be compared to these letters [*d'Espagne*] . . . If you do the same thing for every country, you will have a unique collection in the genre, and a collection which will be of the greatest value, believe me . . . I will do everything within my power to persuade you to also describe Germany, the Italian interior, the North, Prussia. It would be a great work and a great glory."[6] Others perceived only the wish to go and plead Gurowski's cause in person. Custine's more attentive readers were the least surprised because, in fact, he had expressed an interest in that part of the world at the time of his trip to Seville in 1831. "I cannot speak about the Russians," he wrote then, "whom I do not know but whom I would like to know: they are at least as Asiatic as were those people whose blood is mixed with Spanish blood. I would be interested in comparing Russia with Spain. Both are more like the Orient than any other nation in Europe, whose two extremities they form."[7] Was that all? Custine was never a man to explain himself completely; he was even capable of failing to mention whatever was most important to him.

A fact that cannot be disregarded is that just as Custine was writing *L'Espagne*, the first volume of *De la démocratie en Amérique* appeared. Custine interrupted his account of Spain to devote nearly ten pages to refute Tocqueville's theories, revealing once again his curiosity about countries whose origins are European. The United

6. Balzac, *Correspondance*, 5 vols. (Paris, Garnier, 1960–1968), letter of August 1838, III, pp. 424–426.
7. *L'Espagne*, op. cit., p. 258.

States may well be separated from Europe by an ocean, but nevertheless they are closely linked to it by population and political and intellectual life. Clearly a comparison between Russia and the United States had far richer possibilities than one between Russia and Spain. Tocqueville hints as much in his conclusion:

> *There are on earth today two great peoples who, having started from different points, seem to be advancing towards the same end: they are the Russians and the Anglo-Americans. They both grew up in the darkness; and whilst Europeans were busy elsewhere, they suddenly placed themselves in the forefront of nations, and the world learned at almost the same time of their birth and of their greatness.*
>
> *All other nations seem, more or less, to have reached the limits nature has assigned to them and within which they now need only to remain, but those two are still growing . . . America is struggling against obstacles of nature; Russia against men . . . The principal means of action for the one is liberty; for the other servitude.*[8]

It was the right moment in which to write about Russia. Besides, it is easy to imagine that Custine, who rejected Tocqueville's belief in the inevitable victory of democracy, was pleased at the idea of dis-

8. Alexis de Tocqueville, *De la démocratie en Amérique, Souvenirs* and *L'Ancien Régime et la Révolution* (Robert Laffont, Bouquins, 1986), pp. 376–377.

proving it by a symmetrical comparison. Tocqueville's domain was the western extremity of the European universe; his would be its Oriental limits. Custine disliked Tocqueville. "I have met M. de Tocqueville, author of the American Democracy. He is a puny man, thin, small and still young; he has something of the old man and something of the child; he is the most naïve of ambitious men. He has a charming expression but he lacks frankness, his mouth is old and ill-shaped, his complexion bilious; I would be attracted by his lively physiognomy if it troubled me less. It is clear that he will argue along more than one line and that his opinion is a weapon with which he means to attain his ends. This is how the new star in our political firmament has impressed me."[9]

They did have a number of things in common, most particularly, memories of their relatives. It was with Malesherbes, Tocqueville's great-grandfather, that Delphine took refuge during the Revolution; Delphine's great friend was, as we have seen, Tocqueville's aunt who married Chateaubriand's older brother. Both were guillotined; his parents were imprisoned and freed, like Delphine, when Thermidor brought an end to the Terror, but Mme de Tocqueville never regained her emotional equilibrium. Born in 1805, Tocqueville didn't have Custine's terrifying memories but a shadow must have been cast over his early years, as one was over Custine's, by the

9. *Lettres à Varnhagen*, op. cit., p. 420.

melancholy of those who had escaped the Terror and by the financial and political difficulties of a family that failed to rally to the Empire.

Custine and Tocqueville were both conservatives, both convinced of the impossibility of going back to pre-revolutionary principles, and both troubled by the loss of their traditional place in society. In pointing out that he has an "intellectual taste" for democratic institutions but, that as an instinctive aristocrat, he despises and fears the crowd, Tocqueville echoes Custine's asking "whether one shouldn't impose silence on one's antipathies" and accept with good grace a wise and moderate representative government. They both turned to other countries to find answers to the questions they asked about their own society. Tocqueville went to study the effects of democracy on the American republic and Custine hoped to find in Russia "new arguments against the despotism at home, against the disorder that bore the name of liberty."[10] Custine opened his book with a personal account of his father, his mother and himself, because he wanted to underline the point of departure of his own thinking, his obsessive concern with the violence that inevitably results from a society subjected to tyranny and with the delicate balance between equality and liberty.

---

10. *La Russie*, II, p. 420. [See also I, p. 20, "I was going to Russia to find an argument against representative government, I return in favour of constitutions."]

Both succeeded admirably in their undertaking. *De la démocratie en Amérique* is the most important nineteenth-century book about the United States and *La Russie en 1839* is the only contemporary account of the Tsarist Empire that has survived. More remarkable than their immediate success is the fact that these books are still read today. But here there is a distinction to be made between the two. The *Démocratie* is read just as Tocqueville would have wanted it to be. It is studied more in the United States than in France and if the text remains extremely interesting, it is because of the soundness of Tocqueville's reasoning, and the constancy of American principles of government. Tocqueville prepared for his trip; he had learned English and, not only did he spend nine months in the United States, but he also took the trouble to check his sources and his facts. His methods were those of a serious journalist, easily appreciated and understood by academics, whereas the success of *La Russie* is far more complicated. It is neither treatise nor study, but a cry from the heart, a drama, a book of impressions which lead to a verdict. The genius of the book lies in the fact that its judgements are equally applicable to Nicholas I's Russia and Stalin's U.S.S.R.

Today's reader will be amazed by the juxtaposition of such a detailed account of the times due to Custine's acute talent for observation—a court ball is described with the same precision as a street brawl or the agony of going down a steep slope in a four-wheeled telega—and an ensemble of intuitive reflections which might have been written yesterday about the Stalinist régime. Of course, Russia has changed during the course of a century, and of course there has been no uninterrupted continuity between Nicholas I and Stalin. The two régimes were by no means identical. Custine did succeed in analysing the worst effects of despotism, the contagious elements of fear and violence which spread from top to bottom of the social scale, and, in so doing, he wrote a timeless book. The realistic descriptions made the book a success in Custine's day; today it is valued as a prophetic nightmare. All Custine's admirers have delighted in quoting by the dozen aphorisms that apply to both the Tsar's Russia and the Soviet empire.

> *A ruler can be popular in Russia without attaching any importance to human life . . . nothing can discredit authority with a people for whom obedience has become a condition of life.*[11]

> *The more I see of Russia, the more I approve of the Emperor when he forbids Russians to travel and makes it difficult for foreigners to visit his country. The political régime would be unable to withstand open communication with Western Europe for more than twenty years.*[12]

Solid reasons were required of anyone wishing to leave Russia in the nineteenth century—departure for reasons of health was the

11. Ibid., I, p. 155.
12. Ibid., I, p. 203.

easiest—and then, on arrival abroad, Russians were obliged to make themselves immediately known to their embassy. A suspicious report by an informer was enough to have one ordered to return home. Too long an absence was unfavourably looked on and often cut short. Pushkin, for instance, was never given permission to travel abroad. The comte Demidoff, Princesse Mathilde's husband, had to leave his wife and forgo the delights of Paris to return to Moscow at once on the orders of the Tsar.

> *In this country, to admit the existence of tyranny would be progress. Foreigners who have described Russia have conspired with the Russians to deceive the world on this point as on many others. It is impossible to be more treacherously compliant than most of the writers who have rushed here from every corner of Europe only to wax sentimental about the touching familiarity which reigns between the Emperor of Russia and his people. Can the prestige of despotism be so great that it subjugates even the merely curious . . . or do the sincerest of minds lose their freedom of judgement as soon as they enter Russia?*[13]

> *At every step which I take here, I see the ghost of Siberia rising before me and I think of everything implied by the name of that political desert, that abyss of misery and cemetery of the living;*

13. Ibid., I, p. 306.

that world of fabulous colours, a land peopled by vile criminals and sublime heroes, a colony without which this Empire would be as incomplete as a palace without cellars.[14]

Russians are still convinced of the efficacy of lies; this is an illusion which surprises me in a people who have had recourse to them so much . . . It is not that they are lacking in finesse or understanding; but in a system in which the rulers have not yet understood the advantages of freedom, even for themselves, the governed are obliged to retreat before the immediate disadvantages of sincerity.[15]

Ours is the weakness of chatter, theirs is the strength of secrecy: therein particularly lies their cleverness.[16]

Tyranny is the imaginary disease of nations; the tyrant, disguised as a doctor, persuades them that health is not the natural condition of civilised man, and that the greater the danger, the more violent must be the remedy.[17]

Until now Russians have been treated by travellers as spoilt children.[18]

14. Ibid., I, p. 311.
15. Ibid., I, p. 418.
16. Ibid., I, p. 374.
17. Ibid., I, p. 163.
18. Ibid., I, p. 22.

The Russian Journey

Where there is liberty, everything is published and immediately forgotten because everything is seen at a glance; under an absolute government, everything is hidden but guessed at, provoking a keen interest: the slightest circumstance is remembered and noticed, conversation is animated by secret curiosity.[19]

If men remain silent in Russia, the stones speak and they speak in a lamentable voice. I am not surprised that the Russians fear and neglect their old monuments: they bear witness to their history, which more often than not they would like to forget.[20]

In Russia secrecy presides over everything . . . Every traveller is guilty of indiscretion.[21]

Such insight from a passing traveller, deaf to the language around him, is as surprising as the incisive quality of his judgement. Custine, who knew only too well how to hide behind finesse and subtlety, speaks clearly here, with the precision of classical maxims. His detractors—there were some in both Russia and France—chose to dismiss the text on grounds of the author's lack of seriousness. Custine refused to discuss the matter. He replied with one line, "It is true, I looked badly, but I guessed well."[22] André Gide inevitably

19. Ibid., I, p. 287.
20. Ibid., I, p. 167.
21. Ibid., I, p. 418.
22. Ibid., II, p. 437.

comes to mind. Having been invited by Stalin to make an address at Gorky's funeral in 1936, Gide stayed a few days in Moscow, then made a short trip into the country, visited two or three collective farms, watched the games of little pioneers with amusement and interest, one imagines, listened with stupefaction to the theories of the régime's artists, and, alone among the group of Communist sympathisers who travelled with him, returned to write a book devoid of any illusions.

> *In the U.S.S.R. it is admitted in advance and once and for all that, on all matters, there can only be one opinion. The people have their minds so fashioned that conformism comes easily and naturally to them, and so imperceptibly that I do not think hypocrisy enters into the question. Are these really the people who made the revolution? Every morning* Pravda *teaches them what it is suitable to know, to think and to believe, and it does no good to divert from that!*[23]

He was attacked for his lack of statistics, his ignorance of Russian, his inability to appreciate the beauties of Stakhanovism.[24] Nevertheless it is Gide who had looked, listened and made conscious judgements. Perhaps it took outsiders like Custine and Gide, ferociously attached to the freedom of their own ways and more sensi-

---

23. André Gide, *Retour de l'URSS* (Gallimard, 1936).

24. Notably Georges Friedmann in *De la Sainte Russie à l'URSS, André Gide et l'URSS* (Gallimard, 1937), pp. 241 ff.

tive than others to the brutality of orthodoxy, to outfox the mechanism of tyranny so quickly. It is tempting to think so, although Custine's reaction wasn't entirely spontaneous. He had planned his journey and thought about the Russian régime more than he let on.

Despite his Polish attachments, Custine was not hostile to Russia during the 1830s. Under the Empire, depending on whether one was for or against Napoleon, Russia appeared as the enemy or the ally. Custine was a legitimist, and although, unlike many aristocrats, he hadn't taken refuge in Russia, he was aware of his debt to the Tsar. Without him Louis XVIII would never have been restored to the throne. He may well have had a bad memory of the hordes of brigands and flat-faced Cossacks who accompanied the king on the French campaign, but like Molé, Balzac, Lamartine and Chateaubriand, he was a partisan of a limited alliance with Russia. It was susceptible to French influence and had a social system founded on a compact between the sovereign and the nobility that seemed to guarantee an order compatible with progress.

The vicomte de Julvécourt's Russian account appeared in 1834, and Mme Vigée-Lebrun's *Souvenirs* in 1836. They both painted a picture of a tamed Russia likely to strengthen Custine's beliefs. He read what he could of Pushkin, the first "feeble and rare"[25] translations of whose work became available in 1837, but only saw the Eu-

25. *Lettres à Varnhagen*, op. cit., p. 442.

ropean influence in them. "This man has borrowed some of his colours from the new poetic school of Western Europe . . . I do not yet see him as a real Muscovite poet."[26] He missed the other aspect of the poet's sensibility and didn't mention his death in 1837.

Tsar Nicholas had no reason to mistrust Custine, who favoured the traditional order and wore the martyr's crown of his father and grandfather. The formalities were made easy and he was welcomed in palaces with open arms. Nor was he made to feel discomfort on account of his sexuality, whatever his Parisian moralizing friends might have thought. On the contrary, the Emperor received him as a friend, entertaining him tête-à-tête on two occasions. Etiquette was disregarded in order for him to attend the marriage of the grand duchess, the Tsar's eldest daughter; he was invited to the imperial private apartments. Better still, he was allowed to wander through them alone to look at them at his ease.

However grateful Custine may have been, he was not an easy man to influence. In 1843, Saint-Marc Girardin ended his article on *La Russie* with the comment: "Custine was able to see a great deal because he was viewed almost as an accomplice (if M. de Custine will excuse the expression). The accomplice allowed himself to hear everything and revealed all."[27] Had Nicholas I taken the trouble to read his novels, he would have saved himself great disappointments.

26. *La Russie*, op. cit., I, p. 366.
27. In Cadot, op. cit., p. 267.

Who would have believed that this conservative Catholic would denounce the priesthood with a virulence worthy of Stendhal?[28] A traveller like Custine who delighted in infinite subtlety and knew how to listen was not one to be easily co-opted. And in Germany, where he stayed before setting out for the North, he heard things of which he took note.

Custine proved to be very discreet about his contacts. On passing through Berlin, he saw Varnhagen and never mentions it though he recounted in the book his conversation with a Lübeck innkeeper. Having noticed the difference between travellers arriving from St. Petersburg and those embarking for the return journey, the innkeeper tried to persuade Custine not to go, for he felt "that a country which one leaves with so much joy and to which one returns with so much regret is a bad country."[29] Varnhagen was kept informed by his diplomatic contacts and was curious about current intellectual ideas astir in Russia. He was profoundly conscious of the political difficulties faced by Nicholas I which he explained in detail to Custine during their long conversations. At Varnhagen's, Custine met Alexander Turgenev with whom he had already become acquainted in Paris. This Turgenev, uncle of the famous writer, had been sent to

28. The plot of *Le Monde comme il est* is partly based on the wickedness of the "parti-prêtre," the political party of the priests.

29. *La Russie*, op. cit., I, p. 77.

Paris after the Decembrist rebellion of 1825, in order to investigate European archives and, if possible, to spirit away whatever documents most compromised Russians—a curious mission for a man whose own brother was one of the officers implicated in the revolt. He was a liberal and independent man who congratulated himself on living in France rather than Russia. At the same time, he was clever enough to play a complex role, being both an observer—if not a spy—on behalf of the government to which he was hostile, and an intermediary between the most advanced political and literary Russian circles and the French intellectual élite. In Paris he was respected for his culture and open-mindedness. Chateaubriand, who often invited him to Mme Récamier's property at l'Abbaye-aux-Bois (where Custine met him), called him a "man of all kinds of learning."[30] In any case, on seeing Custine again in Berlin, Turgenev decided to direct him towards what was most independent and courageous in Russian society.

He recommended that Custine visit Prince Viazemski, a man close to Pushkin and a great friend of Mickiewicz, whom he had known in Poland; Viazemski had been exiled from court for his opinions and confined to his estates. Better still, he gave Custine a letter of introduction to Tchadaiev. Tchadaiev was an officer who resigned his commission in 1815, stayed in England until 1826 and

30. In Cadot, op. cit., p. 181.

annoyed the Tsar so much by saying that society was becoming ever more abject and servile that he was declared mad. He was ordered to stay in his room and have the doctor visit him every day. The doctor was not the only one to come. The whole of Moscow—generals, princesses, painters and writers—filed through the madman's bedroom, to the joy of Alexander Herzen, who quipped that as the insane captain's power was recognised, the Tsar's insane power was diminished.[31]

Another Russian whom Custine had seen at length in Frankfurt and met again on the boat to St. Petersburg contributed to shaking his confidence in the Tsarist Empire before he had even crossed the border. Prince Kozlovski's character and position unquestionably added weight to his judgement. In 1802, at the age of nineteen, he went to Rome as a young diplomat, where he made friends with his French colleague who just happened to be Chateaubriand. Then he converted to Catholicism. This was tantamount to a political conversion since to leave the national church in order to submit to Rome was a manifest sign of wishing to escape from the Tsar's absolute control. In fact, in 1840 the Tsar was to declare that to leave the Orthodox Church was a criminal offence, punishable by confiscation of the convert's property. The prince stayed abroad until 1836, frequenting all the best salons in Paris, London and

31. *La Russie*, op. cit., II, p. 506.

Berlin. On his return, he proved both his courage and the liberality of his views by intervening on behalf of the Poles. He certainly inspired Pushkin's unfinished poem, dedicated to an unknown man "who loved foreign peoples tenderly, whilst wisely hating his own."[32] He was the only one of his sources whom Custine identified. By the time the book appeared in 1843, nothing more could touch the prince. He had died three years earlier.

Material preparations for a journey to Russia were just as important as the intellectual ones. Despite his delicate health, Sainte-Barbe had accompanied Custine on all his trips, but they decided not to subject him to Russia. The crises of rheumatism that paralysed him would have made the journey too painful. Custine, who was always worried about him, made him promise to send regular news, the least delay in which caused Custine terrible anxiety. He would be accompanied by his Italian valet, Antonio.

Antonio had worked for Custine since 1826. He was totally devoted and as capable of organizing his master's pleasures as of attending to his daily comforts. He was a man of great personal distinction, gifted, according to Custine, "with the political intelligence of a modern Roman and the noble heart of the Ancients,"[33] and who always seemed to have been a wonderfully resourceful

32. In Cadot, op. cit., p. 189.
33. *La Russie*, op. cit., II, p. 239.

travelling companion. On the Russian roads, his capabilities as a blacksmith and wheelwright prevented considerable delays. Furthermore, Antonio was a man who could jump from a carriage drawn by a runaway team, stop the horses terrified by the sight of an elephant, and fall asleep a quarter of an hour later in the back of the barouche. Less dramatically, he often slept in the carriage at staging points, to protect it from thieves. The accessories all tempted the peasants, whose preferred saying was that "Our Lord would steal, too, if his hands had not been pierced." Had they not been careful, the travellers might well have found the barouche "without a hood, stripped bare, with no braces, no curtains, no apron, turned in fact into a primitive tarantass."[34] It is hardly surprising that Custine considered Antonio a really superior person.

As we have seen, Custine didn't travel light, but rather as was customary in the eighteenth century before the train changed travelling. The railway was still a long way off in Russia: the St. Petersburg–Moscow line was only inaugurated in 1858. For this trip, the marquis outdid himself, his most cumbersome piece of luggage being the English carriage he insisted on taking against all advice. The primitive solidity of a sledge was more suited to the Russian roads. What he really needed was a small, portable, collapsible iron bed, "an object of prime importance for a European travelling in Russia, with no wish to accustom himself to spending the night wrapped in

34. Ibid., p. 249.

a rug, lying on a stair or a bench."[35] A bed was as indispensable in Russia as an overcoat in Spain. Custine also regretted not having been able to bring large supplies of linen in his overladen carriage, as the sheets and towels with which he was provided always seemed used and, he said, he could never discover who deserved the honour of dirtying them. Despite the amount of his luggage, he agreed to take for Turgenev a case of Bohemian crystal to Prince Viazemski. An experienced traveller, he also took some padlocks, effervescent powders to purify the water, bouillon cubes made for him by Mme Chevet, the proprietor of the well-known Parisian restaurant, and his Montaigne, without which he never left home.

35. Ibid., I, p. 319.

12

Obsessions

Custine's ambition on embarking for Russia was to act as
a political observer, but unlike Tocqueville who dissociated the quasi-scientific traveller from the romantic
tourist (to the first we owe the *Démocratie*, to the second, *La Course
au lac d'Onéida*), Custine made no attempt to numb his sensibilities.
On the contrary. In Spain, he was already advocating travel as a personal discovery; in Russia, his voyage of discovery soon became, by
his own admission, a confession.

Naturally every visitor observes his surroundings through the
filter of his own past experience. For Custine, whose early childhood was torn apart by the violence of the terrible scenes he witnessed, the filter was particularly coloured. Fear, he claimed, was
the first emotion of which he had been conscious and the observa-

tion of the mores of a country under the sway of an absolute ruler subconsciously awakened these memories. The anxiety which gripped him from the moment of his arrival in St. Petersburg had nothing in common with the exquisite fear, "the voluptuous delight of the traveller's imagination," that he had experienced in Spain. Such fear, inseparable from the love of danger, was a diversion that represented for him not courage but the fear of boredom. In Russia, he experienced a painful emotion which completely took hold of him and from which nothing could distract him. The courage he had shown in Spain and Italy and the way in which he overcame his fear—of brigands, of shipwreck, or of the living dead who peopled the inns—were the product of his education but the anguish that possessed him in Russia sprang from the unappeasable, primitive terror of a child horrified by the sight of his mother being taken away by madmen armed with pikes.

As long as he was on the boat crossing the Baltic, surrounded by the "natural world lit [by] a monotonous pallor [like] the dream of a white-haired poet," he gave way, as a true Romantic, only to "poetic terror . . . an indefinable sorrow,"[1] but as soon as the formalities of landing began, poetry gave way to reality, or at least to *his* reality. Suddenly, with no change and with no real justification, it was the Terror. Why had he ever thought of going to Siberia? From the start

1. *La Russie*, op. cit., I, p. 90.

of his book he used the word Siberia to designate Russia, and Siberia, as he points out, was synonymous with exile, a terrifying exile which leads to a living cemetery. Large boats unable to enter the St. Petersburg canals were anchored just in front of the silent Kronstadt fortress, and an *army* of police and customs officers, "the Empire's jailers,"[2] climbed on board. Custine realised that he was about to enter the *empire of fear.* He was made to go down to the steamer's main saloon for his interrogation. From then on all Custine's vocabulary evokes the horror of a trial and the ignomiy of everyone involved in it.

He likens "the Areopagus of clerks assembled to interrogate the passengers" to a "tribunal, more fearsome than imposing . . . [whose members leaf through] registers with sinister concentration . . . Every foreigner is treated as guilty . . . the passengers are persecuted by this mental torture."[3] This was all taking place in front of the prison-fortress of Kronstadt with its half-buried dungeons in which soldiers and sailors who were insurgents of the Decembrist movement had been immured for nearly fifteen years. "No voice could be heard from this tomb; the shapes which could be seen sailing near it were as silent as the stones they had just left; it was like a funeral procession prepared for a death that kept it waiting."[4] The

2. Ibid., I, p. 143.
3. Ibid., I, p. 140.
4. Ibid., I, p. 141.

processions in reality consisted only of boats intended to take the passengers ashore, but one glance at the miserable oarsmen was enough to remind Custine of the hell of the galleys. "The men who rowed these lugubrious, ill-kept little boats . . . [were] dressed in rags, half-covered by sheepskins worn with the fur on the outside . . . [they were] deeply, oilily dirty . . . with dead eyes."[5] The formalities were over more quickly for Russians than for foreigners. Custine concludes: "*My friends*, treated according to their rank, were freed; they left the prison in which they had travelled, without even bidding farewell to me, whom they left bent under the weight of police and customs irons. What use would it be to say farewell? I was dead."[6]

Finally, after another "session of the court of assizes . . . [during which] an Italian merchant was searched to the bone," Custine was allowed to enter the city, but not before his travelling pistols and, inexplicably, an old travelling clock had been confiscated. More annoying still, he discovered that his carriage had been sent by mistake to a prince who happened to be away, and that he would be obliged to go to endless trouble to establish the customs officers' error. He set out to find Coulon, a French innkeeper, who was said to run the best establishment in town. It might be thought that no

5. Ibid., I, pp. 141 and 142.
6. Ibid., I, p. 146.

hotel could surprise a man who had travelled through Spain, and yet . . .

After a great deal of talk, the innkeeper, "a degenerate French-man,"[7] grudgingly gave him a stifling apartment without curtains or blinds and Custine discovered one of the peculiarities of St. Petersburg inns. If you had no personal servant, no one attended to you. What was he to do about his immediate problem? He could neither sit down nor lie on the furniture, which was covered with a brown material that turned out to be a living blanket of bedbugs. Since Antonio, his valet, spoke no Russian, he could be of little help. Fortunately he managed to discover "in one of the dark corridors of this walled desert . . . this gilded stable hung with velvet and silk . . . known as the Hotel Coulon"[8] a servant seeking employment, who spoke German. This man acquired for Custine the indispensable iron travelling bed, and explained the best anti-bug strategy to Antonio. The mattress should be stuffed with fresh straw, but above all the four feet of the bed should be placed in jars of water, with the bed in the middle of the room and all the other furniture removed. In fact, to avoid vermin, it was essential to prevent the revoltingly dirty servants from sprawling over the furniture in an oriental fashion as soon as the master's back was turned, as was their custom.

7. Ibid., I, p. 165.
8. Ibid., I, p. 166.

A Taste for Freedom

The marquis never travelled after that without his bed and a straw mattress cover for Antonio—which he soon discovered to be all the more necessary because beds were the rarest pieces of furniture in Russia. The greatest noblemen slept on benches. The upheaval of his settling in had the effect of waking him up; instead of resting as he had intended, he set out to discover St. Petersburg.

The intensity of his impressions on arrival may be surprising but in Russia brutality stared anyone of the slightest sensibility in the face as soon as one stepped into the street. Custine couldn't bear physical violence done to men or animals. At a bullfight in Spain, his curiosity turned to disgust and he felt his "pity going over to the animals' side." He was sorry for the horses and sympathised with the bull, and described the women seated in the galleries round the ring as furies or tigresses, applauding the progress of the unfortunate horses' slow death, "their hooves entangled in their entrails," condemned to the most terrible end.[9] It is hardly surprising if in Russia he felt shaken after his first few steps outside in the town.

In the middle of the street at a time of day when it was crowded with strollers, in the most beautiful part of the capital, he saw a coachman who had failed to make way quickly enough for a courier to pass being punched and hit in the face with a whip and a stick. What shocked him most was that this cruelty had no effect whatso-

9. *L'Espagne*, op. cit., pp. 112–114.

ever on the passers-by; they went on their way, no one protested. Worse still, "one of the coachman's colleagues . . . obeying an irritated signal from the [bully] . . . ran to hold his mount . . . for as long as it pleased him to continue the beating. In no other country could you ask a man of the people for assistance in the arbitrary beating of a friend!"[10]

Custine immediately assessed the degree of corruption in a society which accepted such horrific, gratuitous aggression as legitimate punishment: "Thus the spirit of iniquity goes down stage by stage to the very foundations of this unfortunate society which subsists on violence only, a violence that obliges the slave to lie to himself, so as to thank the tyrant . . . and what is called public order here is a mournful quiet, a terrifying peace, reminiscent of the tomb."[11]

From another incident he discovered how quickly men's hearts are hardened by such sights. Two porters started to quarrel on the bank of a canal. A policeman intervened and to escape from him, one of the men climbed up the mast of a boat. The policeman managed to catch hold of his foot and made him fall head first into a pile of wood. He then proceeded to beat him about the body and trample him "as one tramples the grapes in the wine press." The man who was covered in blood began to bellow like an ox. Fifty feet away Custine was watching, hypnotised and, he admitted, these "horri-

10. *La Russie*, op. cit., I, p. 350.
11. Ibid., II, p. 41.

ble cries mitigated my compassion, it seemed he was no better than a beast and that I was wrong to be moved by him as though he were of my kind. The more the man yelled, the more my heart hardened." In the end he left, sickened by the idea that he too could feel "contempt for the weak."[12]

This double theme of violence in society, accepted with terrible calm, and of the moral perversion it brought in its wake was to haunt him throughout the journey. The excesses of the Revolution were the result of a passing frenzy, whereas in Russia, cruelty was methodical, cold, persistent and contagious.[13] Horrified, Custine was to watch the growth of evil within himself. The young postilion who took him from St. Petersburg to Moscow—a very young boy, almost a child—was knocked roughly to the ground and beaten by the head stableman. Custine did not stop him. An unfortunate colt escaped from its enclosure and galloped after his carriage, having mistaken one of the mares in harness for its mother. The coachman refused to listen to the postilion's plea to pull up the horses so as to save the poor animal which was exhausting itself in a race beyond its strength. Custine didn't intervene. There was worse to come, as we shall see, on the road to Siberia, when he dared not show his pity for a group of exiles.

The agonising malaise that Custine felt on arriving in Russia was

12. Ibid., II, p. 73.
13. Ibid., I, p. 372.

exacerbated by the strangeness of everything he saw.[14] Whereas the writer's task is to describe, he felt unable to do so. "Here my words will not tally with things,"[15] he was to say. The inundated country-side around St. Petersburg, the difficulties—worse than in any other country—confronting travellers, the character of the city, at once both new and old, splendid and unfinished, the behaviour of the people: everything seemed to him bizarre and incoherent. He was unable to establish any connection or any point of agreement with what he knew. "In Russia, the names are the same as elsewhere, but things are quite different."[16] The countryside seemed to him "uniform, empty, without variety, without colour, without limits and yet without grandeur . . . a desert of water framed by a desert of peat: sea, coastline, sky all melt into one another, like a mirror, but so lustreless, so mournful as if the glass had not been silvered; it reflects nothing."[17] Worse yet, this physical and historic desert, with its expanses of water, its stunted pines and puny birches, was a land without memories. For Astolphe, the Romantic, Chateaubriand's spiritual heir, a landscape without ruins, with no marks of the past, which evoked nothing, was a land of the dead.

The city, built at the whim of Peter the Great in such an inhospita-

14. Irina Grudzinska Gross, *The Scar of Revolution, Custine, Tocqueville and the Romantic Imagination* (University of California Press, 1984), chap. 5.

15. *La Russie*, op. cit., II, p. 103.

16. Ibid., I, p. 267.

17. Ibid., I, p. 136.

ble position, suffered, in Custine's French eyes, from such lack of harmony that he found it hard to portray. In the first place it was impossible to find a guidebook; the bookshops didn't sell them.[18] He set out haphazardly, but a town centre, which irresistibly attracts the visitor in Paris, Florence or Seville, didn't exist in St. Petersburg. The immense empty city had no heart. On the large square in front of the Winter Palace, Alexander's huge granite column "has the effect on the eye of a stake and the houses around the square seem so flat and so low that they look like a palisade."[19]

This void, which is a characteristic of new countries, is also, or so it seemed to him, a consequence of absolute power; "The absence of liberty creates solitude and radiates sorrow. Only free countries are populated."[20] There are "fewer men than columns in the Petersburg squares which are always sad and silent because of their grandeur and above all because of their imperturbable regularity. The square and the straight line accord so well with an absolute monarch's way of seeing things, that right angles are the undoing of despotic architecture."[21] The only advantage of "this vast plain" which serves as a central square is that one cannot spy on people walking around:

18. Ibid., I, p. 192.
19. Ibid., I, p. 215.
20. Ibid., I, p. 203.
21. Ibid., I, p. 278.

"One can see anybody coming from afar and one can talk here more safely than in a room."[22]

A Parisian like Custine, for whom the city is a paradise for strolling, must have been struck by the lack of gaiety and fantasy in a population of "superior functionaries overseeing inferior functionaries."[23] No one walked for pleasure, head in the air, looking for entertainment. There were no cafés, no newspapers to discuss. It was a town where people didn't talk. "Everything is dismal, regular as in a barracks or a camp,"[24] with a wild element provided by the coachmen and the horses. "Animals and half-wild men run headlong about the town with an air of worrying freedom."[25] Custine could only understand old, solid towns, geographically defined by their walls, by their closely built houses, by a network of streets and by architectural style. There was nothing like that in St. Petersburg, "immense town whose heart is made of stone, its body of bricks and plaster, its extremities of painted wood and rotten planks. These planks are placed, by way of walls, around deserted marshland."[26]

To read Gogol—*The Greatcoat*, for example—is to be convinced that Custine was not exaggerating. "Soon [Akaky Akakievich] en-

22. Ibid., I, p. 362.
23. Ibid., I, p. 163.
24. Ibid., I, pp. 162–163.
25. Ibid., I, p. 283.
26. Ibid., I, p. 240.

tered those deserted streets . . . not a soul was in sight; the only light came from the snow glinting on the street while the low huts slept morosely behind their dark shutters. By now he was near the point where the street opened into a vast square, a terrible void, on the far side of which the buildings were barely visible."[27] Custine was very struck by the empty spaces within the confines of St. Petersburg. "Russian towns enclose whole countries."[28] In Moscow he passed by isolated ponds and through fields like steppes to dine in a faraway district, which was nevertheless within the city walls.

Russian towns, with their dirt roads, their wooden houses and their lack of monuments or old buildings, were more an extension of the surrounding countryside than independent entities, founded, as they were in Western Europe, on distinct privileges, and having given rise to a particular class—the bourgeoisie. (Custine noticed the absence of this group at the theatre. There was no dress circle or gallery, which in Paris would have been reserved for the lower or upper middle class, which proved that the spectators all belonged to the same caste: the nobility in this instance.) The lack of any distinction between the urban and the rural—for a French visitor the negation of the very idea of the city—was one of the difficulties Cus-

27. Gogol, *Récits de Pétersbourg, le Manteau* (Flammarion GF, 1968), pp. 47–48; Gogol, *Plays & Petersburg Tales, The Greatcoat*, translated by Christopher English (World's Classics, 1995), p. 133.

28. *La Russie*, op. cit., I, p. 178.

tine faced throughout his journey. How was he to find the terms of reference to make sense of what he saw? How could he describe this "collection of contrasts so discordant that nature and society would seem to have been created only to unite elements that alone would abhor and mutually exclude one another"?[29] Custine highlights these internal contradictions by repeatedly juxtaposing incompatible ideas. In Russia, he discovers "laziness without leisure" and "solitude without rest"; a cloister of nuns suggested a "women's barracks."[30]

He could not bring himself to identify as a city this jumbled agglomeration, this Kalmuck encampment "surrounding a collection of ancient temples."[31] It was more like a theatrical set used as a backdrop for a real and terrible drama. All other capitals seem to have been built to last. But St. Petersburg, "with no roots in either history or land, might be forgotten in a day; if new policies carried the master's thoughts elsewhere, the granite hidden under the water would crumble, the inundated lowlands regain their natural territory, and the hosts of solitude reclaim their lair."[32] No one believes that the absurd capital, which seems to deny both the water lying in wait and the enveloping cold, will last.

29. Ibid., I, p. 290.
30. Ibid., I, p. 180; II, p. 444; I, p. 428.
31. Ibid., I, p. 280.
32. Ibid., I, p. 181.

In Morocco, Spain and Italy, life was made tolerable by the fact that the architecture, the materials and the layout of rooms suited the climate. A simple addition, like shutters in a room where in summer the oblique rays of the sun beat down twenty-two hours a day, would be enough to make a bedroom more pleasant. The innkeeper, Coulon, who had become decidedly Russian, didn't think of such a thing. The heat was easier to bear in Seville than it was in St. Petersburg. Under the gentle Roman sky buildings were constructed of stone and marble. On the banks of the Neva, there was no harmony, no agreement between architecture and nature. What folly to have built flat-roofed houses in the Italian style in a country where there is so much snow. Why were there no arcaded streets? The foolishness such inconsistency proved shocked Custine because what he most admired were "the affinities between nature and artistic creation."[33]

Subjected to the worst possible climate, the Russians built "palaces of wood, houses of planks and temples of plaster; therefore the Russian workmen spend the summer redoing what the winter has destroyed . . . stone lasts here as long as mortar and whitewash do elsewhere."[34] That wasn't written for effect. In summer there were thousands of plasterers, as every building needed to be resurfaced. It was a dangerous job because, with such a short summer, the men

33. Ibid., II, p. 16.
34. Ibid., I, p. 217.

had to hurry, seated precariously on nasty planks attached to loose ropes by which they were hauled up the façades of buildings, like "hundreds of spiders hanging from the threads of webs blown apart by a storm."[35]

The malaise Custine qualified as indefinable may well have been exacerbated by his inability to make sense of what he saw. It also explains his turning inward and his fundamental fear, the years of the Terror, when life and liberty depended more on chance than on justice. The Tsar's absolutism brought him constantly back to the Revolution, because the Terror had been just as tyrannical and arbitrary as despotism appeared in St. Petersburg.

Throughout his journey he was obsessed with prisons and prisoners. Although St. Petersburg had no real centre, on the first day, before he even visited the Imperial Palace, Custine went straight to the citadel as if he felt that an explanation of the country lay in the Tsar's absolute power over his people. At Kronstadt he had already thought about the prisoners. As he approached the fortress on this initial walk through Petersburg, he did not notice the pointed steeple, so rare in this land of cupolas, that looked like a monumental heron, "brilliant as the scales of a lizard,"[36] covered in gold thanks to Dutch ducats presented to the Tsar, and typical of Peter the Great's new style of architecture; nor was his attention drawn to the

35. Ibid., I, p. 295.
36. Ibid., II, p. 15.

low pink brick surrounding wall, or the imperial tombs. Only the prisons interested him.

"They did not let me see the prisons: there are dungeons below the water level and cells under the roof; they are all full of men."[37] The walls of the citadel, converted from the beginning into a political prison, did indeed exude fear, blood and horror. There Peter the Great had his own son tortured and assassinated, there the Decembrists were incarcerated in 1825 when their plot failed, and there, ten years later, Dostoyevsky would be imprisoned. Thus the sight of the Romanov sarcophagi inspired only revulsion in Custine. He suddenly felt physically ill.

> *In this funereal citadel, the dead seem freer than the living . . .*
> *were it a philosophical idea to enclose in the same tomb the pris-*
> *oners of the emperor and the prisoners of death, the conspirators*
> *and the sovereigns against whom they conspire, I would respect*
> *it; but all I see here is the cynicism of absolute power, the brutal*
> *confidence of well-assured despotism . . . A Russian emperor is*
> *so full of what he owes to himself, that his justice does not efface*
> *itself before God's justice . . . If I enter the filthy palace of a*
> *great nobleman . . . if I smell vermin under the roof of opulence*
> *. . . I immediately imagine the stench in the dungeons of a coun-*
> *try where rich men do not fear dirtiness for themselves; when I*

37. Ibid., I, p. 173.

*suffer from the humidity in my room, I think of the unfortunate
fellows exposed to the humidity of the inundated dungeons in
Kronstadt.*[38]

Custine was afraid throughout his journey. Objectively his fear was
unjustifiable, but it tormented him all the same. No expression of
politeness, no form of protection was strong enough to reassure
him. He couldn't rid himself of the image of Alexander flattering
one of his ministers before having him seized and sent to Siberia. "I
shivered to think that neither the most scrupulous loyalty nor the
utmost probity could protect a man from the underground prisons
of the St. Petersburg citadel."[39]

The fact that he was a foreigner did not seem sufficient guarantee:
if his curiosity were considered annoying, it would be easy for the
authorities to eliminate him. They had only to tell the ambassador
that by some unforeseen accident, his boat had sunk in a lake. One
would look for his body in vain; the search would soon be called off
and he would be forgotten. From the moment he set foot in Russia,
he was aware of being followed. Under the pretext of helping him to
move about, he was given a guide who, in Custine's eyes, was there
merely to supervise him and who might become his executioner. Far

38. Ibid., I, pp. 273 and 311.
39. Ibid., I, p. 174.

from coming to terms with this, he envisaged the most extreme of all possible consequences: "They will prepare an ambush for me in some forest; they will attack me, they will fleece me, take my letters, and they will kill me to silence me."[40] He was carried away by his imagination: in any case, wouldn't death be preferable to being buried alive like the wretched people, crouching since Alexander's reign in the Kronstadt dungeons, "forgotten by everyone, alone, abandoned in the darkness of captivity, where imbecility becomes the fruit and last consolation of endless boredom ... Even the crimes of some of the prisoners have been forgotten, although they are still there because no one knows where to send them back to and it seems less inconvenient to perpetuate the punishment than to make public knowledge of the matter."[41]

He might tell himself in vain that his preoccupation with danger was bordering on madness, insist that neither his person nor his remarks could in any way trouble the Russian government; he was still unable to rid himself of his fear. Everything seemed tinged with blood. Troubled by his obsession with deportation and incarceration, he would make every effort to see the inside of a fortress. What could explain such mania?

More than by fear, he was driven by one question. How would he have reacted in adversity? Would he have had his parents' courage?

40. Ibid., I, p. 437.
41. Ibid., I, p. 454.

What would he do if he were arrested? He liked to think that his worries were children of the night and that his fears were dreams; he liked to imagine himself "reckless in action"[42] and pusillanimous only in thought, but he had not put himself to the test. These thoughts turned his mind to Delphine more so because 13 July was the anniversary of her death. Every year, wherever he found himself on that day, he had a Mass said for her, and so he made his way to the Dominican convent. When he had finished praying, feeling his mother still there, ready to urge him on and with a lighthearted gesture frighten away his demons, he hurried to the French ambassador. If the Tsar alone counted, he might as well go to court where he was invited for the next day, 14 July 1839, to attend the marriage of the grand duchess and Eugène de Beauharnais's son. It was exactly fifty years after the fall of the Bastille. By a strange coincidence this marriage was to recall Les Carmes and General de Beauharnais, who before leaving for the scaffold gave Delphine his ring, a talisman that Custine always wore.

42. Ibid., I, p. 438.

13

The Empire of Fear

Nicholas I, the eighth child of Catherine the Great's son, Paul I, was not destined for the throne. He was only five years old when his father was assassinated in 1801. His older brother, Alexander, then became emperor. Educated as he was, by a narrow-minded Baltic squire called the baron Lambsdorff, who failed to arouse any curiosity in his pupil, Nicholas would have made an excellent, conscientious officer, simple and honest. He was noted more for his scrupulous severity than as a strategist, or for his leadership qualities, when given the command of a brigade of guardsmen. Since both Alexander's legitimate children predeceased him, he had no direct heir. The succession should then have been assured by his younger brother, Constantine; but as viceroy of Poland and morganatically married to a Pole, Constantine had no intention of leaving Warsaw. He hadn't announced his decision officially, though he had told Alexander and a few intimates. Nicholas, curiously, was not included among this group.

Alexander's death therefore caused great confusion. Nicholas, ignorant of Constantine's wishes, declared him emperor. When he eventually learnt of his brother's refusal to return to Russia, he hesitated to accept the crown without a formal renunciation from the ex-tsarevich, only too conscious of his own lack of popularity with the army. For three weeks couriers rode back and forth from Poland to Russia; meanwhile a group of officers, members of different secret societies and in favour of a constitutional monarchy, attempted a military revolt. Supported by a small percentage of St. Petersburg regiments, they refused to swear allegiance to Nicholas, whose absolutist ideas were well known, and invaded the capital's main square with cries of "Constantin Konstitutsia." It was claimed afterwards that the soldiers shouted all the more enthusiastically because they didn't understand the word constitution and thought that Konstitutsia was the name of Constantine's wife. Nicholas confronted the men bravely, then, faced with their refusal to back down, gave his loyal troops the order to shoot. The demonstrators dispersed but the ringleaders were known. Five officers were executed. After a speedy trial the other Decembrists—the name recalled the date of the uprising, 26 December 1825—were deported or thrown into prison. The tone for Nicholas's reign was set.

The new Tsar grudgingly accepted Louis-Philippe's accession, mobilised an army to help the king of Holland quell the Belgian revolution in 1830, and the following year suppressed the Polish insurrection with great cruelty. For him, the world was divided into bad revolutionaries and good conservatives, preferably royalist. The marquis de Custine, descended from the Sabrans, the son and grandson of martyrs, in no way connected to the citizen-king's government, was not only one of his own, but might as a writer be of service to Russia. So the Tsar received him with unusual and exquisite urbanity.

He made the exception of ignoring etiquette on Custine's behalf. The marriage of the Tsar's daughter was to take place on 14 July. Custine had been invited but to appear at court before having been presented was against all protocol in St. Petersburg. He hadn't yet been presented. As soon as the Emperor heard of the problem, he decided that the rule was not applicable. From the first evening on, both he and the Tsarina had some long, substantive conversations with their visitor. Custine was clearly delighted. He was extremely curious about the court and the personalities of both the Tsar and the Tsarina.

"Far from putting me off, these things attracted me," he wrote.[1] It amused this man, who had lived in a circle that still remembered the splendours of Versailles with emotion, to penetrate a real court, and one where the sovereign was absolute. "It is a journey into old

1. *La Russie*, op. cit., I, p. 223.

times: I imagine myself at Versailles, a century ago." He was more than amused; in the chapel where the marriage was celebrated, and where he saw the imperial family for the first time, he admired the Greek profile of the Tsar and succumbed to the charm of this man "taller than ordinary men, by half a head"[2] and of remarkably noble bearing; he was also moved by the Tsarina's[3] indefinable attraction with her sweet, penetrating voice and by the beauty of the young bride, full of grace and purity. He was enchanted by the poetic luxury of the evening reception, embellished, it seemed to him, "by all the respect and all the care directed towards the empress. A queen is necessary at elegant entertainments."[4]

The Tsar constantly singled him out at different soirées (the festivities continued for nearly a week), leading him to one side, staying with him at length. He asked about his plans, explained his own political views and described the dramatic start to his reign. The Tsarina arranged for him to visit her private apartments. Astolphe was conquered. He forgot all his ideas about liberty and independence to become like "the bourgeois at home when they feel themselves about to be taken in by the grace and artfulness of old-fashioned men; their good taste tempts them to give way, but their

2. Ibid., I, p. 200.

3. She was the daughter of Queen Louise of Prussia, Napoleon's beautiful enemy.

4. Ibid., I, p. 246.

principles resist . . . I was battling with a similar struggle."[5] He defended himself with all his might against the power of Nicholas's attraction: he wanted to preserve an open mind.

Without the others, he might have yielded—the others being the courtiers. "It is not the prince who embarrasses you when he does you the honour of speaking to you, it is his court." Custine's idea of the role and responsibility of an aristocracy was too lofty for him not to be shocked by the submissiveness and servility of the grandees. He was surprised by these "kind of superior slaves,"[6] who were to be seen walking the streets in winter without a frockcoat to please the emperor, who liked it thought that the climate in his capital was temperate. He could not fail to notice that the Tsar's attentions brought instant celebrity. All the most important people at court threw themselves shamelessly at him. They admitted that the Tsar "supplanted their reason, their will, imagination, passion; under his onerous rule, no creature is free to breathe, to suffer or to love, outside the framework designed in advance by the supreme wisdom."[7] It was impossible not to be affected by the complete lack of any interesting conversation, except the Tsar's.

Custine was not a man of the Ancien Régime, but he had listened

5. Ibid., I, p. 264.
6. Ibid., I, p. 25.
7. Ibid., II, p. 197.

and read—notably Saint-Simon—and wasn't so naïve as to be unaware of the subtleties that could exist between respect, politeness,
subservience and servility. He also knew that in France nobility
was based on birth, thus guaranteeing the aristocracy's independence. The Russian system was quite different. Civilian society was
divided into fourteen classes—this quasi-military hierarchy was
known as the *tchinn*—and the passage from one to another could
only happen at the Tsar's behest. This institution nullified the nobility by making everyone equal before the Tsar: "It is divine right applied to the mechanism of social life."[8] Although the favours of ad-
vancement may not have been solicited, they were still fought for,
hence "the immense power to arouse passions at the disposal of the
head of state."[9] These noblemen, eaten away by ambition, paralysed
by the fear of displeasing, were both anxious and inert, totally dependent on the sovereign, and ignorant of any dignity that might
accompany their position. "Flattery is an industry like any other,
but like any other, and more than any other, it allows for only a pre-
carious existence."[10] Observing them, Custine had the impression
that the court in which they moved was "a theatre where the actors
spent their lives in dress rehearsal. Not one of them knows their
part, and the day of the performance never arrives because the di-

8. Ibid., I, p. 301.
9. Ibid., I, p. 413.
10. Ibid., II, p. 273.

rector is never satisfied with his subjects' acting."[11] The despicable sight of fear inspired by an all-powerful Nicholas stifled any desire he had to laugh. Had he nourished any illusions as to the position of the nobility or the way society worked, he would have been disabused of them by the festivities to which the Tsar invited him at Peterhov—the Marly of the tsars—built in a large park dotted with pavilions and cottages, on the Baltic coast.

The Tsar's hospitality was magnificent; every evening seven or eight hundred people dined in the English palace, a residence close to the Tsar's where the ambassadors and their suites were lodged. Custine's place was laid for these dinners, but he had no room there. A number of people envied him when two dressing-rooms in the theatre were put at his disposal, and where, thanks to his bed, which he had had the good sense to bring with him, he lacked for nothing. The ball, in the superb setting of the park embellished with fountains and waterfalls like Versailles, was simply dazzling. The trees festooned with Chinese lanterns were invisible beneath their diamond-bright decoration, making the illumination magical. The lanterns, arranged with amazing artistry, in the shape of flowers or suns, columns or walls, created a fantasy world. The wide canal resembled an "immobile stream of lava in a blazing forest."[12] It wasn't Europe or the real, modern Asia, but "the fabulous Baghdad of a

11. Ibid., I, p. 222.
12. Ibid., I, p. 318.

Thousand and One Nights." Custine admired it, but again he was afraid.

It was a rather peculiar reception. Twice a year a few carefully chosen merchants and peasants were invited to the palace with the courtiers for a masked ball which masked nothing, certainly not the social differences. At Peterhov, the noblemen wore uniforms and carried a little piece of silk under their arms, known as a Venetian coat. The mujiks—or beavers, as Custine called them—were dressed in Russian style with long Persian robes, and the merchants wore kaftans. But what troubled Custine more than anything was the silent, solemn crowd. No one laughed, no one raised a voice, silence was de rigueur and the polonaises, which were "just walks to the sound of instruments," seemed more like processions than dances. Animation and gaiety, the essentials of any fête, were lacking. Nicholas dominated the crowd from his great height, and the sea of guests divided as he passed. He crossed rooms without so much as anyone brushing against him. The political fiction that he was *opening* his palace to all his subjects, rather than raising those subjects, lowered them all to the same level. The purpose of these receptions was not to tell the peasant that he was equal to his masters but to establish by means of some despot's cruel joke that the nobleman, like the serf, was a slave in the eyes of the sovereign. From these details and from the impressions he noted at the time, Custine was to draw his conclusions.

What did absolute power imply? That is, Russian absolute power. It must be stressed that in Custine's mind, Louis XIV's absolute power and that of the Tsar's had nothing whatsoever in common. The authority of the first was limited by customs that everyone accepted and endorsed, and was, furthermore, exercised alongside the authority of an independent church and within the framework of ancient institutions, whereas the Tsar, as head of a national church ruling over a nation of children, was not even held in check by a respect for legitimacy. In France, legitimacy was "blind as necessity . . . [in Russia] it floated like a passion."[13] In St. Petersburg, where "government is despotism mitigated by murder," the master was himself afraid, which made him even more formidable. So it was impossible to compare the two régimes.

One of the most curious consequences of the Tsar's absolutism was that the sovereign was responsible for everything, including natural disasters that were completely outside his control. Hence the secrecy—incomprehensible to a Westerner—surrounding the slightest accident. "It would be inappropriate to speak of the Flood, had that catastrophe occurred under the reign of a Russian emperor."[14] Thus, during the festivities at Peterhov, a violent gust of wind capsized a large number of boats that were crossing the gulf. How many casualties were there? Two hundred? Five hundred?

13. Ibid., I, p. 314.
14. Ibid., I, p. 347.

Two thousand? How could they be counted? No one knew, no one mentioned it. To do so would have been to "hurt the empress and to accuse the emperor."[15] It was said, in spite of evidence to the contrary—at the Emperor's ball, the Sardinian ambassador lost his watch and Custine lost his purse—that there were no thieves at Peterhov. Never "would a mujik steal a flower from the garden of his Tsar."[16] The police never mentioned a murder, the slightest disorder, the merest incident, for they, too, were afraid and applied themselves "with all their power to maintaining [the master] in his tutelary gaiety."[17] No one wanted to risk the Tsar's displeasure, particularly since it was so easy to say nothing. Besides, "of all the faculties of the intelligence, the only one valued here is tact. Imagine an entire nation bent beneath the yoke of this drawing-room virtue. Picture a whole people as prudent as a diplomat with his fortune to make, and you will have an idea of the pleasures of conversation in Russia . . . Russia is a nation of mutes."[18]

For a man like Custine, who spent his life in salons, conversation was one of the essential pleasures of living. Such a pastime, however, involving curiosity, irreverence and knowledge can only flourish in a climate of freedom. It was no accident that the eigh-

15. Ibid., I, p. 322.
16. Ibid., I, p. 312.
17. Ibid., I, p. 346.
18. Ibid., I, p. 347.

teenth century—the century in which everything was called into question—saw the salons at their finest, or that the art of conversation waned in France after the Revolution: too great a social variety made inference impossible; for a conversation to be brilliant, all the participants must share the same vocabulary and have no need to spell things out. Everyone recognised Custine's prodigious talent in this field. Barbey d'Aurevilly admired the way he talked "like a man who had known Mme de Staël and who has retained the perfume of this fiery rose of conversation. He is the fruit tree of anecdote! Shake it and the anecdotes fall, tracing a divine curve as they do so! He should be seen at dessert! Pulling the whole of Europe person by person, out of his pocket..."[19] Imagine, then, his dismay in this country where "one neither writes nor speaks ... [where] no one ever proffers a word which might really interest anyone ... where all the resources of the language are worn out by erasing ideas and sentiment from conversation,"[20] where aptitude in lying was natural and openness dangerous since the questioner became responsible for what he had heard. It was this constant presence of fear which made of Russia the empire of facades.

There was only an appearance of civilisation in this country where duplicity triumphed, and Custine's malaise, which he always declared himself unable to define, was exacerbated by the fact

19. Barbey d'Aurevilly, op. cit., letter to Trébutien, March 1854.
20. *La Russie*, op. cit., I, pp. 202–209.

that no one spoke spontaneously, for fear of expressing what they thought and also because no one—at least among those he frequented—spoke their mother tongue. There was no mother tongue in Russia, because Russian wasn't spoken in sophisticated circles, and the French, which was generally used, was stiff and inaccurate.

This Frenchifying bothered Custine. In the first place, it was deceptive. "The sensitivity of their ear, the various sounds of their vowels, the multitude of consonants, the different kinds of hissing which need to be exercised in order to speak their language, all accustom the [Russians] from childhood to conquering the difficulties of pronunciation. Even those who know only a few French words pronounce them as we do. Thus they create for us a perfidious illusion."[21] It was misleading because it made it impossible to know if the speaker was making mistakes on purpose or through ignorance. Misleading, also, because the use of this foreign language, even by those who knew it well, was like an added disguise. The savagery of the country's mores was masked by an idiom that didn't correspond to reality. The words changed their meaning—thus "to give permission" to live in Siberia meant to send into exile—which facilitated lying; and this contrived vocabulary gave the impression of two nations struggling with each other: "Russia such as she is, and Russia as she would like to be seen in Europe."[22] Custine suffered

21. Ibid., II, p. 230.
22. Ibid., I, p. 303.

particularly from these questions of language because they added to the detachment that he found so disagreeable, making it all the more difficult to place the Russians with whom he was in contact. For him language was an essential element of a person.

He had already been irritated in 1829 by certain writers who Anglicised or Germanised French, and by fashionable women who engaged English nannies to look after their children who "speak English as if they were wearing powder."[23] Where there is no language, there is no thought. "How can natural intelligence come to light in a society where one speaks four languages before knowing one? When you have to translate into your own language, as the Russians for whom their language is a foreign one must, this borrowed style hampers spontaneous thought and destroys simplicity of expression . . . The confusion of languages favours obscurity of thought; mediocrity takes advantage of this and superiority is offended."[24]

Custine judged Russian writers unfairly whose works he couldn't read in the original. Pushkin, to whom he devoted only a few dismissive lines, seemed to him too subjected to foreign influence, less Slav and less interesting than Mickiewicz; he doesn't mention Gogol, his contemporary, though he should have been attracted by his fantastic imagination, his taste for satire, and his torment in the face

23. Ibid., I, p. 367; *Lettres à Varnhagen*, op. cit., p. 320.
24. Ibid., I, pp. 366 and 368.

of the forces of evil, made all the more acute by secret desires to which, unlike Custine, he never dared admit.[25] Dostoyevsky had not yet published, and Tolstoy was eleven years old at the time of Custine's visit. Custine would never read *Anna Karenina* or *War and Peace*. He would never meet Tolstoy's creation, Levin, so uncompromising, determined to be Russian and exasperated by the way waiters stuck a French name on every dish, and the French lessons his sister-in-law imposed on her children. It was not in Tolstoy, however, that he would have encountered the extreme violence he feared, or his own revulsion from the political régime. He would have had to turn to the pages of Dostoyevsky, for whom the image of the autocratic hierarchy was epitomised by an imperial messenger whipping his coachman on the back of the neck, while the coachman in turn lashed the horses into a full gallop.[26]

Custine hadn't been in Russia for a month before his ambivalence towards the Tsar, the two-faced Janus, had turned to open hostility. Even before he left St. Petersburg, he had begun to see only the side of the Tsar on which were engraved "the words violence, exile,

25. Gogol was translated into French and English after Custine went to Russia, in the early 1850s. Although Mérimée may have praised his work, I do not know of Custine having written anything about it. Besides, there is nothing to indicate that he read Turgenev or that his curiosity was aroused by Dostoyevsky.

26. Dostoyevsky, *Journal d'un écrivain* (Gallimard, 1951), p. 267.

oppression, or Siberia, the equivalent to them all." What brought about this hardening of attitude was a letter written by Princess Trubetskoy that he came to read. The fate of this unfortunate woman shook him as only a tragedy which touches a person closely can. His memories of the Revolution, the Princess's letter and Telenev's account—a story which Custine pretends to have been given by a young writer, but which is undoubtedly from his own pen— are, as it were, in parentheses in *La Russie en 1839*; in them, Custine reaches into the very depths of his own soul. In these digressions, he doesn't describe Russia, he describes himself. Sometimes the two themes are interwoven, most particularly in his telling of the Trubetskoy tragedy.

Sergey Trubetskoy, scion of a princely family going back to the fourteenth century—a family with which Custine could therefore identify—was one of the instigators of the Decembrist uprising. Nicholas condemned him to fourteen years of forced labour in a mine in the Urals, and to live the rest of his life in a colony in Siberia. His wife was the daughter of a French emigré, a baron Laval, attached to Alexander I's court as a reader of the French papers and whose wife held a well-known salon in St. Petersburg. She asked for the "favour" of following him. In order to join him, she travelled thousands of leagues by telega, an open carriage without springs, primitive enough to withstand the Russian roads. The prince himself had made the journey with his feet in irons. The couple, "quite distantly united" in happier times, were drawn together by their terrible trials and the first of their five children was born in Siberia.

The Decembrists' children were taken in as serfs to the Crown. They had only a number instead of a name since their parents had lost theirs along with their civil and political rights. They could be given a new name, made up of their patronym; this name was only sanctioned if the child was separated from its parents and brought up by the state. The Trubetskoys, like all political exiles (only one of them allowed his daughter to be brought up in a national institution), kept their children with them. When the oldest was seven, the princess "humbly begged" the emperor to allow him to be sent to the town to be properly educated. The Tsar refused: "The children of galley-slaves, galley-slaves themselves, are always sufficiently knowledgeable."[27]

Seven years later, having served his sentence, Prince Trubetskoy was sent to a remote colony, more than a hundred leagues from any other dwelling. The princess, despairing at the thought of her fragile, sickly children growing up in this snowy solitude, surrounded by ice and spongy heathland, wrote a second letter to the Tsar, asking to be allowed to live near Tobolsk, Irkutsk or Orenburg, if only to be near an apothecary. A copy of this letter, sent to her family, was passed to Custine. When Nicholas I heard about it, he replied

27. *La Russie*, op. cit., II, p. 28.

that he was surprised anyone dared still talk to him about this family.[28] Custine's indignation at such disdainful cruelty is not surprising but the intensity of his sympathy for the mother is fascinating.

He doesn't mention the father's distress or the children's misery. Only the mother strikes his imagination, a mother who could have been his, for hadn't the princess something of Delphine? A woman indifferent to her husband but able to draw from within the courage to risk suffering in order to look after him evoked Delphine going to La Force to comfort her husband, knowing full well that in so doing she might be arrested. Princess Trubetskoy, in despair at being unable to look after her children's health, is again Delphine, powerless in prison to come to Astolphe when he fell seriously ill.

The rage which overcame Custine when he read the princess's letter was hardly rational. After all, he was fully aware of the fate of political prisoners. During a conversation with Nicholas I when the Tsar mentioned the uprising at the start of his reign, Custine was not particularly shocked by the energy with which it had been suppressed. Now suddenly, he is disgusted and horrified by the harshness of a man whose will and character he admired a few days earlier: "No more hesitation, no more uncertainty; for me the Emperor

28. The princess's fate was also mentioned by Vigny in his poem *Wanda*. The unfortunate woman died in Siberia, whereas her husband survived long enough to benefit from Alexander II's favour on his accession, and he was able to end his days in Moscow.

Nicholas has finally been judged . . . May God forgive him; fortunately I will not see him again! I would tell him what I think about this matter which would be the last degree of insolence . . . Besides, by such gratuitous boldness, I would give the final blow to the unfortunate people whose defence I go to unsolicited, and I would lose myself."[29] This declaration—rhetoric, since Custine was clearly not going to confront the Tsar—in which he oscillates between attack and withdrawal, illustrates his torment. Whenever he turns inward, he comes up against the fundamental problem of how to face up to violence. With what weapons? What are the risks one can take for oneself or for others?

The same question is examined in a short story, included in *La Russie*, about a savage peasants' revolt. The serfs slit the throats of men, women and children before they in turn were massacred or deported. Custine evokes the most terrifying image of his early childhood: bloody human remains hanging from sabres, pikes bearing the heads of women, hair flying, bits of bodies pierced by pitchforks. There is also Xénie: the gentle, compassionate daughter of a sadistic steward of the estate. She is threatened by the mere fact of being her father's daughter. A young peasant, Fédor, who secretly loves her, protects her. She too reminds one of Delphine. During the course of the story she stares down the mob to save Fédor's child. Fédor, of course, is inspired by Jérôme, Delphine's humble admirer.

29. Ibid., II, p. 33.

A Taste for Freedom

This story, which is entirely unexpected in the middle of Custine's book, is interesting not only because of its autobiographical overtones, but also because of its terrifying impartiality. Everyone is cruel: noblemen, stewards and peasants. Human evil is absolute. The exception, Xénie, who represents the good, goes mad. Custine had to go to Russia, a country where merciless order was imposed at the cost of human lives, in order to admit to himself a certain justification for the Revolution, excusing its excesses. This creates an inner tension which makes the beauty of *La Russie*.

Before going to Russia, he wondered what he would have done during the Revolution; after a month in Russia, the question took on broader dimensions. What would he have done had he been persecuted? Would he have been a complaisant victim, a despicable, unworthy martyr, or would he have stood up heroically? It was of little importance whether the executioner represented the people or a despot. He suddenly realised it was not the political side or the constitutional arguments that counted, but the dignity of man. A dignity he saw nowhere in Russia: not in the Tsar, degraded by his inability to forgive, not in his subjects, drunk on slavery. On leaving St. Petersburg, to travel further into the country, he would have eyes only for persecution which he detected everywhere. He had already mourned the political régime. What he was to describe now was the misery of oppression in all its detail; his subject was Siberia.

A reader with some idea of geography might be surprised that, for Custine, Siberia began at the gates of St. Petersburg. To put too fine a point on it would be to fail to understand Custine, the passionate observer. Siberia to him wasn't a province, but a state of mind. Siberia begins as soon as one enters the empire of fear. As we have seen, he had felt fear ever since his arrival in the capital, not only in the streets but in the salons and even at court, where uniformity was imposed on everyone and the identical slavishness of rich and poor alike proved the all-powerfulness of the superior authority.

One might think that once he was out of the city, rejoicing in the freedom of nature, Custine would have breathed easily at last, but he did nothing of the kind. Quite the contrary. He was always watched, in this instance by the *feldjaeger*. The *feldjaeger*, both indispensable and unbearable, represented power. His job was to transmit the emperor's orders. His life was spent on the roads, and occasionally a distinguished foreigner—like Custine, for instance —would be granted the favour of the services of this "living telegraph"[30] for the duration of his journey. He wore a uniform. His obvious prestige made it easier to get new horses at the coaching inns, guaranteed the service of postilions whose wages he negotiated, and his presence alone was evidence of the importance of the traveller he was escorting. He exasperated and frightened Custine, who, far from being flattered by such a mark of consideration, understood

30. Ibid., I, p. 286.

only too well that his every movement, his every reaction, his every sign of interest would be immediately reported. He realised that the presence of this guide-spy-protector "with frail limbs, a wasp waist, an upright, military bearing, sharp grey eyes, pinched lips . . . both timid and frightening, like hatred crushed by fear,"[31] denied him any real freedom of action or thought.

Before analysing Custine's impressions, it is important to consider what he called "the material life," by which he meant the appalling travelling conditions; they must have contributed to his pessimistic vision. If Dumas's and Gautier's descriptions appear to be written about a different country it must be because they came to Russia twenty years later and were able to travel by railway. Russian trains were surprisingly comfortable. In France passengers were threatened by asphyxia, by hunger or by a burst bladder, whereas in Russia the toilets at the end of every carriage and more elaborate ones with running water *à l'anglaise* in each first-class compartment meant that the passengers could take advantage of the well-provisioned buffets at all the stations with no anxiety. To watch the landscape unfolding through the window as the train travelled peacefully along made the countryside seem tranquil and cheerful, whereas poor Custine, shut up in his carriage, not only had difficulty seeing but also was in constant fear of hitting his head on the hood,

31. Ibid., II, p. 292.

so violently was he shaken about. Had he had the hood removed, he would have risked being thrown out; all this amidst the postilions' wild cries and the whiplashing rained on the poor horses by the coachman.

When they stopped, there were no inns, "no beds, not even straw to lie on."[32] He had to have his mattress filled with strong-smelling hay, which aggravated his headaches. The food was foul; there was neither white bread nor wine, or even water to drink. It was necessary to travel with large pitchers of seltzer water, a real inconvenience because despite being wrapped in straw, the pitchers often broke. Russians travelled huge distances at a time precisely to avoid these difficulties, but Custine had such bad migraines that he was obliged to stop every twenty-four hours. Conditions alone are enough to explain the traveller's lack of enthusiasm, but worse still was the journey Custine was taking in his head, nourished by boredom and constant fear.

The infinite space unfolding in front of him did nothing to liberate him. He felt captive in a dreary, sad, funereal desert. Travelling under a heavy sky, like a lid overhead, through cold, harsh landscapes, he gave a cry of despair: "What a country . . . where nature counts for nothing, for nature must be forgotten in a limitless plain, with-

32. Ibid., II, p. 246.

out colour, without shape, without line apart from the never changing horizon traced by the leaden circle of the sky on the iron surface of the land . . ."[33] He is immediately caught up again with his obsession about the impossibility of applying words to things: "One cannot say road about a ploughed field, a rough stretch of grass, a furrow in the sand, or a chasm of mire . . ."[34] A nest of insects or a pile of dung could not be described as an inn. Clusters of dilapidated little houses reflected in grey ponds could not deserve the name of town.

Not only did the sterile landscape so lacking in majesty, this "immense swamp,"[35] bore him, and the discomfort of the journey destroy the poetry of the steppe, but the landowner in him was shocked by the sickly woods, the meagre pine trees and the waste of natural resources. Most of all he suffered from the fact that Russia seemed to him an intellectual desert. There was nothing to stimulate the mind. There were no sites to visit in the countryside, no works of art to study in the cities. The immensity of the country caused isolation and impoverishment. "A vast expanse of land is and always will be the greatest obstacle to the circulation of ideas since the earth cannot be furrowed in every way like the sea; water, which at first

33. Ibid., II, pp. 256 and 293.
34. Ibid., II, pp. 246–247.
35. Ibid., II, p. 52.

glance seems destined to divide the men of this world, is what unites them. Marvellous problem . . ."[36] In the midst of all this nothingness, every twenty or thirty leagues identical little towns would appear with no distinctive characteristics; every entity needed to be self-sufficient and always consisted of a group of huts, simple heaps of grey planks, offering the traveller no distraction. Arrival in Moscow broke the monotony of the journey although Custine's initial enthusiasm was short-lived. "At first sight, the effect of Moscow is prodigious; it would be the most beautiful town for a dispatch rider galloping around the walls of all the churches, convents, palaces and fortresses . . . ,"[37] but as soon as he reached the heart of the city— for unlike St. Petersburg, and despite its size which enclosed fields, lakes and woods, Moscow did have a centre—that is to say, as soon as he reached the Kremlin, he was gripped by the now familiar terror. The Kremlin appeared to him like "the citadel of ghosts." The present had frightened him at the Tsar's court; the past, as he understood it in Moscow, expressed "war supported by fear . . . everything in the architecture of the Kremlin has a symbolic meaning, intentional or not; but the reality that remains when you have overcome your first fear and penetrated to the heart of all this savage magnificence is a heap of pompously named palaces and cathedrals

36. Ibid., II, p. 179.
37. Ibid., II, p. 164.

and dungeons. The Russians, however hard they try, never leave their prison. The climate is tyranny's accomplice. The cold in this country does not allow the building of vast churches where the faithful would freeze as they prayed . . . the dark cathedrals of the Kremlin with their narrow vaulting and thick walls resemble cellars; they are painted prisons just as the palaces are gilded jails."[38]

Although it is summer, his description is one of winter. In order to illustrate the sinister uniformity of the countryside, he wrote: "The snow always looks the same; the shroud in which the earth is wrapped is white whether it is six inches or six feet deep . . . For a man who knows only icy plains with sparse evergreens, every cold, deserted land represents his land."[39] In the middle of August, he felt "winter and death hovering over these sites: the northern light and climate lend things a funereal hue; after a few weeks, the horrified traveller thinks he has been buried alive; he would like to rip up his shroud and flee this unenclosed cemetery which has no limits but the horizon; he struggles with all his might to raise the leaden veil that separates him from the living."[40] How can this fantastical vision be explained? In Custine's mind, Russia was Siberia and Siberia was a

38. Ibid., II, p. 102.
39. Ibid., II, p. 354.
40. Ibid., II, pp. 293–294.

place of exile. Real and imaginary images clashed. His obsession with exile and its accompanying icy train of pain and death triumphed over reality. Not surprisingly, because it is quite true, there is something lugubrious about the limitless expanse of the vast Russian plain.

There is a real difference of character between American space, symbolising freedom, and Russian space, symbolising punishment. To go to America, to travel around America is symbolic of hope, optimism and discovery. To take the road to Russia is to embark on "the empire of profound silence," to cross "great empty spaces, barren countryside, solitary towns," and only see "prudent physiognomies."[41] In Russia one travels east to be deported. Siberia has been colonised by political prisoners or criminals. There is no such thing as going east for pleasure or adventure. Custine succumbed to fear even though he was travelling freely, because he wanted to, out of curiosity. The mere fact of displacement evoked the hell of Siberia which "with all its ghosts . . . had the effect on him of a basilisk's stare on a fascinated bird."[42] This obsession churned in him a constant feeling of guilt. He was no longer tormented by doubt about his own moral strength; now his sin became that of insensibility, of indifference and lack of solidarity with the victims of torture. "I am

41. Ibid., II, p. 440.
42. Ibid., II, pp. 292–293.

making this journey for my own pleasure . . . but what were the feelings and thoughts of so many unfortunate people who made it before me? I am seeking distraction and entertainment in the wake of other people's despair."[43] He felt this most acutely on meeting a group of six Polish exiles, who, chained together and guarded by twelve mounted Cossacks, were advancing along the road to Siberia. Because of the arbitrary nature of judgement, the absence of witnesses, anonymity and the inevitability of being forgotten, these men were victims of a far worse fate than French convicts would have been. An exemplary death has meaning; to disappear in the Siberian desert without a trace seemed to Custine to add the whole weight of the imagination to the severity of the law. From the shelter of his closed carriage, he saw them, observed them and proceeded without stopping, without offering the consolation of even a look or a word to these unfortunate men who would die, abandoned by everyone.

Why didn't Custine stop? Because he was afraid of the *feldjaeger* who was watching him, staring at him, with his very presence reminding him that he wasn't free to criticise the autocracy by expressing compassion. Humiliated by and ashamed of his fear and submission, he felt contaminated, infected by the effects of despotism on its victims. He went on his way tortured by the presence of

43. Ibid.

his grey-eyed tormentor with the thin, pale lips and sugary voice who was as "frightening as a monster."[44] This feeling of guilt wasn't an affectation. In various degrees it haunted Custine throughout his life, and the visit to Russia summed up all the nuances of his discomfort but gave him, at the end of the journey, the chance to regain his dignity through an awakening of courage and effective action.

Back in Moscow, after his stay in Nizhni, Custine was preparing to take the road back to St. Petersburg before returning home via Berlin when, on the day of his departure, his servant awoke him at four o'clock in the morning to tell him of the arrest of a Frenchman, a young man called Louis Pernet. Pernet had just returned from a trip to the north of Russia with another Frenchman whom Custine had met earlier with the governor of Nizhni. The first thing Custine did was to go to Pernet's companion, to whom he always refers as M.R., who prudently refused any kind of intervention: the unfortunate Pernet was in prison. It would be impossible to reach him. It would be best to do nothing. Custine immediately decided that the matter was even more serious than he had imagined.

At the risk of displeasing his *feldjaeger*—he was reassured by the fact that he was defending a Frenchman—he put off his departure and went to see the French consul. The consul, having become more

44. Ibid., II, p. 338.

Russian than the Russians, refused to intervene on the pretext that Monsieur Pernet hadn't bothered to register at the consulate on passing through Moscow. Far from letting the matter drop, Custine then set all his intelligence and energy to helping his compatriot. He made "courage out of fear."[45] Just as he had often pictured his mother in jail, so he imagined the torment of the "poor unknown man gripped by the phantoms of solitude and prison" to the point where he eventually identified with him; "I too was guilty, exiled, beaten; I shared the prisoner's madness."[46] Wherever he turned he encountered inertia and cowardice. People warned him: he was laying himself open "to a lot of trouble; perhaps to something worse," they added with a knowing air.[47]

Realising that he was getting nowhere, Custine decided to ask for the help of the ambassador, M. de Barante, and so left for St. Petersburg. Barante, very close to Mme de Staël and Mme Récamier, was an old friend. He listened with attention and strongly assured Custine that he would deal with the situation. The meeting heartened Astolphe and, in his words, "dissipated the phantoms of his imagination."[48] Having at last regained his moral integrity, Custine spent

45. Ibid., I, p. 205.
46. Ibid., II, p. 385.
47. Ibid., II, p. 387.
48. Ibid., II, p. 391. As if to prove that the whole thing was not imaginary, Custine tells the end of the story at length: the release of Pernet and, more particularly, a description in the greatest and most awful detail of his detention.

a few more days in St. Petersburg before leaving, and by October was delighted to find himself at Ems, surrounded by calm and the graceful Rhineland country. He took the waters to recover from his exhaustion and by year's end launched himself once more into the activity, luxury, gaiety and elegance of Saint-Gratien.

14

The Evidence

Custine didn't set to work immediately. In the first place, it wasn't his style. He claimed, in some kind of coquettish, authorial way, that his slowness was due to laziness and it has to be said that writing this kind of travel book did require lengthy reflection. In the case of *La Russie en 1839* there was an additional twofold problem. There was the question of correctness: despite his indignation, did Custine have the right to betray the hospitality and trust of the Tsar and all the different people who had received him and helped him? Furthermore, wouldn't the appearance of the book, which could only be critical, damage the interests of his friend Ignatius Gurowski by giving Nicholas I a pretext for refusing him pardon and the restitution of his rights?

In 1840, Custine made a last effort on behalf of the young man. He took him to Ems, where he would have the opportunity of presenting him to the Empress, and to ask, once more, for justice. He failed completely. He then realised the uselessness of his attempts. Nothing now stood between him and the writing of the book; his conscience demanded it and he went to the trouble of justifying himself in the introduction. He did so with the assurance of one who knows himself right, and stressed that he was not tied to the state by duty, sentiment or social custom.

To write a book of the scope which he envisaged required a certain calm, and Ignatius's escapades (his public attack on a peer of France and his elopement with the infanta) kept Custine in a state of extreme agitation. As we have seen, the years leading up to the book's publication weren't happy ones for him. The *ménage à trois* disintegrated. To entertain his far-off friends, Custine may well have boasted of the repercussions of Gurowski's idyll, but he could not hide the irritation and sadness caused by the attractive young man's defection. Besides, all the fuss rebounded on him and tarnished his name. "Custine has fled to Italy, having helped *his friend*, the Pole Gurowski, to carry off the Infanta of Spain,"[1] Balzac wrote to Mme Hanska. To be sure, there was no scandal to compare with the one of 1824, but Custine was too sensitive not to feel a certain animosity building up around him. Mérimée's mocking remarks

1. Balzac, *Lettres à Mme Hanska* (Robert Laffont, Collection Bouquins, 1990), I, p. 570.

about the incident were repeated in every salon. "I am tired of taking the trouble to amuse a crowd of people who delight in all that hurts me, and who are hurt by all that I rejoice in," he wrote to Sophie Gay. "I am not so foolish as to expect friendship from a large number of people, but however indifferent you may feel, when you go regularly to someone's house, you owe him consideration and I have been unable to obtain from them what everyone has a right to expect." After the commotion of Ignatius's marriage to the infanta, Custine resigned himself to leaving France.

He rented the rue de La Rochefoucauld and put Saint-Gratien up for sale. It was "too much of a Paris house" to be a refuge. In fact, when, after a shouting match, the valet Antonio's sister left her husband—one of the Saint-Gratien "moneybags"—even the village people began to talk and to make life unpleasant for the inhabitants of the château. Custine felt implicated in the incident because he treated Antonio as a member of the family. Officially—according to the detailed account he gave in a long letter to Victor Hugo, a cautious financial expert—his decision to leave Paris resulted from money troubles. He had lost half his fortune. "In the first place," he explained, "I began by spending more than my income: no fortune can withstand this prolonged disorder"; then the minister Thiers shook "his old confidence in France's destiny." He placed his capital in Holland but the two men, recommended by his bank to pay the money into the account, were crooks. One shot himself, the other ran away to America. Custine came to the conclusion that he must

"sell Saint-Gratien before people think I am obliged to be rid of it
. . . I am accused of being bizarre, of having manias, it little matters:
you think I am reasonable. I prefer to be seen as an imbecile of a
traveller than to expose myself to the pity of fools . . . the compassion of a superior man is a blessing from heaven, that of mediocre
men is like the kick of an ass, which does not mean that I take myself
for a beaten lion: not all the donkey's kicks are aimed at lions."[2]

He wanted to change his way of life. The departure of Ignatius
brought calm and order back into his existence, "part willingly, part
forcibly."[3] The young man had stirred up the old couple's ways
and brought movement and gaiety to their establishment, attracted
new faces and facilitated their spicier entertainments. Without him
Saint-Gratien would mean suffering "the inconveniences of an existence that has lost its advantages," he explained to Sophie Gay. Better the dignity of a serious life than to drag on with a "boringly frivolous" one. Besides, Custine was now determined to write his book.

The two friends left together for the shores of Lake Annecy, taking with them their dog, Galaor, mistaken for a little white pig by
their Savoyard neighbours, and their copy of Rousseau's *Confessions*. Perhaps due to the influence of the bishop of Annecy and the
authorities of the region who came to visit them, Custine saw his
exile as penance for his free-and-easy life. Despite immense inner

2. Letter from Custine to Victor Hugo, Victor Hugo Museum, Paris.
3. *Lettres à Varnhagen*, op. cit., p. 423.

resources, and without really being able to admit it to himself, he suffered considerably from being out of the swim during this long retreat. For the first time, comparing himself to an old horse put out to pasture, he mentions the effects of age and complains of the isolation inherent in long trips. But to recover from the Pole's leaving him, to lick his almost unmentionable wounds, about which he wrote openly to Varnhagen, he needed to be further removed from the Parisian gossips.

In the autumn, the two friends left Savoy for Italy, "neutral terrain between the earth and the sky,"[4] and settled in Milan where in a monotonous existence free from surprises, "sterile as a journey through moorland,"[5] their only entertainment was the opera. They spent seven months there which was to seem like a long, long convalescence; in a state, Custine wrote to Varnhagen, "which resembled sleep; a reverie between memory and hope . . . this sojourn is for me a kind of remedy for the soul and the body; it is like the old Parisian cure which prescribed chicken broth when you were agitated."[6]

His book, meanwhile, was progressing. He worked hard to "unmask the colossus" with what little ammunition he had at his disposal, as he explained to Victor Hugo, and often, when he mistrusted his memory, he asked for old letters back from his friends. (He had

4. Ibid., p. 431.
5. Ibid., p. 435.
6. Ibid., p. 431.

sent his letters from Russia via diplomatic pouch to be able to write freely.) Back in Saint-Gingolphe, near Evian, he wrote the last line of his book on 10 September 1842 and announced to Sophie Gay: "It needs to be revised, pruned, corrected but the edifice is standing." He could return to Paris and rediscover with pleasure, as he wrote to Varnhagen, "my paving stones, . . . my language, my changing sky . . . and a number of people to whom I have no need to explain myself."[7]

His book, called simply *La Russie en 1839*, was published by Amyot in 1843. To his surprise and great joy, it was an immediate commercial, although not critical, success. This proved a far better remedy than chicken broth. Custine's ambition had always been to occupy a place among the respected writers of the day and to be counted by them as a peer. He had never quite succeeded: the greatest—Hugo and Balzac, for example—always treated him like a little boy. He often had to be satisfied with condescending reviews and it pained him not to be recognised. For, at bottom, and he knew it, he was the marquis de Custine, the famous marquis, not Custine, the writer. In 1843, the doors of the club were finally opened to him.

People interested in Russia awaited his book all the more impatiently because, on coming home, Custine hadn't disguised his disappointment. In a letter to an old friend, Mme de Courbonne, after

7. Ibid., p. 443.

his return, he announced, "Everything seemed new, instructive, surprising and above all calming; I assure you that when you have seen Russia, you thank heaven for living anywhere else."[8] Well before publication, Balzac, predicting that Custine would produce a "terrible" book, ordered Mme Hanska not to write to him for any reason: "That is absolute and you will soon know why,"[9] and he must have congratulated himself that Custine hadn't made the detour to visit his beloved. It was much worse when the book came out. Terrified for the woman he loved, who was still living under the Tsar's authority, and fearful lest his friendship with the marquis might become known in Russia, Balzac struck his intended dedication to Custine from *Le Colonel Chabert*. Had he been able with one stroke of the pen to eradicate any trace of his friendship with Custine, he would have done so with a light heart.

The book was bold, accessible and persuasive and caused such a commotion that it would have been impossible to ignore it. The evidence carried results, and not only in Paris. Translations were immediately put on sale in England, Germany and Sweden. "Paris," Custine explained, "was full of Russians who started to screech like eagles, or rather like geese—imagine the noise!! They forced everyone to read it . . . My fear, when the first edition was printed, was that the book would fall like a stone to the bottom of the water; I

8. Letter dated 4 November 1842, *Revue de France*, op. cit., p. 737.

9. Balzac, *Lettres à Mme Hanska*, op. cit., p. 507.

dreaded the clever silence of the men I was attacking: but I am reassured on that point, their clumsy rage surpasses all my hopes!"[10] People fell on the four volumes, costing 30 francs. The first edition, with a run of three thousand copies, was sold out in a few months. "The craze is a rare good fortune. Given the present state of the bookshops, and a work as long and expensive as this, I rejoice in it, as a man little accustomed to public approval,"[11] the happy author admitted to Varnhagen. In November the three thousand copies of a second edition, cheaper by half and in a smaller format, went just as quickly despite silence from the press and the existence of four Belgian pirate editions. Two editions were sold in two years in Great Britain and three in Germany. The success was sustained as further editions appeared regularly until 1854, a year in which the Crimean War lent the text an added topical interest. Custine was then asked to produce a popular edition to be used as propaganda for Napoleon III's foreign policy. It would be the last one of the century.

The French critics may have been slow to declare themselves, but the Poles, especially those living in Paris, expressed their enthusiasm as soon as the book appeared. "This book is done to console us for all our sufferings . . . it is written to detach forever from Russia good men of every country and every opinion, even those who put

10. *Lettres à Varnhagen*, op. cit., pp. 456 and 470.
11. Ibid., p. 463.

their hopes in absolutism,"[12] wrote Mickiewicz's translator. The reaction in Poland itself was more lukewarm: Custine didn't disguise his contempt for a nation that had been unable to protect its own liberty, and his friendship with Mickiewicz and Chopin had failed to convince him of the very real originality of Polish culture. The English, finding a certain pleasure in this attack against a rival power, warmly welcomed *La Russie en 1839*. In France, instead of taking the lead, journalists followed the public, and even then only gave a very one-sided view of the work: some were only interested in the religious questions the book raised, others in the occasion and suitability of publication. The most serious, like Saint-Marc Girardin in *Le Journal des débats*, wrote an exposé of their own opinions on Russia, so that Custine seemed to be more a point of departure for their digressions than a subject for discussion.

Obviously Russian reactions were the most interesting. The Russians in Paris, as Custine remarked, were unanimous in their indignation. How could they not have been? Even if they had agreed with Custine, they were too concerned about keeping their properties and their jobs to risk provoking the Tsar by applauding the severity of his critic. Reforming Russians and, even more to the point, revolutionary ones, like the philosopher Alexander Herzen, were of course unable to publish their opinions. Herzen noted secretly in his

---

12. Christian Ostrowski, *Lettres slaves* (P. Amyot, 1857), pp. 119–120, in Cadot, op. cit., p. 253.

diary that Custine's book was the most interesting document and the most intelligent book written by a foreigner about his country. "He acts on me like torture, like a stone crushing my chest; I do not see his mistakes because the basis of his judgement is sound."[13]

In Russia, "this book . . . provoked terrible anger," according to the duchesse de Dino, Talleyrand's niece and a friend of Custine from youth. "The Emperor reads it attentively, speaks of it with disdain, and is, at bottom, outraged."[14] Another witness confirmed that the Tsar ended by throwing the book violently to the ground shouting, "He is despicable . . . M. de Custine, you present yourself to me as a legitimist, you win my confidence by deceit, then you deliver me and my people as a sacrifice to Louis-Philippe."[15] To add insult to injury, this Custine had had the audacity to claim that Nicholas was developing a paunch.[16] In revenge, Nicholas banished Ignatius Gurowski's sister from court and exiled his brother, Adam, who went to live in New York where he became a journalist for the *New York Herald*.

No refutations were published in Russia, as if to prove Custine right. The Tsar initially even wanted to allow the book to circulate in Russia "to show what little importance he attached to it," then

13. Cadot, op. cit., p. 255.

14. Ibid., p. 230.

15. Ibid., p. 238.

16. Princesse Mathilde, quoted by the Goncourts; *Journal* (Robert Laffont, Collection Bouquins, 1989), II, p. 43.

changed his mind and ordered all copies to be seized from the book-shops. The usual silence fell. Naturally the book was read clandestinely, but this serious and therefore dangerous subject was never discussed except in whispers or tête-à-tête. Even Balzac, the cautious lover, couldn't resist getting a copy to Mme Hanska whilst warning her to be very careful—neither to lend it nor talk about it.

Abroad the Russian government waged a lively campaign against the insolent marquis, albeit without upsetting him because, as we have seen, he was delighted by all the noisy protests which were hardly hurtful, coming as they often did from doubtful characters. "It is a pity that Custine has not yet encountered intelligent or appropriate criticism," Turgenev admitted.[17] To counter his opinions, it was most often argued that he had spent too little time in Russia and didn't speak the language. Many years later, Dostoyevsky, in turn, condemned "books written on returning from Russia by viscounts, barons and above all marquis, tens of thousands of copies of which circulate in Europe . . . [in which] the French traveller decides to study Russia in depth and in detail and sets out at once for Moscow. There he glances at the Kremlin, thinks about Napoleon, sings the praises of tea, of the healthy beauty of the people, anguishes over their corruption . . . protests against Peter the Great and takes the opportunity to tell his readers the story of his own

17. Quoted by Nora, in *Lettres de Russie*, op. cit., p. 406.

life, full of the most extraordinary adventures."[18] Nevertheless Custine's and Dostoyevsky's opinions coincided with remarkable frequency. Dostoyevsky was writing more than twenty years after Custine's journey, but basically—at least until the emancipation of the serfs in 1861—little had changed during that time within the empire.

Dostoyevsky was too much of a nationalist not to be wounded by Custine's contempt, if only for Russian literature, and too politically minded not to protest the blindness of a visitor who, having seen only boyars and peasants, had nothing to say about the activities of the small circles of intellectuals bubbling with ideas and plans for reform, to which the apprentice novelist belonged at precisely the time of Custine's visit. This was unfair criticism since it would have been quite impossible for a foreigner to infiltrate these semi-clandestine meetings. All the same, on matters of language, behaviour, cruelty towards men and animals, or even about architecture and urbanisation, the two men were in complete agreement, which adds weight to Custine's arguments. It also goes to show that if his

18. Dostoyevsky, *Journal d'un écrivain*, op. cit., pp. 12 ff. Dostoyevsky doesn't mention Custine by name—and it must be remembered that although Arlincourt and Julvécourt were both viscounts, Dumas was also a marquis (de La Pailleterie)—but the reference to the number of copies can only apply to Custine.

text can be applied in the abstract to Stalin's U.S.S.R., it is, above all, a judgement of nineteenth-century Russia.

It has been seen how the artificial use of French irritated Custine. Dostoyevsky also reacted violently to this Franco-Russian jargon exclusive to Russia: French as spoken by Russians was "a dead language, unnatural and contrived, a mad, fanciful language," he declared, and he explained the lack of original thought among Russians—especially society people—by the fact that they were not born into a living language. "They acquire a kind of artificial one by learning Russian at school"; "language is the form, the body, the clothing of thought . . . the richer it is" the stronger, the more tranquil and intelligent the person.[19] Custine himself wrote: "Where there is no language . . . there are no thinkers . . . Originality of thought is more closely connected than may be supposed to the integrity of idiom."[20] Custine deplored the general mistrust which killed all conversation in Russia. Like a distant echo, Dostoyevsky confirmed this impression in his account of a meeting on a railway train with a Russian who was going abroad. The first look was already a suspicious one. The man "eyes you, he fears you, he is ready to lie to you . . . in short, insincerity and enmity develop on both sides, and all of a sudden, the conversation stops dead."[21] Custine's

19. Dostoyevsky, *Journal*, op. cit., pp. 354–356.
20. *La Russie*, op. cit., I, p. 366.
21. Dostoyevsky, *Journal*, op. cit., p. 345.

comments on the plastered buildings of St. Petersburg come to mind; Dostoyevsky's view of them was no more indulgent; on the contrary, walking in summer through "streets covered in dust and lime, [he is distressed by] the architecture which expresses the town's complete lack of character and personality . . . Architecturally it reflects all the architecture of the universe, of every epoch and every style; everything in turn has been borrowed and systematically spoilt."[22]

Both writers express the same horror and fascination with the daily occurrence of violence in the empire. They both describe in the smallest detail flogging by the birch. Unlike Custine, Dostoyevsky had suffered physically and mentally from cruelty. Condemned to death for having read a subversive text aloud at a gathering, he was subjected to a mock execution, then sent to a Siberian camp made hellish by the cruelty of the prisoners and the sadism of the guards, but the experience neither hardened him nor accustomed him to injustice. After ten years of Siberia,[23] his disgust at the outrages committed against humanity remained just as acute, and once again he joins Custine in his compassion for the victims. The two of them were equally shocked by the barbaric treatment of animals and experienced the same despair at the contagiousness of violence. On

22. Ibid., pp. 191 and 193–194.

23. Dostoyevsky spent four years in a forced labour camp, and a further six years, first as a soldier, then as an officer, in a regiment stationed in Siberia.

the twenty-fifth anniversary of the Society for the Protection of Animals, Dostoyevsky wrote: "When the mujik learns to have compassion for his animals, he will begin to have some for his wife," and he was horrified that children should be brought up among peasants who whipped their horses across the eyes when they were stuck in the mud.[24]

Why this animosity against Custine? A foreigner's merciless observation is bound to cause some irritation. There was as well the exasperating blindness of the French man of letters towards Russian literary genius, a blindness springing straight from the conviction, so deep-rooted in Custine, of the cultural superiority of Western Europe. That conviction led him to take a paradoxical stand: he deplored the fact that most Russian (or Polish) writers were imitators, while refusing to recognise the originality of Slav talent. Custine had raised a real problem that would trouble Dostoyevsky all his life.

Western literature was admirable. For all his Russianness—real and desired—Dostoyevsky had a sophisticated knowledge of French and English literature, and did not disguise his enthusiasm for the century's great writers. In his journal he tells of the shattering effect

24. Dostoyevsky, *Journal*, op. cit., p. 265. The theme of violence towards animals can also be found in Tolstoy. In *Anna Karenina*, Vronsky reveals his bad character when he kicks Froufrou, his dying filly.

of reading George Sand's first works in the 1830s—a lasting effect since, in *The Brothers Karamazov*, there are curious similarities to be found with *Spiridion*, a somewhat forgotten book by George Sand. Furthermore, the first time Dostoyevsky's name appeared on the cover of a book was in 1846, as the translator of *Eugénie Grandet*. How movingly he exclaimed, faced by the firing squad, on discovering that his death sentence had just been revoked, "One can see the sun," Victor Hugo's quotation that few Frenchmen could recognise today. Reading Dickens in the Siberian camp—an officer had acquired a copy of *The Pickwick Papers*—he was so overwhelmed that he was unable to finish it. He could appreciate Western culture without being tempted to identify with it.

Unable to return to their national roots—the movement which Dostoyevsky called *development*—Russians, according to him, remained servile sheep. Turgenev, who preferred France or Germany to Russia, was a despicable example of that way of thinking, whereas Tolstoy, whose inspiration came largely from national tradition, represented a renewed Russia. True, Custine hadn't understood Pushkin, but he had anticipated the main points of the debate which would concern Russian intellectuals towards the middle and end of the century. The fact that such clear-sightedness annoyed the more thoughtful Russians in no way diminishes its merit.

To conclude, let us return briefly to Tocqueville. The success and long-standing regard in which his book has been held are not surprising. Tocqueville studies the function of democracy in a given society and describes its mechanism with the talent for which he is renowned. Those questions which fascinated the contemporary reader are still relevant, particularly since American society has retained the same constitution and the same fundamental principles. There need be no break in communication between Tocqueville and today's reader. Tocqueville, the man, does not feature in the book. The book's only subject is political procedure.

Custine's method was entirely different. The subject of his book was himself, in Russia. *La Russie* is neither a classical essay nor a conventional political study, but a *journey of analysis*, allowing for both his astonishing insight into a society that offended his sensibilities and the lacunae which, paradoxically, contributed to his future success by preventing the book from becoming dated. Had Custine been interested in agrarian reform, the functioning of the administration, manufacturing methods and precise statistics rather than fear, secrecy and the arbitrary nature of things, the book would never have been revived a hundred years later and read as a predictor of the Soviet régime. The differences between the tsarist empire and the Soviet empire would have been more striking than the analogies. The five executions ordered by Nicholas I would have been compared to the millions of Stalin's victims; and the Gulag would have been contrasted to Katorga, where prisoners didn't die of hunger but borrowed Dickens from passing officers. *La Russie en*

1839 would have stood on our dusty shelves next to Dumas and Gautier or the historian Leroy-Beaulieu.

Custine's acuity, his originality and lucidity—as the Russian poet and diplomat Fyodor Tyutchev was the first to remark—all spring from the fact that he reacted to the most serious things less with his reason than with his emotions.[25]

25. Cadot, op. cit., p. 239.

15

"Half of Myself"

C ustine did not rest on his laurels after the much-hoped-for, long-awaited success of his book. Like a journalist who has handed in his copy, Custine never returned to the subject of Russia except once, in the middle of the 1848 revolution, wondering whether he had been right to side with what he called the anarchic movements. A growing detachment and physical weariness were barely disguised by the pleasure of seeing his talent recognised, added to a certain irritation at his dwindling income. Not dramatic, this loss of income was enough to put a brake on his taste for extensive alterations. He could still afford to run Saint-Gratien, but not to improve it, which made him wish to be rid of it. The sale of the property, always discussed but never pursued with determination, was like some melancholy leitmotiv. Since no one had offered to buy it, he offered it in 1846 to Balzac for 150,000 francs. Their so-called quarrel about *La Russie* hadn't damaged their friendship. Having heard that the property had cost Custine 300,000 francs and that no buyer had been found for 200,000, Balzac was quite tempted. "It is a delicious dwelling," he wrote to Mme Hanska, "and a fine deal . . . You would buy it in your name. I will offer him 120,000 francs payable over three years at three per cent interest . . . It is all done, only one's nightcap remains to be carried in."[1] Unconvinced by her dear Honoré's "enormous good sense," reasonable Mme Hanska refused the château.

As Custine's back was not against the wall and he didn't want to further lower his price, he resigned himself to keeping Saint-Gratien. Bored by the role of landowner, he seemed equally to have lost his enthusiasm for travel: it no longer amused him. "The railways stop me," he would write to Varnhagen, "I knew how to walk but I am afraid of wings which drag along the ground."[2] He divided his time between France and Italy, Italy having become as familiar to him as his native land. In 1845 he bought a little property at Ciampino near Rome: "What they call here a vine, with all its picturesque and rural accessories."[3] He was to spend the tumultuous political years following the events of 1848—years which saw the fall of

---

1. Balzac, *Lettres à Mme Hanska*, op. cit., 5 July 1846, II, p. 244.

2. *Lettres à Varnhagen*, op. cit., 16 October 1855, p. 507.

3. Letter to Sophie Gay, 6 June 1845, in Luppé, op. cit., p. 250.

Louis-Philippe, Europe shaken by a wave of revolutions and the establishment of the Second Empire—examining his conscience, broadening and deepening his religious thinking. He remained within familiar boundaries. Saint-Gratien and Ciampino were to be the two poles of his existence.

His allegiance to the Catholic religion had always worried him. As a man tormented by desire, unable to submit the flesh to the spirit, for whom pleasure and sin were absolutely as one, he found that, far from bringing him serenity, his faith forced him to question himself ceaselessly. He felt only too strongly "that one can think well and behave badly . . . Passions are in the blood, flesh makes beasts of men; thank heaven, the spirit is not always choked by the flesh; the body ends with death, and even in life, the immortal being execrates its tyrant."[4] How could he turn his back on the certainty that to attain moral beauty, sublime enough to satisfy God, it would be necessary to make "the voluntary sacrifice of the appetites of the flesh"?[5] A sacrifice that he was not yet ready to make. Another point to which he returned constantly was the difficulty of accepting the idea of a perfectly good, all-powerful being whose works produced such cruel results. Did the Christian idea demand evil in order to attain virtue? He wanted to write a novel that dealt with all these

4. Custine, *Romuald, ou la Vocation*, 4 vols. (Amyot, 1843), in Luppé, op. cit., p. 274.

5. *Lettres à Varnhagen*, op. cit., p. 493.

questions which he treated so admirably in his letters to his old friend Varnhagen. He set to work as soon as *La Russie en 1839* was published.

This novel, *Romuald*, which ultimately ran to 1,300 pages, with a subsequent sequel, is neither easy to read nor simple to analyse. Let Custine speak for himself. "My novel is unfortunately something quite other than a novel," he wrote to Varnhagen, telling him of his plan, "It is a treatise on theology and practical philosophy, framed in the story of one man's life." The hero, Romuald, born Anglican, "after [a series of] failures reminiscent of Saint Augustine," means to become a clergyman.

> *[F]rom failure to failure, fallen into despair, abandoned by everyone, he is at death's door when his wife comes to his help. She represents the ideal of woman, man's guardian angel and she has never lost sight of him. She has followed him from afar, she has watched over him during his greatest misdeeds. Facing death and, having lost the power of speech, he is unable to confess. It is then that his wife, insulted, abandoned, repudiated, thinks that she should, out loud, make the dying man's confession . . . Resuscitated by the healing of his soul, he feels that he owes everything to his wife and wishes to return to her. But she knows him too well to accept such a sacrifice: far from stopping him from following the career into which she believes God calls him, she decides to become a Catholic and a cloistered nun in*

order to give the repentant sinner back his freedom. He then becomes the greatest preacher of the century . . . The mystical idea of the sacraments dominates the book, especially the denouement.[6]

Throughout the book, Custine stresses repeatedly that only Rome can save Christianity. Only Catholic institutions make men big enough to give them "colossal dimensions." Protestants are deprived of this help and, furthermore, he thinks that the Reformation has despiritualised religion. In reply to Varnhagen, who blamed the Catholic church for disregarding science and for confusing superstition with faith, he wrote, "where the mystery is adopted as a basis for belief, of what use is it to question the apparent unreason of certain practises."[7]

The writing of such a novel wasn't easy and Custine weighed the difficulties carefully: "If it were not an invention, I would feel comfortable."[8] In fact, once his theory, which had been so clearly explained in letters, was written for a wider public and artificially incorporated in a *story*, it lost both its verisimilitude and its power. Custine admitted the lack of clarity in his book, deplored the tangled muddle of this convoluted novel and bewailed: "What bram

6. Ibid., pp. 482–483.
7. Ibid., p. 485.
8. Ibid., p. 483.

bles, what petrification, what extinguished volcanoes, what sterility gather under my pen (my pickaxe)."⁹ Quite unable to cut the book himself, he told Sophie Gay that it needed "the scissors of friendship" before being published. But he was in a hurry to give the public a text so important to him. He was afraid that his ideas would become stale, or that others would appropriate them, and he chose not to wait, even though it meant publishing his book at the worst time, in September 1848; the French were again busy taking sides, calculating risks, and trying to find a balance between security, progress and justice.

Launched "on a sea of fire" and hailed by only a few insignificant articles, the novel sank without a trace. No one bought it, no one read it, no one talked about it, although it was immediately translated and reprinted twice in Germany. Had there been a debate, it would certainly have been pointed out that the events rocking Rome at the time—of which more later—blatantly belied the writer's theories.

Custine faced the third revolution of his lifetime with a certain indifference, quite in tune with "this land of railways" that France had become, where the grossest materialism triumphed. "The dominating passion of those who live in the provinces is . . . will you believe

9. Tarn, op. cit., p. 552.

it?" he wrote to Varnhagen, "greed combined with a strong dose of conceit. One lives to eat better than one's neighbour whom one despises from the bottom of a heart shrunk by the stomach."[10]

He hadn't given way to panic during the June demonstrations although he was aware of the dangers involved: "We have been through sad times; the ambitions to which the word Republic opens the door placed us within an inch of our downfall, we did not go to bed without thinking that the insurgents might come and shoot us in the night, in the courtyard, in the name of the enemies of family property."[11] He decided to leave Paris as quickly as possible and take refuge at Saint-Gratien, with a gun which he didn't know how to use, there to set up a "phalanstery of idlers" with Sainte-Barbe and Mme Merlin, but he came back on 8 July to attend a service for Chateaubriand who had died a few days earlier.

Victor Hugo was struck by the lack of crowds and the mediocre emotion at the funeral celebrated in a stupified Paris: ". . . All this noise of fusillades, of cannons and of the tocsin prevented there being heard, on the death of M. de Chateaubriand, that kind of silence which marks the departure of great men."[12] It was a sign of a certain detachment that the death of this man who had been so important to him hardly affected Custine. He was even quite ironic in the account

---

10. *Lettres à Varnhagen*, op. cit., pp. 497–498.

11. Ibid., p. 503.

12. Victor Hugo, *Choses vues 1847–1848* (Gallimard, 1972), p. 349.

of the funeral he sent to Sophie Gay: "What is left of France [attended]: he would come to life again if he could see the effect of his death."[13] The coldness that may have been justified a posteriori by the cavalier treatment of Delphine in the *Mémoires d'outre-tombe* was nevertheless shocking, and went unexplained by Custine. His indifference seemed to extend from politics to his old friends. Even the failure of his book left him unmoved. He wrote to Sophie Gay, by way of explanation, "It is my fate to have no more success and to compensate for this by a resignation which at life's close is perhaps better."

Before leaving for Rome with Sainte-Barbe, he took the trouble of having a copy of *Romuald* bound by Simier, who made the most exquisite Romantic bindings. He had it stamped with the arms of the pope in order to present him with it at a private audience. Barbey d'Aurevilly, as usual too mocking to let that pass, wrote to his friend Trébutien, the Norman bookseller: "This spiritual Gomorrhean of a Marquis de Custine . . . is on very good terms, despite his vices, with Pius IX . . . The Church has never damned men of spirit except at the last."[14] In 1848, when the unfortunate pontiff received Custine most agreeably, he had no heart for either damnation or literature. He had a revolution on his hands.

13. Letter to Sophie Gay, 22 July 1848.

14. Barbey d'Aurevilly, *Correspondance*, op. cit., letter of 18 September 1851, III, p. 95.

To everyone's surprise, and most particularly to his own, Pius IX had been elected in June 1846 by a conclave so violently divided between liberals and conservatives that the cardinals had been reduced to voting for an almost unknown man whose strongest suit was his absence of political passion. Responsibility only made him hesitate more; Pius IX took indecision to a point of absurdity. He had sent an armed corps to support the revolt against Austria in Milan and Venice, while refusing to order the soldiers to fight, thereby provoking fury in the Papal States. The murder of his minister, the comte Rossi, provoked the Roman crowd to attack his residence in the Quirinale Palace. Uncertain of the outcome, and with little confidence in his Swiss Guard, Pius chose, on 25 November, to run away, disguised as a priest, and to ask the protection of the king of the Two-Sicilies at Gaeta.

The Republic of Rome was then instituted. According to the new constitution, the pope retained his spiritual power but was divested of all temporal power. Pius then appealed to France for the return of his Papal States. Louis-Napoleon Bonaparte, the president of the recently formed French Republic, was obliged because of internal political pressure to agree to send troops, under the command of General Oudinot, to crush the Roman republicans. He could not manage without the backing of the French Catholics, whose leader, the comte de Montalembert, had demanded help for the pope in return for his support. After an initial setback, Oudinot besieged and bombarded Rome. The pope would have liked the French to severely repress the rebellion before his return, but Louis-Bonaparte imposed a general amnesty and on 12 April 1850, Pius IX finally returned to Rome.

What had become of Custine meanwhile? Fascinated by the spectacle of what was happening and as reckless as he had been in Spain and Calabria, he felt a resurgence of youthful curiosity and was able to display his natural courage in a city given over to anarchy. He walked through every district and in perfect Italian—he was no longer taken for a Frenchman—he questioned strangers, joined conversations and silently deplored the plunder all around. "A calm disorder reigns in the city, an anarchy without violence of the most singular kind."

Although gangs of hooligans harmed property more than people, it was dangerous, and Rome seemed horribly sad to him. "I weep for Rome and her villas: the Pamphili and the Borghese pines have been cut down . . . and all the marvels of art and nature carried away by the revolutionary storm have ended up in a field of potatoes."[15] The pope's departure created an enormous void for the new men in power to fill and, he wrote to Sophie Gay, "we have the usurper (Canini), the sophist (Mazzini), the condottiere (Garibaldi), the desperadoes (or armed cowards); all the mercenaries and rabble of

15. To Sophie Gay, 13 June 1849.

Europe have hurried here to participate in these Saturnalian politics."[16]

Rome became impossible for a Frenchman, so Custine took refuge at home in Ciampino, where, thanks to Antonio, nothing had been touched. Having become what he called "an amateur emigré," he lived on false news and false hopes. He had brought with him, almost by force, a French bishop, Mgr de Falloux, and his old friend Mme de Menou, widow of the general who had only distinguished himself by defeat in Egypt and the Vendée and ending his career as governor of Venice. Both the bishop and Mme de Menou refused to acknowledge the most obvious danger. The bishop irritated Custine enough to excite his wit: "[Mgr] is a cross between a parrot and a man, one cannot tell if he is still a young man or a somewhat elderly woman. He is not a fool although he has the makings of one, nor a bird although he has the beak, he is not wicked although he would like to be . . . he is active but not mobile, he is changeable, but none of the changes help him in any way . . . he is a frozen chameleon."[17] The politics of Oudinot and his diplomats seemed pointlessly complicated to Custine. "They use their minds," he said, "like lorgnettes the wrong way round."[18] Obliged to leave Ciampino, which

16. To Sophie Gay, 23 December 1849, in Tarn, op. cit., p. 685.
17. *Lettres à Mme de Courbonne*, op. cit., p. 59.
18. To Sophie Gay, June 1849.

was too isolated for the troubled times and, furthermore, unhealthy during the summer months, he headed for Naples.

He was tempted by the idea of spending the summer alone with Sainte-Barbe at Sorrento, but afraid of solitude, "even [the solitude] of paradise, in a time when one only lives off news."[19] In the furnace of Naples where he vegetated like an over-heated plant, he didn't work on the sequel to *Romuald*, as planned. He was exhausted: "The heat of the sun and the coldness of the people cause my idleness to triumph. I am old," he concluded, "and I make myself older so as to excuse my indolence."[20] Finally, overcome by the confusion in which he lived, he decided to return to France, and more determined than ever since he was threatened with expropriation of his property at Ciampino to make way for the railways. "The political sky," he wrote, "is like an autumn fog: every now and then the point of a building is perceived, a ray of light falls on a cross; then the wind blows and covers everything in an impenetrable veil." Suddenly feeling old, Custine didn't fancy living without a house of his own. "I will come back to Saint-Gratien in the spring," he wrote to Mme de Courbonne, "I plan to die there, you will help me."[21] This lassitude may have been encouraged by the fact that Italy, agitated, worn

19. Letter to Sophie Gay, 13 June 1849.
20. To Sophie Gay, August 1849.
21. *Lettres à Mme de Courbonne*, op. cit., p. 742.

out and divided, no longer constituted a haven for him, whereas the future of France, since the coming to power of Louis Bonaparte, looked more stable and peaceful. He returned home just before Louis-Napoleon's coup of 2 December 1851, an event which left him with no reaction. He had lost all political passion. In his private life, however, he was shattered by a series of deaths.

His closest friends were dying: Sophie Gay, the confidante to whom, on 31 December 1850, he had sent flowers to celebrate their fifty years of friendship, died aged seventy-four on 5 March 1852. Three weeks later, it was Mme Merlin, the constant visitor to Saint-Gratien whose voice and musical taste enchanted her host. Mme de Menou died next, Balzac had been dead for two years and the good doctor Koreff collapsed on a patient's doorstep in 1851. Under the circumstances, how could he fail to contemplate his own end, not metaphysically, but literally? Custine would spend a great deal of time putting his affairs in order. It could almost be said that he devoted his final years to the task.

The material organisation of his life was centred around Saint-Gratien. By constantly talking of sales and failed sales, Custine disguised the fact that for the past ten years of his life, he had divided, partitioned and rented Saint-Gratien. He lived in various dependencies converted into comfortable houses where he continued entertaining, while the princesse Mathilde who had occupied the main house since 1853, was little by little buying up the estate. At the start of their negotiations, Custine asked too much money to settle the deal at once, and in any case, because of his strong attachment to the property, he really preferred putting it off.

The princesse Mathilde was about thirty when she first met Custine. She was the daughter of Jérôme, the youngest of the Bonapartes, and Napoleon III's first cousin. Through her mother, Catherine, daughter of the king of Wurtemburg, she was a descendant of the old European dynasties. All three pretenders to the French throne —the comte de Chambord, the duc d'Orléans and Louis-Napoleon —had thought of marrying her. But nothing came of these plans: the smell of the Revolution was too strong for the legitimists, the lack of fortune too painful for Louis-Philippe and Louis Bonaparte's arrest put an end to a burgeoning idyll. She finally married a Russian parvenu, Count Demidov. He was enormously rich, but brutal, jealous and uncontrolled to the point where one day he slapped his young wife's face in public. Unlike Custine, princesse Mathilde had, with good reason, great admiration for the Tsar. With a wave of his wand, Nicholas settled the problems of his new subject very favourably: he announced the couple's separation and ordered the count to give his wife an annual income of 500,000 francs.[22]

Rich, beautiful and lively, she returned to Paris where she made

22. This was a considerable sum. Only a few families in France enjoyed so large an income.

a very influential position for herself because of her excellent relationship with her cousin. Until the Emperor married Eugénie de Montijo, she acted as mistress of the house at the Elysée. Chance and the summer season brought her into contact with Custine. In summer, the princesse often visited a friend, Mme de Reiset, who owned a house in the Montmorency valley and regularly attended the marquis's soirées. She was also greatly attached to another habitué of Saint-Gratien and an old friend of her mother's, Mme de Courbonne. Knowing how much Custine wanted to sell his property, these women put him in touch with the princesse. The two immediately took to one another.

Custine's exquisite politeness attracted Mathilde. She was delighted by the charm and intellectual interest of his receptions and concerts where Princess Czartoryska "resurrected her master, Chopin," and to which Verdi came as a neighbour. Her enthusiasm was all the greater because of the aura of the First Empire that surrounded Saint-Gratien. She must have known that the house's first owner, the comtesse de Luçay, had been designated by Napoleon to accompany her mother, the Princess of Wurtenberg, from Stuttgart to Paris where her marriage to Jérôme took place. The princesse expressed "with fire" her wish to buy the property, but according to Custine, the plan was never taken any further. Custine remarked on his surprise to Mme de Courbonne: "Where does this icy silence come from? I have upset my summer, changed my plans, arranged my house and then . . . nothing?" But he later admitted that he hadn't known how to take advantage of the opportunity.

Throughout their discussions—it took them years to settle the matter—they continued to see each other with pleasure. He was obviously charmed by "the august neighbour, utterly entertaining, good, charming, wicked . . . in fact everything most pleasing in its unaffectedness, in the exercise and originality of conversation, accompanied by a pantomime which brings every word to life."[23] He often visited her in Paris where she arranged an audience for him with the Emperor who proved most agreeable. If Custine had been able to accept the slightest commitment, there was no doubt that he would have been made very welcome at court. Who knows what he might have become—chamberlain or senator?

Political ambition in a man who had for so long refused to participate in public life was not going to develop so late. Besides, what could he accomplish? "I have reflected on the profound opposition of my Catholic ideas to the new philosophy. Admiration can fill many a gulf, mine for this talent is sincere, the first of the times, but its direction distresses me, have I the authority to say so?"[24] It did not suit him to be in the limelight which, in the official world, would be inevitable. He knew it. Without the complete freedom of his private life, he would have been lost.

23. *Lettres à Mme de Courbonne*, op. cit., p. 51.
24. Ibid.

Not that his intimate soirées were peopled with youths; the seductive Gurowski with all his extravagances hadn't been replaced. When Barbey d'Aurevilly arrived unexpectedly, he found Sainte-Barbe and Custine ensconced with their friend Foudras and that "Vitellius sodomite of a Lerminier." Lerminier was an influential literary critic, a lawyer "as witty as Fontenelle and [who], despite the belly, the guts and hiccups due to perpetual indigestion, has, like all the eighteenth century, a grace in conversation and a touch of champagne"[25] (*sic*). Marquis and novelist, Foudras was twenty years younger than Custine. According to Astolphe, Foudras was the personification of talent and charm. This judgement has hardly been confirmed by posterity for, despite their alluring names—*Un caprice de grande dame, Diane et Vénus*, and *Viveurs d'autrefois* in four volumes—Foudras's novels are forgotten. His attraction lay elsewhere: although burdened with a wife and children, his taste leaned towards gentlemen. "[He] looked like a large parrot with a big red head eating a cherry, and now he only looks like a magpie who has stolen a spoon."[26] An anecdote about Barbey d'Aurevilly would, if necessary, confirm the company's regrettable appearance. During a dinner with old friends, he turned to Coppée and said, "Look here, Coppée, they say I am a pederast! Pederast! Every-

25. Barbey d'Aurevilly, *Correspondance*, op. cit., letter to Trébutien of 8 November 1844, I, p. 205.
26. Ibid., letter to Trébutien, 10 December 1853, III, p. 173.

thing attracts me in that direction, my tastes, my nature, the pleasure of the thing . . . The ugliness of my contemporaries has long
since made me disgusted with this particular pleasure."[27] As for
Custine, he overlooked the ugliness because Foudras and Lerminier
amused him and besides, there was always his close friend, the indispensable Sainte-Barbe.

The years had strengthened the ties that united Custine and
Sainte-Barbe. "[Separated] we are no more than a half of ourselves
. . . with the most delicate touch, he knows how to soften all the
bitter blows of fate."[28] Custine's refusal since youth to become involved had not been without doubts or anxiety, but throughout his
unconventional life, in which the shadowy areas and the solitude
were balanced by the pleasures of society, he had found peace with
his friend, the gentle, patient Edward. Now a childless man without
responsibilities, he would devote a large part of his remaining time
to carefully looking after Sainte-Barbe's future.

In order to appreciate the provisions of his will, a clearer picture
of Custine's remaining relations is needed. Since the death of his
uncle, Elzéar, his family consisted of a distant cousin, Robert de
Custine, and his aunt Dreux-Brézé; she was the one who hadn't had
the courage to accompany Delphine in support of her own father be-

27. Philippe Berthier, *Barbey d'Aurevilly et l'imagination* (Geneva, Librairie
Droz, 1978), p. 174.

28. *Lettres à Mme de Courbonne*, op. cit., p. 68.

fore the revolutionary Tribunal. Astolphe had always remained on good terms with his sister-in-law, Mme de Maussion, whose husband died in 1846. Custine had remarked cruelly at the time to Sophie Gay, "his poor wife nursed him as if she adored him. The feelings one does not have are often easier to handle than those one has."[29] There was no question of making her his heir, particularly since she was very rich.

Although she had never shown him the least sign of affection, the old Dreux-Brézé aunt had her eye on her nephew's fortune and was bold enough to suggest an heir to him. He replied in jest that he was unable to decipher the letter with the proposed name. Then breaking off further negotiations, he concluded, "That is enough said about a matter that is painful to deal with and perfectly useless to discuss; so let us say no more about it, unless it suits you to make me repeat the thing without any result."[30] He had long since made his choice. The impropriety of his aunt's suggestion persuaded Custine that he had better take every precaution to protect Sainte-Barbe's rights, because it was to him of course that he intended to leave what remained of his fortune.

Then Custine, the poet, the dreamer, inhabitant of another planet, came into his own as a lawyer, and a very competent one. In 1852, he drew up a will in favour of "Monsieur Edward Sainte-

29. Letter to Sophie Gay, in Luppé, op. cit., p. 267.
30. In Tarn, op. cit., p. 702.

Barbe, my best friend, who for thirty years has never left me, and who in all circumstances has given me proof of the sincerest devotion." It could not have been clearer, but what would happen if he, Custine, sank into his dotage? Sainte-Barbe would obviously be threatened if Custine's aunt or some distant cousins whom he "practically never saw . . . and from whom [he] had received no sign of affection" became his guardians. In the circumstances of his losing his reason and having to suffer "all that old age and decrepitude can bring by way of misery," Custine asked the court to name as guardians his lawyer and Sainte-Barbe. Edward would hate being unable to look after him, for even "in imbecility, one has flashes of reason and stirrings of memory." He specified that Sainte-Barbe should be authorised to withdraw the necessary money for the upkeep of the house and the servants' wages.

Another matter of concern was where Sainte-Barbe would live if he was left alone. The rue de La Rochefoucauld had been sold for a life annuity of 30,000 francs, partly reverting to Sainte-Barbe. After the sale, the couple had moved to a wing of the hôtel Foudras, in rue Blanche, but Custine was not sure that Foudras would continue to rent it to Sainte-Barbe alone. In any case Sainte-Barbe might not want to stay in that big apartment. In doubt and anxious "for the health, for the life perhaps, of a man without whom [he could not] live,"[31] Custine decided to buy his friend a small house nearby, in

31. Letter to Lerminier, 25 December 1856, in Luppé, op. cit., p. 296.

what was to become the rue Ballu. As a final precaution, he filed a document in which he had enumerated his reasons for deciding to disinherit his family in 1844, reasons "which a quite natural delicacy" prevented him from explaining in the will, but which he authorised the lawyer to reveal in the case of litigation. Having put his affairs in order, Custine, relieved, continued to lead the life he loved, dividing his time between his friends, the Sunday soirées to which "the regulars" came, reading and working in a chalet he had restored by the lake.

In 1857, readers in France had much to look forward to. It was the year in which both *Madame Bovary* and *Les Fleurs du mal* were published. Did Custine read Flaubert? He must have. The publication of *Madame Bovary* with its ensuing scandal could not have failed to attract his attention but there is no reference to his reactions, either in Barbey d'Aurevilly's correspondence or in Custine's last letters to Varnhagen. We do know that he was moved by *Les Fleurs du mal*. "Like a faithful mirror, you reflect the spirit of the times in a sick country and your powerful words often make me cringe from the objects which you choose to paint . . . You are new in an old literature," he wrote to the unknown poet to thank him for his book. Baudelaire included the letter in the 1868 complete edition of his works.

Barbey d'Aurevilly suggested that Baudelaire send Custine his poems, knowing full well that both men were haunted, just as he was, by the "insoluble and sterile problem" of reconciling goodness and passion. All three men sustained themselves with a rigorous and unorthodox Catholicism and, in varying degrees, chose to disguise the bitterness of their lives under a veil of dandyism. At the time of Baudelaire's trial, which ended in the suppression of six poems judged to be obscene, Custine wrote to Barbey d'Aurevilly: "I share your opinion on *the poet condemned but not judged* by our morality police, and your last word is a superb warning.[32] Our black-robed puritans stubbornly wish to make this world a nunnery devoted to the education of young girls . . . If the depiction of vice is to be excluded from literature, not only art but religion will have to be sacrificed; the Bible will have to be impounded . . . in it vice is horribly characterised, and with such crudity that it would revolt the courts were they to find that style in a modern writer."[33] Baudelaire admired Custine for having created characters whose only "requirement is to cultivate the idea of beauty in their person, to satisfy their passions. They have at their disposal vast quantities of time and money without which fantasy, reduced to passing reverie, can hardly be transformed into action."[34] In an article written in Au-

32. "After *Les Fleurs du mal*," Barbey wrote, "the poet who made them blossom can do only one of two things, either blow his brains out . . . or become a Christian."

33. Claude Pichois, *Lettres à Baudelaire*, Etudes baudelairiennes IV–V, at La Baconnière, Neuchâtel, p. 48.

34. Baudelaire, *Oeuvres Complètes*, op. cit.; *Peintre de la vie moderne*, III, p. 483.

gust, he named Custine with Balzac and Flaubert among those who had tried to bring new life to the novel. But the praise, published on 18 October, came posthumously. On 25 September 1857, as night fell at Saint-Gratien, Custine died from a stroke.

He was buried in the chapel near Fervaques, under an unmarked stone, next to his mother, his wife and his son. Eight days later, the marquise de Dreux-Brézé attacked. She had the house in rue Blanche sealed. The case came to court in July 1858. The family accused Sainte-Barbe of improperly soliciting a legacy "with perseverance and by the most reprehensible means," but Custine's depositions were irrefutable and although the magistrate was puritanical and had been picked to judge both Flaubert and Baudelaire, he decided in Sainte-Barbe's favour. The marquise appealed. Meanwhile the unfortunate Sainte-Barbe died in October, thirteen months after Custine, having converted to Catholicism on his deathbed, as if to pay his last respects to his friend.

He named Foudras as legatee. The only changes he made to Custine's will concerned bequests to the servants. He doubled what had been left to Antonio, who received 40,000 francs, which was a very large sum of money.[35] Foudras then inherited the estate and quickly

35. Twenty thousand francs was considered enough for someone to belong to the middle class. In 1850, 80 percent of Parisians survived on 500 francs a year. Adeline Daumard, *La Bourgeoisie parisienne de 1815 à 1848* (Paris, SEVPEN, 1963).

sold Saint-Gratien and the little house in Paris. More damaging to Custine's literary reputation, he allowed all the papers, letters and unpublished manuscripts to fall into the hands of Custine's hostile family. Much was destroyed or lost.

At the beginning of the twentieth century, Custine was more than dead. The beautiful park at Saint-Gratien had been divided up, the house razed, Custine's papers and letters dispersed and his books nowhere to be found. It would take the political upheavals of this century and the curiosity of a few specialists before this original writer could be rehabilitated. He was the enemy of every school of writing. He heralded the alienation of the twentieth century because he felt that he didn't entirely belong to either his time or his country. "I have always been considered strange here, particularly in my way of writing. The French describe what they see and generally concern themselves with what is, without thinking about what has been and what will be . . . anyone who does not have in front of their eyes a world before ours and another world to come does not see clearly: there is nothing noticeably *present* for us which is not complicated by this triple relationship, and generally in France people concentrate only on their moment in time."[36]

36. *Lettres à Varnhagen*, op. cit., p. 152.

INDEX

Index

Index

Index

Index

Index

ABOUT THE AUTHOR

Anka Muhlstein was born in Paris in 1935. Having taken refuge with her family in New York during the war, she returned to France in 1946, where she continued her studies and graduated with a degree in history and geography from the Sorbonne. She worked for a number of publishers in France, then she settled in New York for good in 1974, after marrying Louis Begley. It was in New York that she began her career as a writer in French. She has published six books: La Femme Soleil *(a study of women at the court of Louis XIV) in 1976 was followed by biographies of Queen Victoria and* Baron James *(the first Rothschild to settle in France),* Manhattan, *a book-length essay on her adopted home, and a biography of La Salle (published in the United States by Arcade). Her books have been translated into several languages, and she has twice been awarded the History Prize of the French Academy. The French edition of her biography of Astolphe de Custine was awarded the prestigious Goncourt Prize for biography in 1996.*

ABOUT THE TRANSLATOR

Teresa Waugh was born in England in 1940 and learned French at an early age. She studied both French and Italian at Exeter, and has translated numerous books from both languages, most recently, Madame du Deffand and Her World *by Benedetta Craveri. She has also written and published seven novels and numerous short stories. Her novel* A Friend Like Harvey *was just published in England by Victor Gollancz.*